Jamestown

THROUGH TIME

AMY WATERS YARSINSKE

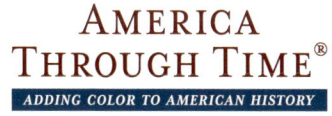

America Through Time is an imprint of Fonthill Media LLC

First published 2016

Copyright © Amy Waters Yarsinske

Unless otherwise indicated in the caption, the pictures in this book are courtesy of the author.

ISBN 978-1-63500-036-8

All rights reserved. No part of this publication may be reproduced, stored in a retrieval system or transmitted in any form or by any means, electronic, mechanical, photocopying, recording or otherwise, without prior permission in writing from Fonthill Media LLC

Typeset in Mrs Eaves XL Serif Narrow

Published by Arcadia Publishing by arrangement with Fonthill Media LLC
For all general information, please contact Arcadia Publishing:
Telephone: 843-853-2070
Fax: 843-853-0044
E-mail: sales@arcadiapublishing.com
For customer service and orders:
Toll-Free 1-888-313-2665

Visit us on the internet at www.arcadiapublishing.com

CONTENTS

Introduction	4
SECTION 1: The First English Settlement in America	7
SECTION 2: Jamestown Rediscovered	25
SECTION 3: Exploring Jamestown Island	47
SECTION 4: Preserving the Past for the Present	69
Select Bibliography	95
About the Author	96

Introduction

On May 13, 1607, three small English ships—the *Susan Constant*, the largest of the ships under the command of Captain Christopher Newport and carrying seventy-one persons, the *Godspeed*, commanded by Captain Bartholomew Gosnold and carrying fifty-two persons, and the *Discovery*, a pinnace and the smallest of the ships, under Captain John Ratcliffe and carrying twenty-one persons—approached a spit of shore at what was soon named Jamestown. During the day, as George Percy, one of those to arrive that day, later writes, they maneuvered the ships so close to the shore that they were "moored to the Trees in six fathom of water." The next day, May 14, he continued, "we landed all our men, which were set to worke about the fortification, others some to watch and ward as it was convenient." These events would take place roughly twenty years after the fated attempts to establish the colony at Roanoke Island and thirteen years before the Pilgrims landed at Plymouth, in New England.

The Jamestown settlement was the manifestation of England's determination to establish its imprint in the New World. The overthrow of Spanish seapower during the reign of Queen Elizabeth I paved the way for England's colonization plan. Enterprising Englishmen had already colonized and influenced far and wide at that time, to include India, the Near East and Russia. Sir Walter Raleigh had made several unsuccessful attempts to set in place a permanent settlement on what is today the North Carolina coast at Roanoke Island, and Sir Walter Gilbert made his attempt farther north, to no avail, at Newfoundland. Success would come for the Virginia Company of London, operating under its April 10, 1606 charter. This joint stock company, a commercial enterprise, was instrumental, under its charter provisions, in guaranteeing to settlers of the New World the rights, freedoms and privileges they would have had in their native land. The first to land here in May 1607—the first Virginians—built homes, a fort, planted crops, fought off disease from maladies they had never seen, and were intermittedly friend and foe of the Powhatan. These men—and women—brought with them their church

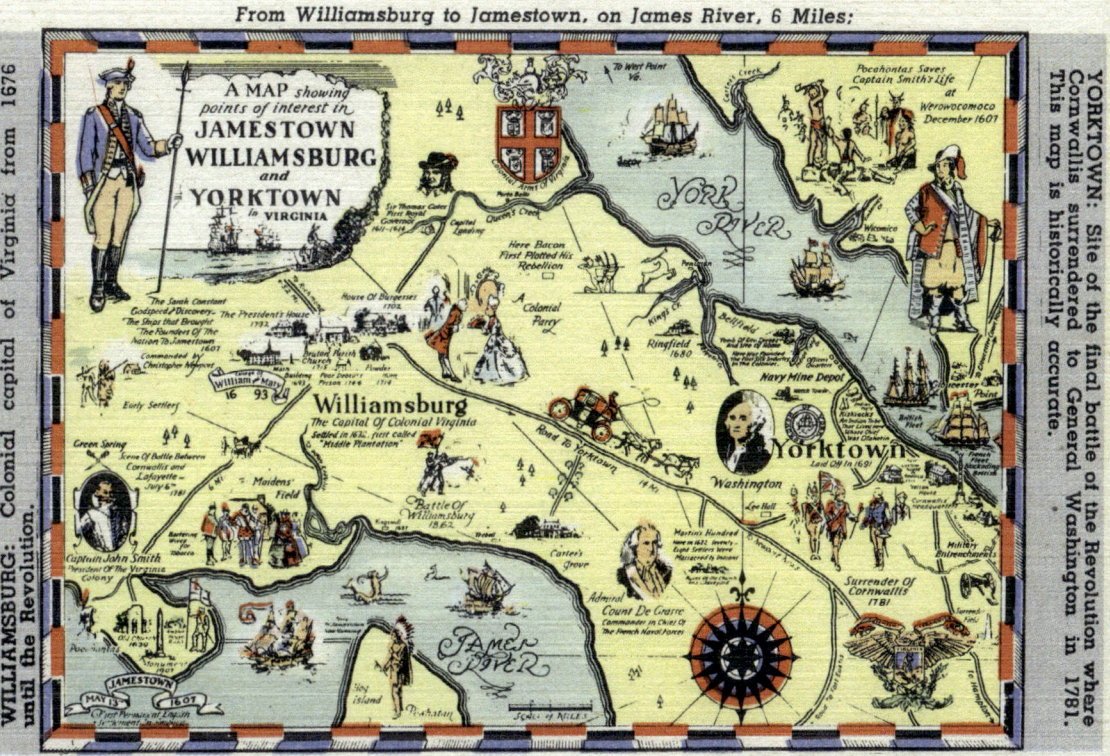

HISTORIC TRIANGLE OF COLONIAL VIRGINIA: The map shown on this linen postcard was made from a larger version on display at the Sign of the Bull's Head, a privately-owned hostelry located, at the time, on Duke of Gloucester Street in Colonial Williamsburg. The postcard dates to the mid-twentieth century.

and reverence for God, maintained trial by jury and their rights as freemen, according to those who would later document the history that took place there. Soon, they would craft representative government.

    The Jamestown we know today is an island, the site of the first permanent English settlement in America in 1607; the point at which the first representative legislative assembly convened in 1619 to set a pattern for self-governance in America; the scene of the dramatic events surrounding Bacon's Rebellion of 1676/7, and capital of the Virginia colony for almost a century, from 1607 to 1699; it grew from the first settlement in 1607 into a town, more village than the formal towns and cities that would follow it, and then it declined as the plantation system flowered, scattering the population of the colony far and wide along the shores of Virginia's deep rivers and many tributaries. Yet in the seventeenth century, this island of marshlands and pine-oak forests was a peninsula between the James River and Powhatan Creek, connected to the mainland by a narrow isthmus that eroded in the eighteenth century.

Jamestown was abandoned as the capital more than three centuries ago, after the burning of the fourth statehouse in 1698. All attempts to force its development and to continue it as the chief town in Virginia had failed. The capital was relocated to Middle Plantation, the unincorporated town established in 1632 that became Williamsburg in 1699. The Jamestown site eventually became farm land and little remained above ground to show later generations that it had once been the center of government in Virginia until subsequent discoveries made from the early twentieth century changed what we now know about it. This account of Jamestown is not an attempt to write a comprehensive history but a substantive glimpse into a place many consider one of the most significant sites—if not *the* most important—in American history.

How much and how well we understand and appreciate what took place at Jamestown more than 400 years ago is dependent on the nation's educational institutions, from primary grades to colleges and universities, and our own desire to read about and, if possible, visit this sacred place in our nation's past. In the words of James Bryce, British ambassador to the United States at the time of the Jamestown Tercentenary, the settlement of "Jamestown was one of the great events in the history of the world—an event to be compared for its momentous consequences with the overthrow of the Persian Empire by Alexander; with the destruction of Carthage by Rome; with the conquest of Gaul by Clovis; with the taking of Constantinople by the Turks—one might almost say with the discovery of America by Columbus." Here was born the great English-speaking nation beyond the seas, of which so many had dreamed before 1607, and here, too, was the cradle of our Republican institutions and liberties.

Today, Jamestown is one of three locations—along with Williamsburg and Yorktown—that comprise the Historic Triangle of Colonial Virginia, and it is home to two heritage tourism sites related to the original fort and town: Historic Jamestowne, the archaeological site on the island a cooperative effort of Jamestown National Historic Site, part of the Colonial National Historical Park, and Preservation Virginia, formerly the Association for the Preservation of Virginia Antiquities (APVA), and the Jamestown Settlement, a living history site and museum, originally Jamestown Festival Park, built for the celebration of the semiseptcentennial anniversary and operated by the Jamestown-Yorktown Foundation in conjunction with the Commonwealth of Virginia. Visitors to Historic Jamestowne can tour the site of the original 1607 James Fort, the seventeenth-century church tower and town, as well as walk through the archaeological museum called the Archaearium and see the close to two million artifacts uncovered by Jamestown Rediscovery.

Section 1

The First English Settlement in America

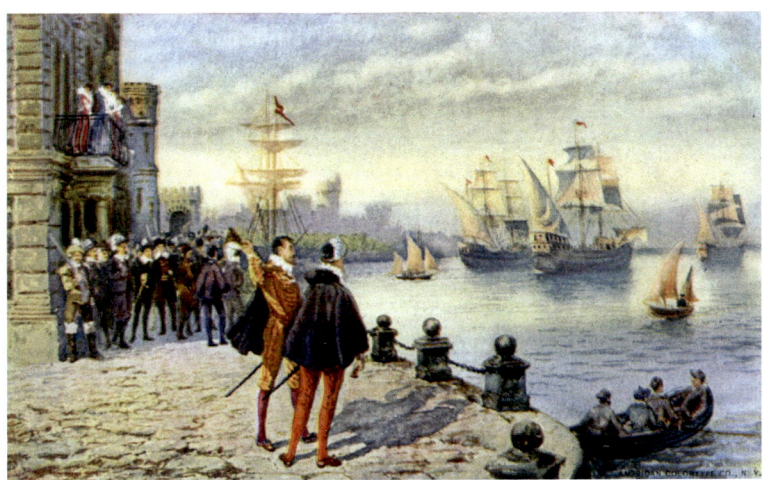

LEAVING BLACKWALL: On December 19, 1606, the journey to Virginia began from Blackwall, England, aboard three ships—the *Susan Constant*, the *Godspeed*, and the *Discovery*; the event is depicted on this Jamestown Amusement and Vending Company, the official concessionaire of the 1907 Jamestown Exposition, postcard.

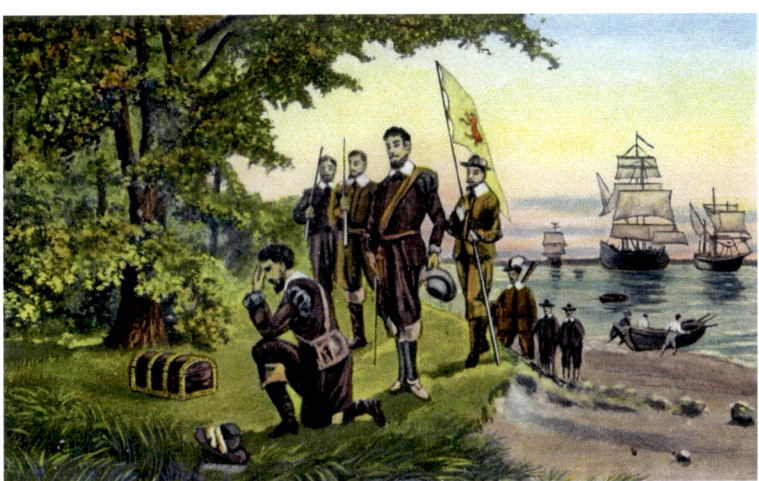

ARRIVAL AT JAMESTOWN: The first English settlers arrive at Jamestown on May 13, 1607. This event is depicted on this Louis Kaufmann and Sons postcard that dates to 1907. The first president of the new Virginia colony was Edward Maria Winfield. The other six council members were: Captains Bartholomew Gosnold, Christopher Newport, John Ratcliffe, and John Smith, and George Kendall, and John Martin.

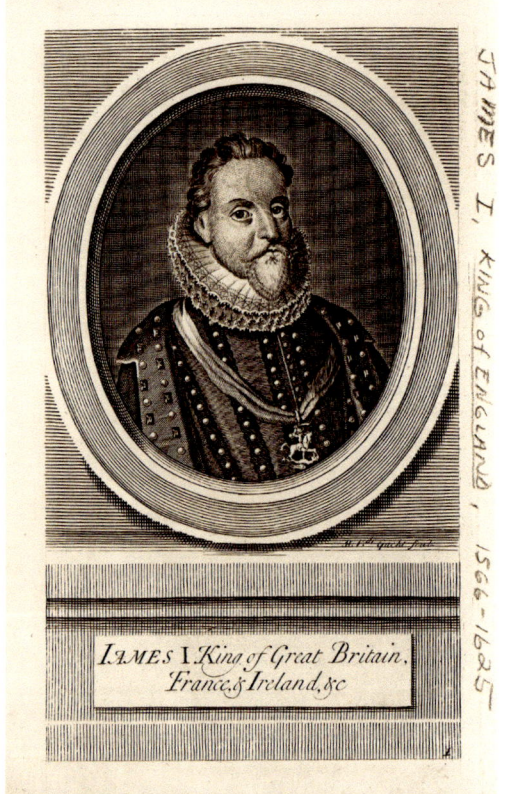 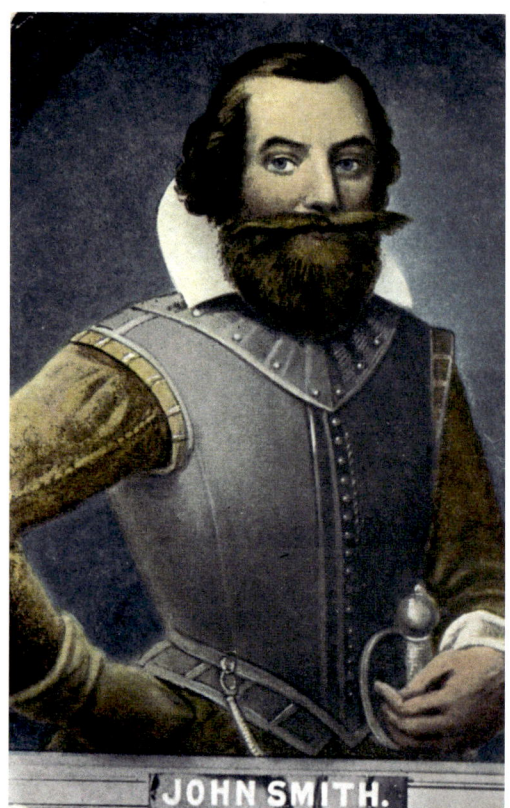

KING JAMES I (LEFT): This head and shoulders engraving of King James I was the work of Michael van der Gucht (1660–1725), and likely rendered toward the end of Gucht's career. James I signed the first of three charters in 1606, granting the Virginia Company the right to control an area extending fifty miles north, fifty miles south, and one hundred miles west of the settlement on the east coast of America. The second charter in 1609 granted the Virginia Company of London an "able and absolute governor" and extended the boundaries of Virginia from those set in the 1606 charter. In 1612, a third charter incorporated Bermuda and established lotteries for the purpose of raising funds. A new set of instructions was written by officials of the Virginia Company in 1618. Commonly called the "Great Charter," these instructions created a council of state, whose members were chosen by the Virginia Company, to assist the governor in his duties, and a "generall Assemblie" that included the council and two "burgesses" from every town, hundred, and particular plantation, "chosen by the [free] inhabitants." Thus, began the first representative government in the European colonies. *Library of Congress.*

CAPTAIN JOHN SMITH (RIGHT): This portrait of Captain John Smith (1580–1631) appeared on an early divided-back postcard. Smith was an adventurer, soldier, explorer and author. After he was elected president of the colony in September 1608, the colonists relationship with the surrounding Powhatan paramount chiefdom deteriorated, largely due his penchant for violently taking food and destroying villages. The final meeting of Smith and Powhatan occurred in January 1609 at Werowocomoco, Powhatan's capital; it was here that each leader plotted to kill the other while conducting civil negotiations. Ironically, Powhatan's plan to kill Smith and his party failed after Smith was warned by Pocahontas. Smith did not witness the First Anglo-Powhatan War (1609–1614) or the Starving Time (winter of 1609–1610) having suffered a severe injury from a gunpowder explosion in the fall of 1609 that forced his return to England; he would never return to Jamestown.

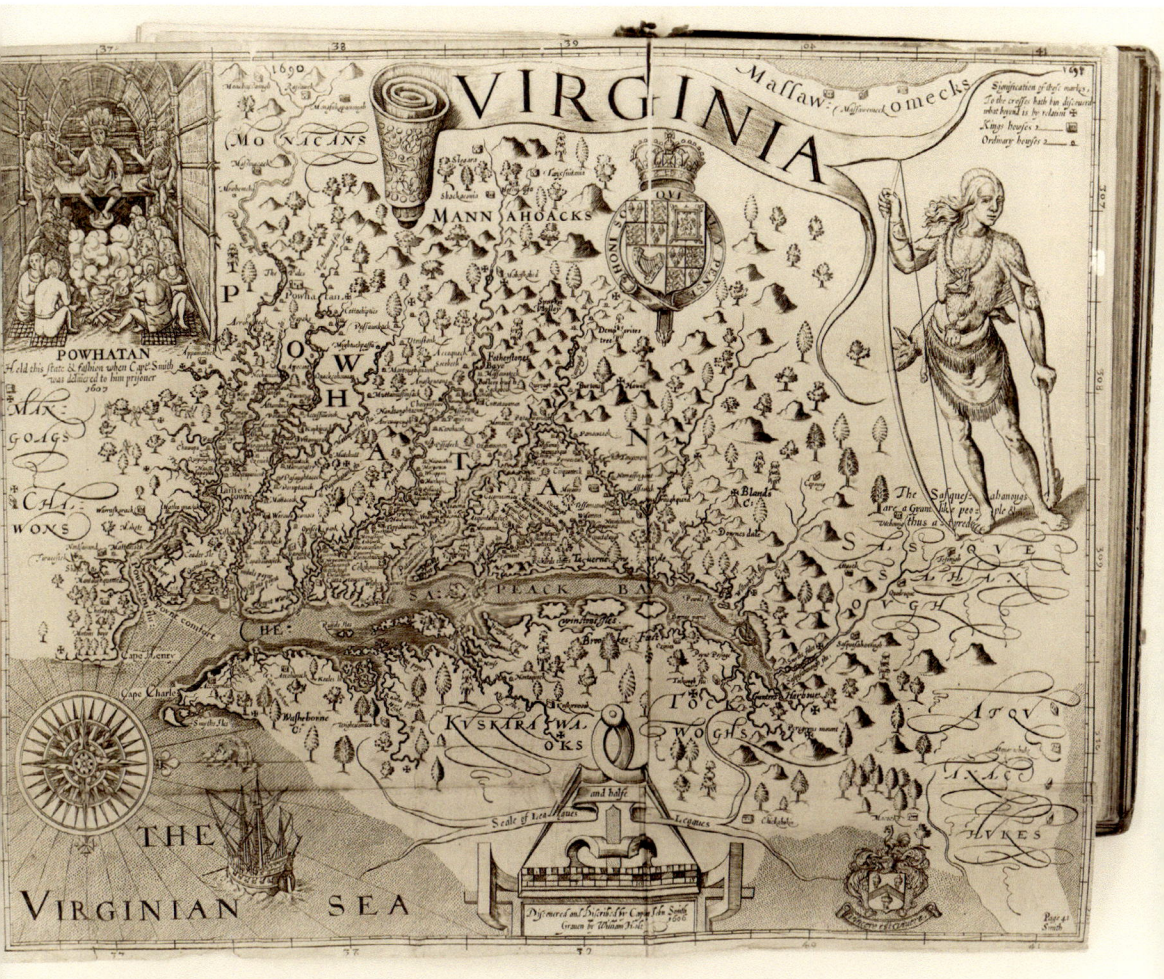

MAP OF THE CHESAPEAKE BAY: Based on a three-month exploratory survey by boat in the summer of 1608 under the direction of Captain John Smith, this map is the earliest published of the entire Chesapeake Bay region. It not only shows the location of Jamestown, the first English settlement in the region, but also the location of Indian villages along the bay and its numerous tributaries. The map is oriented with west at the top, drawing attention to the approaching ships from England at the bottom of the sheet. This engraved version of the Smith map was published in *Virginia, Discovered and Discribed by Captayn John Smith*, sixth state, by William Hole of London, and dates to 1624. *Library of Congress Geography and Map Division.*

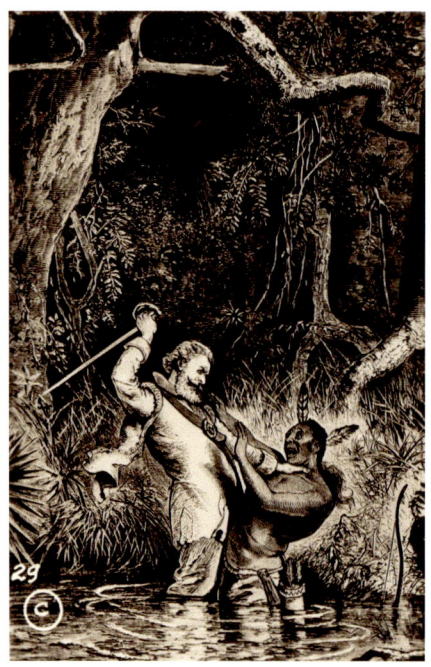

PASPAHEGH INDIANS: This early postcard depicts Captain John Smith's fight with the king of the Paspahegh Indians at Powhatan Creek in 1608. Smith's tenure as president of the colony exposed his less-than-diplomatic approach to governance and relations with the surrounding Powhatan paramount chiefdom, of which the Paspahegh were a tributary. The tribe, which spoke the Algonquian language, formed about 1596 and was among the first to interact with the English newcomers to the Virginia colony, which was in their tribal territory. Unfortunately, due to conflict with the English, as depicted on this early postcard, and exposure to infectious diseases contracted from the settlement, the tribe was eradicated by early 1611 and thereafter disappeared from the historic record.

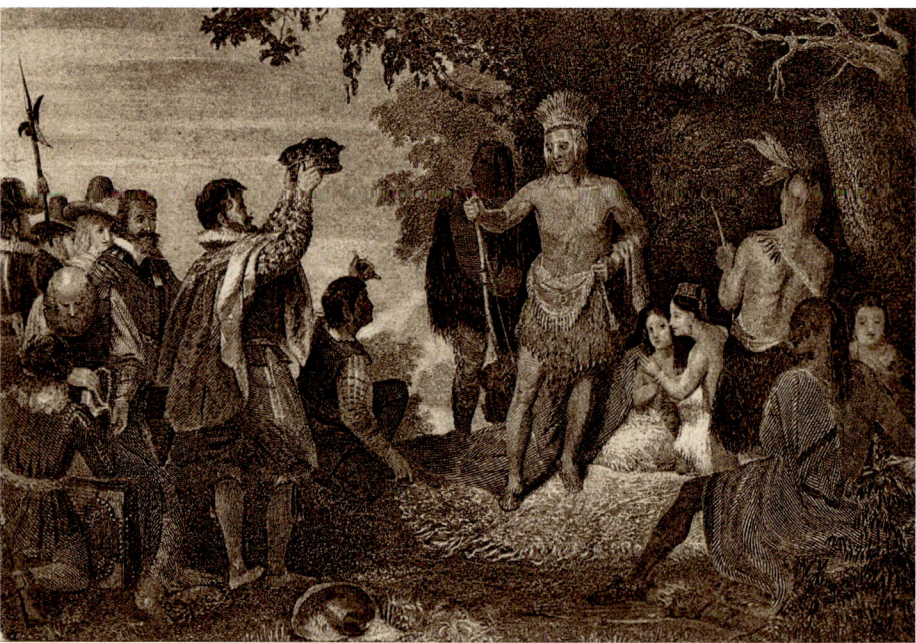

CHIEF POWHATAN: Wahunsenacawh, commonly known as Chief Powhatan of the Powhatan people, was the paramount chief of most of the indigenous tribes in the Chesapeake Bay region in 1607. At its height, his realm known as Tsenacomoco extended across 10,000 square miles from the banks of the James River north to the Potomac River and from the Atlantic Ocean west to the rolling hills of the Piedmont, at the fall line near present-day Richmond. The crowning of Powhatan, at least what historians at that time supposed it to be, is shown on this 1905 postcard but in truth little is known about his life prior to the arrival of the English settlers at Jamestown.

LORD DE LA WARR: Thomas West, third and twelfth baron De La Warr (1576–1618), served as the first governor of Virginia appointed by the Virginia Company of London, arriving at Jamestown in 1610. Though he lived in the colony only a short time, he held the title until his death. De La Warr ran the colony with a firm hand but, importantly, instituted a brutal campaign against the Indians of Tsenacomoco before returning to England due to illness in 1611. The engraving of De La Warr shown here, which names him the third baron De La Warr, appeared in Samuel H. Yonge's *The Site of Old 'James Towne' 1607–1698*, published in 1907. The barony De La Warr (pronounced "Delaware") was created first in 1299 and then again, due to a legal dispute, in 1570. As such, the baron's number depends on a willingness to recognize the second creation, which started its count again at one.

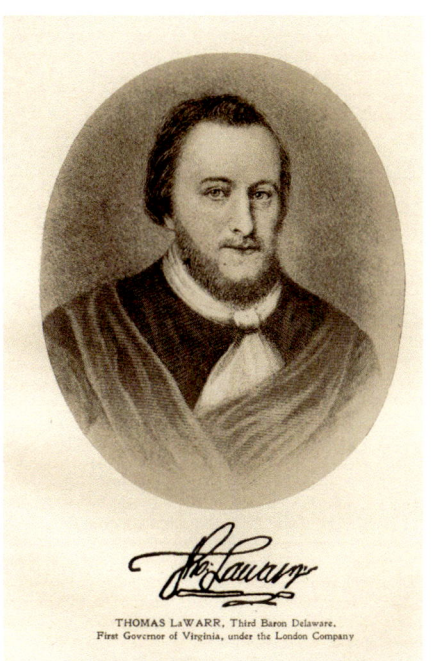

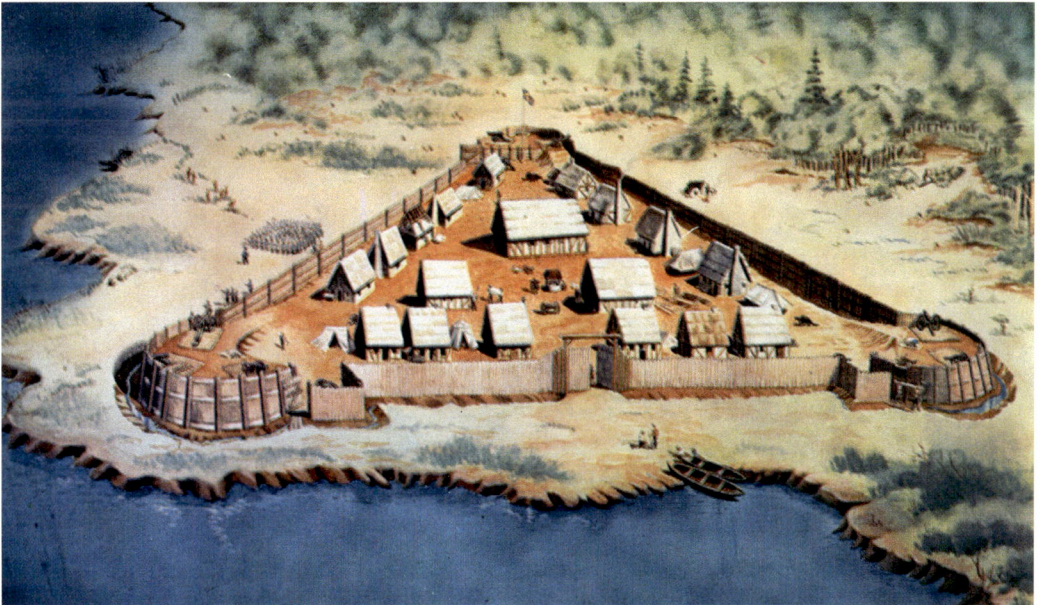

JAMES FORT: William Strachey, who arrived at Jamestown in 1610 and became the recorder for the colony, reported "the fort growing since to more perfection, is now at this present in this manner: …about half an acre…is cast almost into the form of a triangle and so palisaded. The south side next the river (howbeit extended in a line or curtain sixscore foot more in length than the other two, by reason the advantage of the ground doth require) contains 140 yards, the west and east sides a hundred only." Artist Sidney E. King's painting of James Fort is a rendering of what was built for the Jamestown Festival in 1957 and reproduced on a postcard for the event. The replica fortification was erected about a mile from the original location in Jamestown Park.

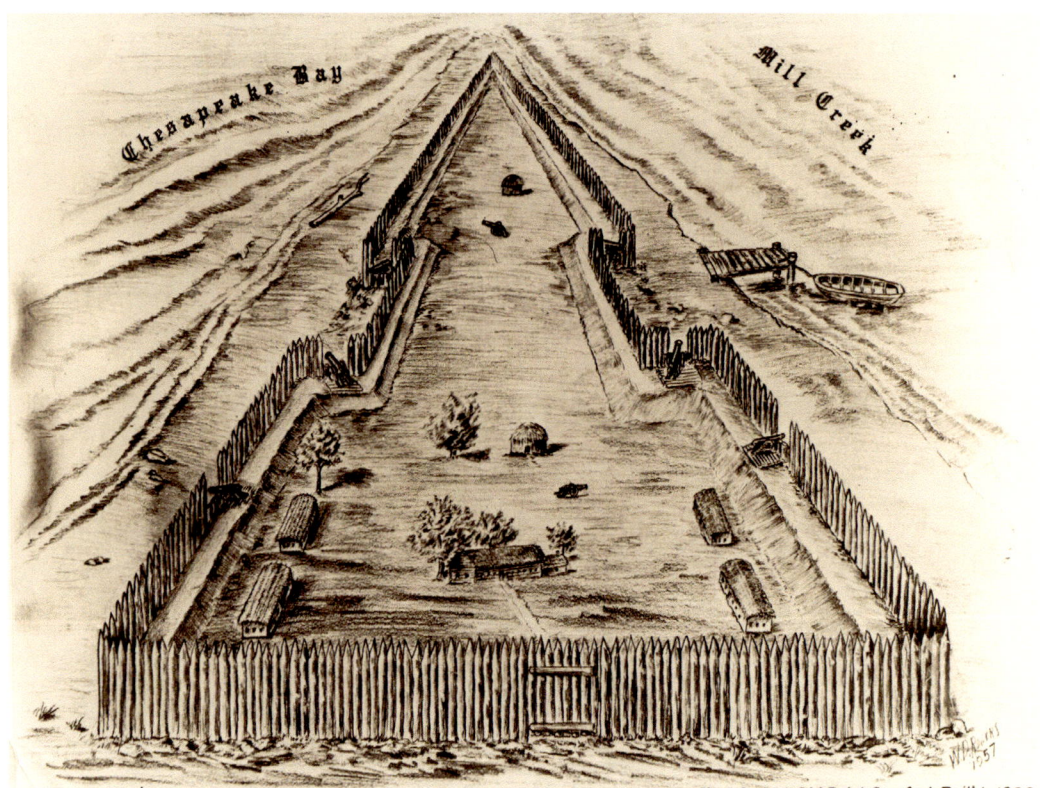

An artist's conception of the probable appearance of Fort Algernourne, the first fort at Old Point Comfort, Built in 1609

FORT ALGERNOURNE: As the presence of English settlers on the banks of the James River became known to raiders of competitor European nations, Captain George Percy, president of the Common Council at Jamestown, ordered Captain John Ratcliffe to Cape Comfort in October of 1609 for the purpose of building a fort, similar in layout to James Fort, but not intended as an outpost to protect a colonial settlement within the fortification. Instead, Fort Algernourne was built to guard English commercial and naval ships passing through Hampton Roads and the colonial towns which eventually dotted the James River. Percy correctly perceived Cape Comfort, as it was called just then, to be a strategic point; one which commanded the channel and served as an excellent observation point. Percy named the new fort Algernourne in honor of his ancestor William de Percy, the first Lord Algernourne and founder of the distinguished line of Earls of Northumberland at the time of the Norman Conquest in 1066. Ratcliffe supervised the fort's construction by a detachment of men from Jamestown. The drawing of the fort shown here was rendered by W. D. Rogers in 1957 and depicts the stockade-type fort built between the Chesapeake Bay and Mill Creek.

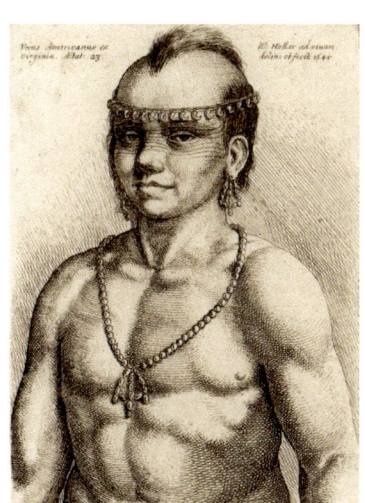

ALGONQUIAN MAN: This engraving of a twenty-three-year-old Virginia Algonquian man by etcher Wenceslaus Hollar (1607–1677) illustrates typical head necklace and ornaments, but also facial markings. The etching was published in 1645. *Library of Congress*.

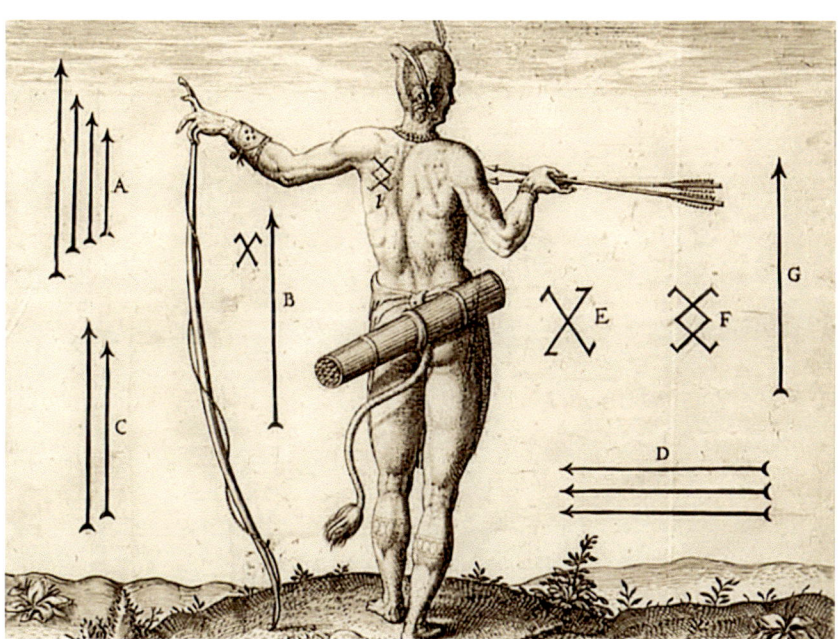

BODY ART: The tribal groups of Virginia, of Algonquian origin, used symbols, particularly body tattoos, to denote affiliations and status within their respective groups. This Theodore de Bry engraving, likely from a John White watercolor (though a White artwork has not been found to match it) is from *Admiranda Narratio fida tamen, de Commodius et Incolarum Ritibus Virginiae*, published in Frankfurt in 1590, with text from Thomas Hariot. The translation of this title is *A Briefe and True Report of the New Found Land of Virginia*. The engraving shown here, titled "The Marckes of sundrye of the Cheif mene of Virginia," was plate number twenty-three. The long title of the book was *A Briefe and True Report of the New Found Land of Virginia: of the Commodities and of the Nature and Manners of the Naturall Inhabitants: Discouered bÿ the English Colonÿ There Seated by Sir Richard Greinuile Knight In the ÿeere 1585 : Which Remained Vnder the Gouernment of Twelue Monethes, At the Speciall Charge and Direction of the Honourable Sir Walter Raleigh Knight Lord Warden of the Stanneries Who therein Hath Beene Fauoured and Authorised bÿ Her Maiestie and Her Letters Patents/This Fore Booke Is Made in English by Thomas Hariot seruant to the Aboue-Named Sir Walter, a Member of the Colonÿ, and There Imploÿed in Discouering. Library of Congress*.

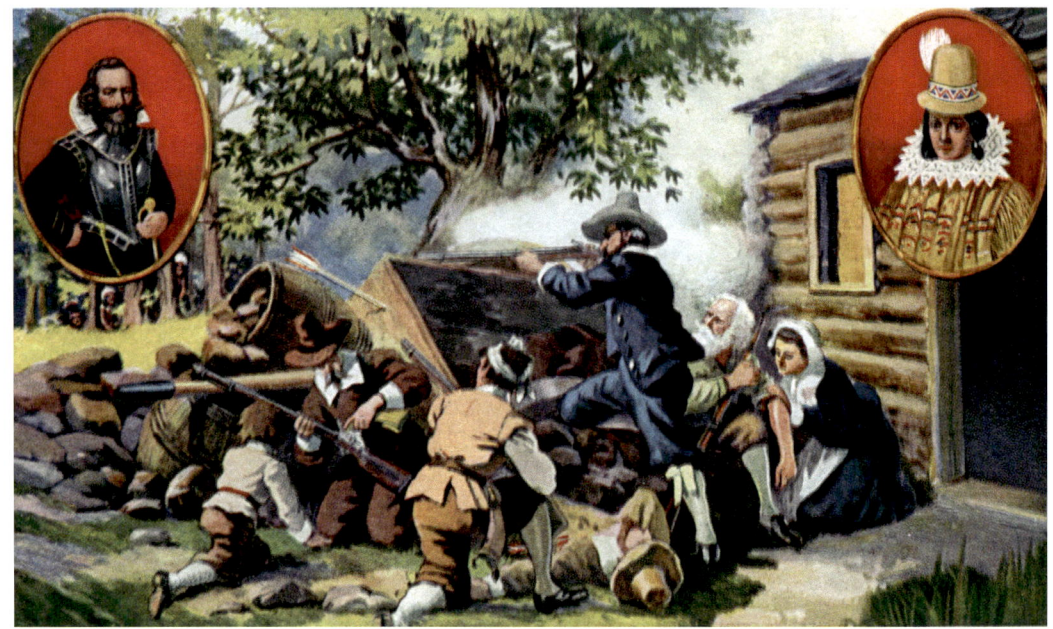

SETTLERS REPELLING AN INDIAN ATTACK: When the hundred or so English settlers sailed into the Chesapeake Bay in the spring of 1607, they encountered one of the most powerful Indian chiefdoms on the Atlantic seaboard. Powhatan, the paramount chief, or mamanatowick, ruled 28 to 32 Algonquian-speaking groups that resided from north of the Rappahannock River to south of the James and west to the fall line. The Indians called their land Tsenacomoco and were intent on defending it from invaders either through diplomacy or war, according to historian Brendan Wolfe's narrative[1] of the First Anglo-Powhatan War. During much of the time between 1609 and 1614 the colonists saw themselves to be, in the words of a 1624 report, "at warre with the natives…" This report was issued just two years after the March 22, 1622 start of the Second Anglo-Powhatan War, which began when Indians under Opechancanough unleashed a series of violent attacks on the colonists. The assault was originally planned for the fall of 1621, to coincide with the redisposition of Powhatan's bones, suggesting that the attack was to be part of the final mortuary celebration for the former chief.

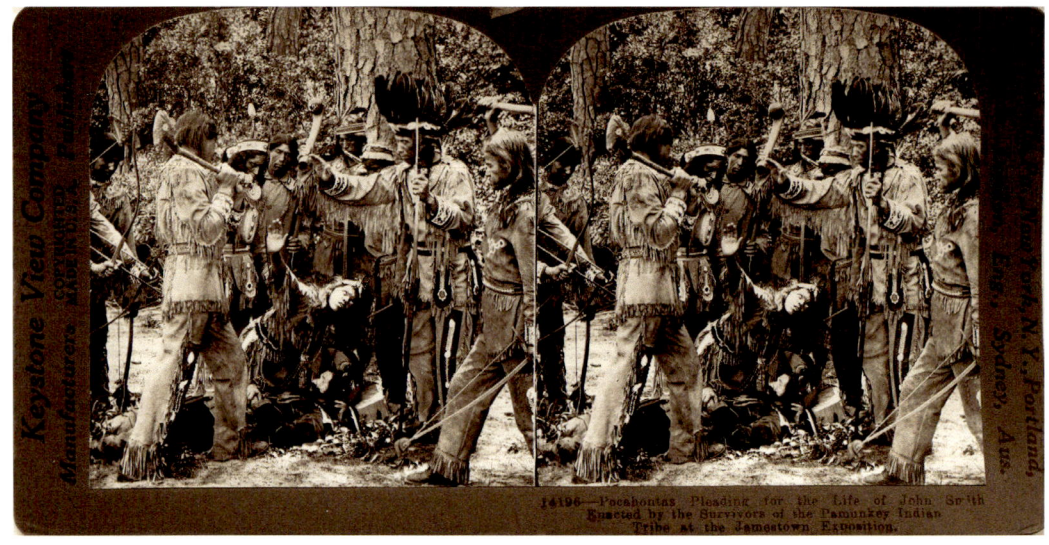

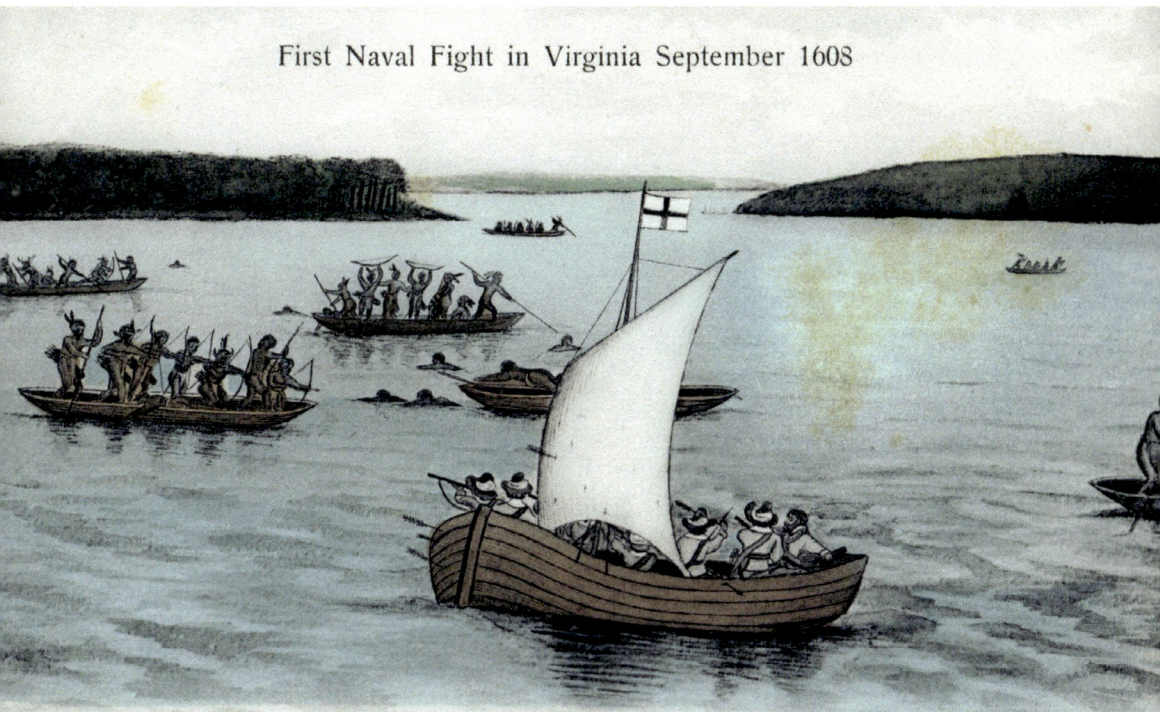

First Naval Fight in Virginia September 1608

Capt. John Smith in open barge of 3 tons burthen, 6 gentlemen including surgeon and 6 soldiers was attacked by eight "canowes" lled with warriors armed with bows and arrows in Nansemond river. Sailing back to the bay, with his muskets he killed or drowned all the Indians save 2 or 3 who swam ashore. He destroyed or captured all "canowes" and he had one wounded".
The Historie of Virginia by Capt. John Smith, Book 3 Chap. 4

FIRST NAVAL FIGHT: Published by William Lamb and Company of Norfolk in 1907, the artwork on this postcard depicts what has been called the first naval fight in Virginia, which took place in September 1608 and involved a barge occupied by Captain John Smith attacked by eight canoes of warriors armed with bows and arrows in the Nansemond River. Smith would later report that he and his six men, including a surgeon, succeeded in repelling the attack, killing Indian attackers by musket or drowning.

OPPOSITE BELOW:

POCAHONTAS SAVES CAPTAIN JOHN SMITH: This scene of Pocahontas pleading for the life of Captain John Smith was reenacted at the Jamestown Exposition, held at Hampton Roads, Virginia, in 1907, by survivors of the Pamunkey Indian tribe. This is view number 98 of the rare 600-view Keystone "Visual Education" book box set. Naval Station Norfolk now occupies the site where the exposition was held to commemorate the tercentenary of the Jamestown settlement.

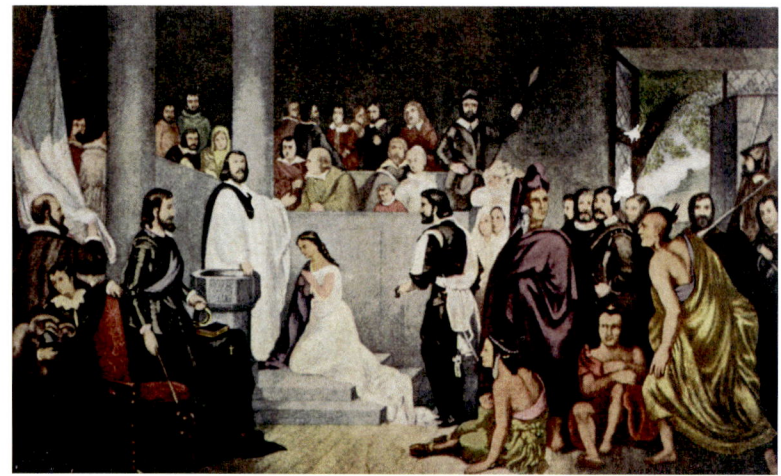

BAPTISM OF POCAHONTAS: John Gadsby Chapman's painting *The Baptism of Pocahontas* was printed by Jamestown Amusement and Vending Company as a souvenir postcard for the Jamestown Exposition held at Hampton Roads (now the site of the Norfolk Naval Station) in 1907. As Powhatan's favorite daughter, she was also leverage to the English who might use her to get more food and other concessions from her powerful father. Such was the case in 1613 when Captain Samuel Argall set a trap to take her prisoner aboard his ship. After her capture, Pocahontas was brought to Jamestown and, eventually, possibly Henrico, a smaller English settlement near present-day Richmond, where she was placed under the tutelage of Reverend Alexander Whitaker, who taught her the English language, religion and customs. During this time she met widower John Rolfe, who became famous for introducing the cash crop tobacco to the settlers of Virginia; they fell in love and wanted to get married. Powhatan agreed to the marriage. In 1613 or 1614, she converted to Christianity, taking the name Rebecca, and in April 1614, she married Rolfe and went by the name "Lady Rebecca Rolfe." *Library of Congress*.

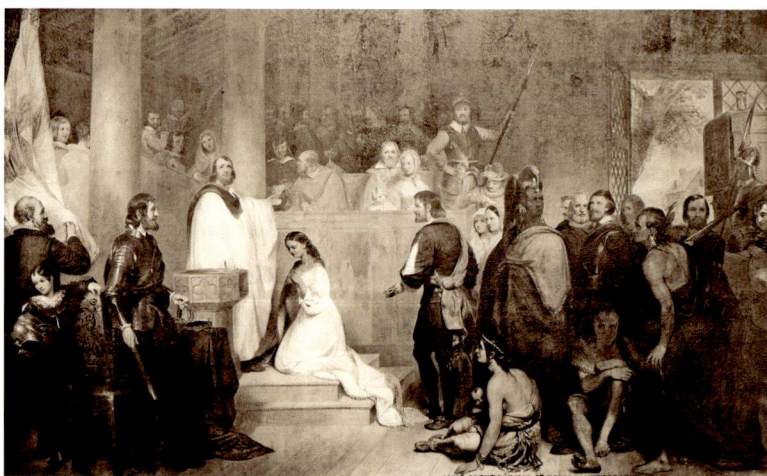

CHAPMAN'S PAINTING: John Chapman was made famous for *The Baptism of Pocahontas*, commissioned by the United States Congress sometime in February 1837, and unveiled on November 30, 1840, in the United States Capitol rotunda. Pocahontas is thought to be the earliest native convert to Christianity in the English colonies; this ceremony and her subsequent marriage to John Rolfe helped to establish peaceful relations between the colonists and the Tidewater tribes. The painting is 12 feet by 18 feet. *Library of Congress*.

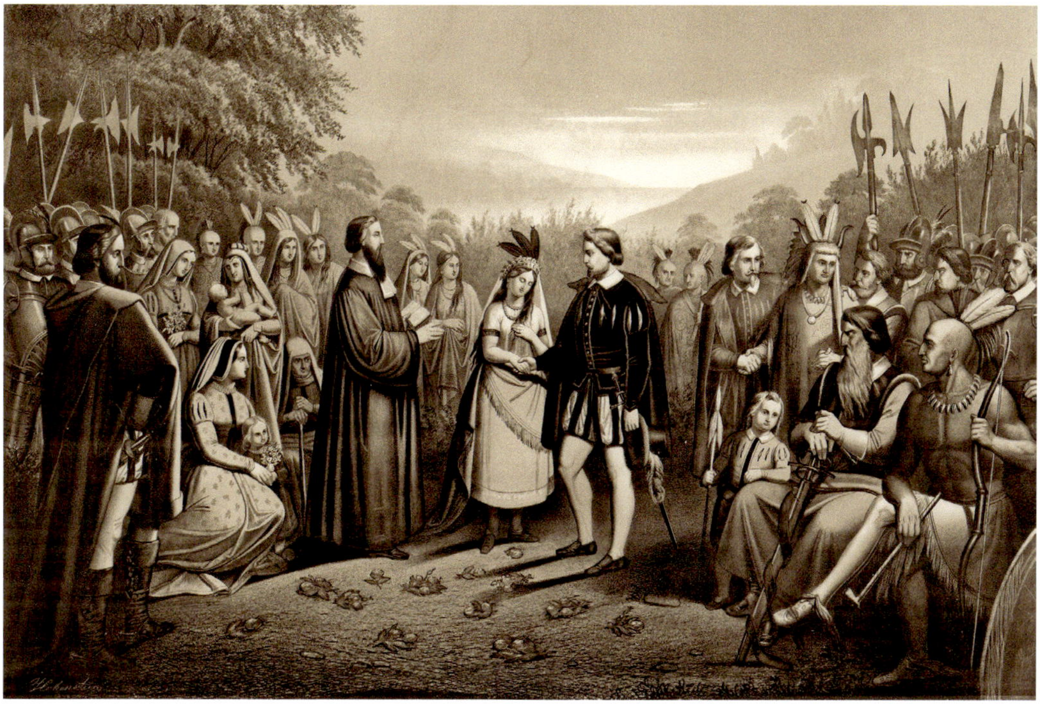

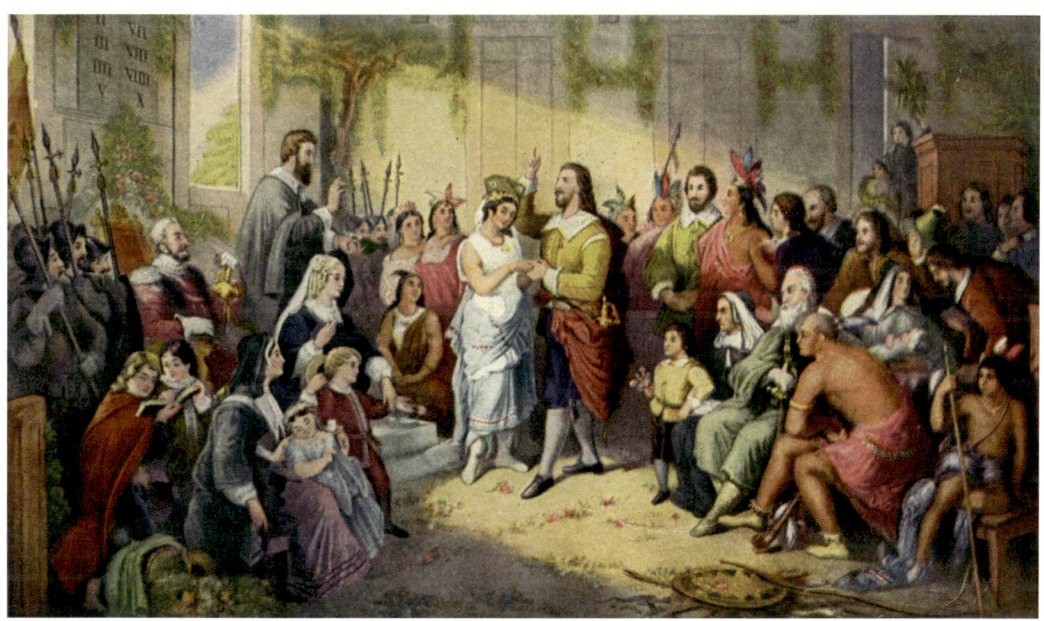

POCAHONTAS MARRIES: The wedding of Pocahontas to John Rolfe is depicted in lithographer George Spohni's 1867 work first published in Philadelphia by Joseph Hoover. *Library of Congress.*

PROMOTING THE LEGEND OF POCAHONTAS: Most depictions of Pocahontas, such as this rendition of her wedding to John Rolfe on an advertising postcard for Prudential Insurance Company of America, and which dates to 1907, were highly romanticized to play up England's great enthusiasm for the daughter of an American "King."

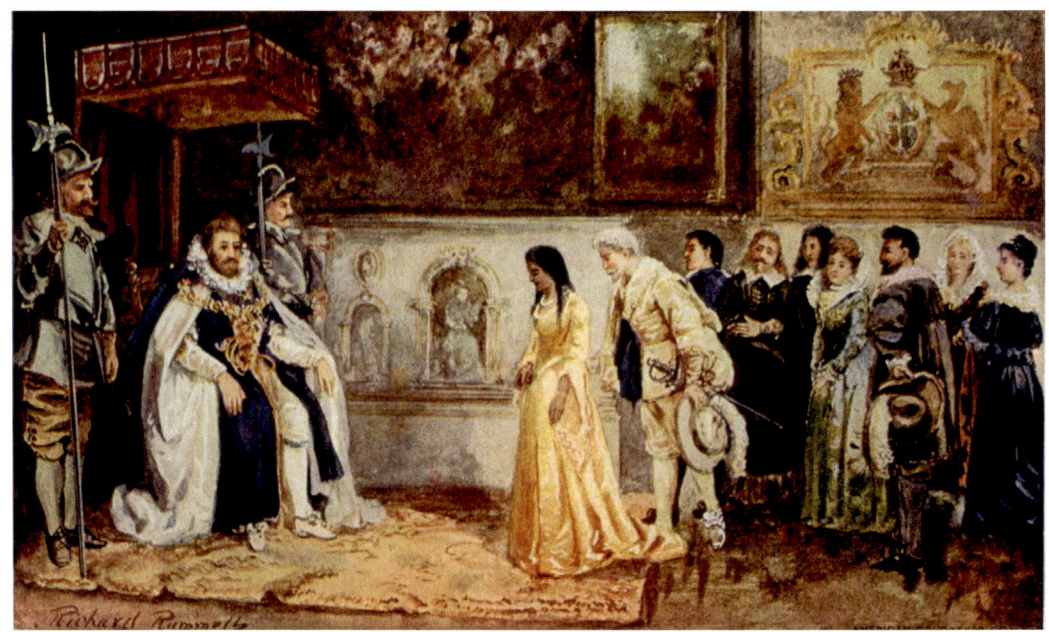

THE ROLFES: The Rolfe family traveled to England in 1616, paid for by the Virginia Company of London. By then Pocahontas was known as Lady Rebecca Rolfe. Though she continued to be attended in her travels by at least a dozen of Powhatan's men and women, they are not shown in this Richard Rummels depiction of her presentation to the court of King James, published on a souvenir postcard for the Jamestown Exposition in 1907. Pocahontas and her entourage would tour England, and she attended a masque where she sat near King James and Queen Anne. *Library of Congress.*

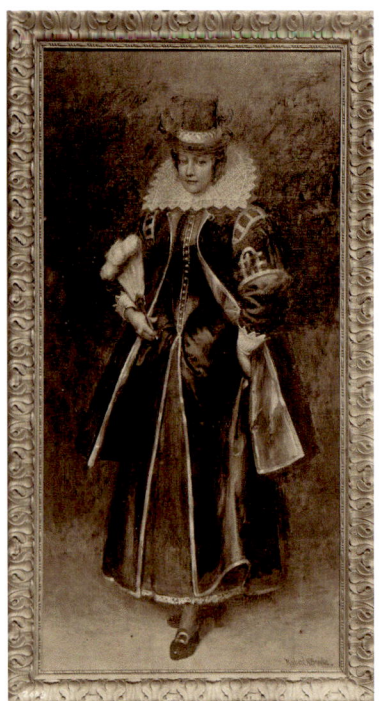

PORTRAIT OF AN INDIAN PRINCESS: This painting titled *Portrait of Pocahontas* by American artist Richard Norris Brooke (1847–1920) is in the Virginia Museum of Fine Arts. The full-length portrait depicts Pocahontas in English court dress. Brooke wrote of the painting that "the court costume of an Indian type is not pleasing" thus he opted to rectify this issue by giving his subject European features, including white skin. The painting was completed in time for display at the Jamestown Exposition held at Hampton Roads starting in 1907; it was photographed (shown here) by Harry C. Mann.

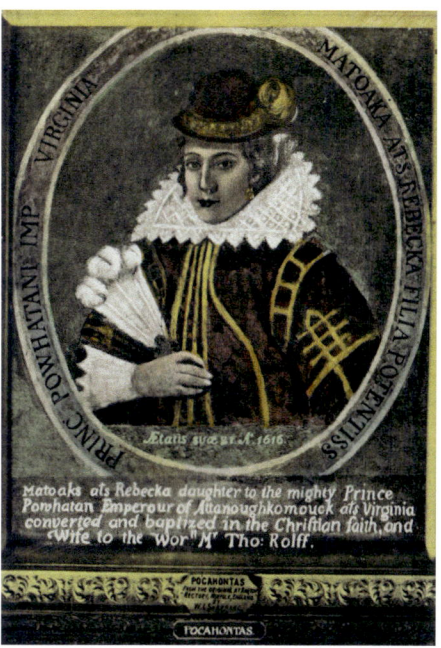

POCAHONTAS DIES IN ENGLAND: The Detroit Publishing Company published this postcard of Pocahontas in 1905, which also shows her in English dress. The Rolfe family, which included son Thomas, settled in Brentford. In March 1617 just as she and her family were to return to Virginia, Pocahontas fell ill; she never made it past the Thames River. Taken ashore at Gravesend, she died and was buried there at Saint George's Church on March 21; she was about 21 years old.

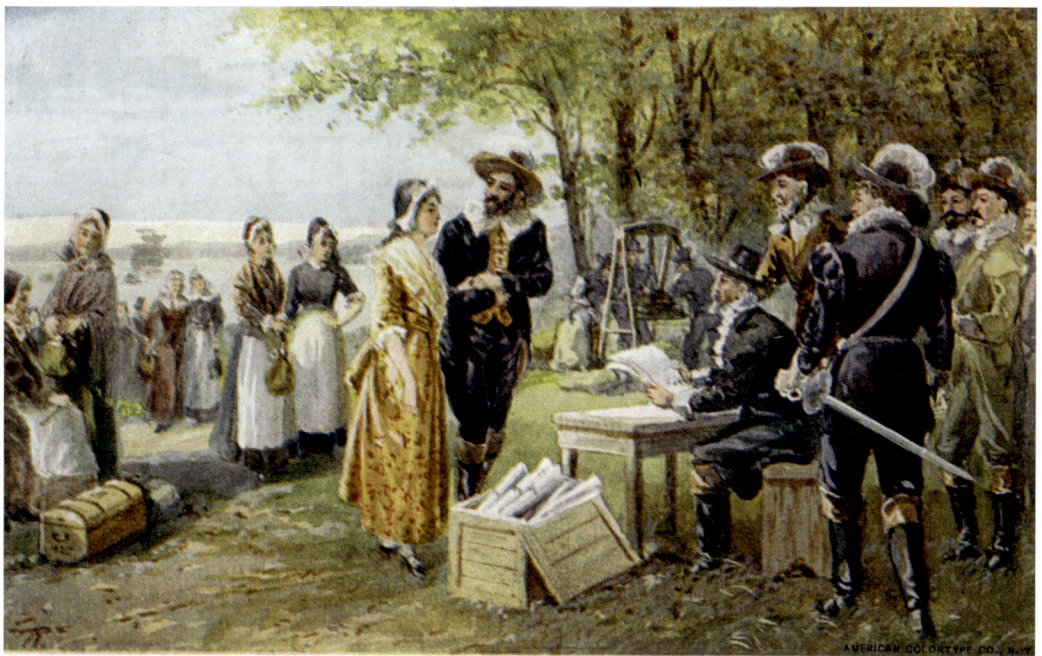

JAMESTOWN WOMEN: The *Landing of the Maidens* was printed by Jamestown Amusement and Vending Company as a souvenir postcard depicting a greatly romanticized portrait of the arrival of this group of ninety young women to the colony in 1619. When the colony was first established there was an initial lack of women, perhaps because their presence was not yet necessary. The first priority of the Virginia Company of London was to build an outpost, explore the territory and determine the best use of Virginia's resources to turn a profit. Women would eventually foster the stability that played a significant role in Jamestown's survival and, ultimately, its success.

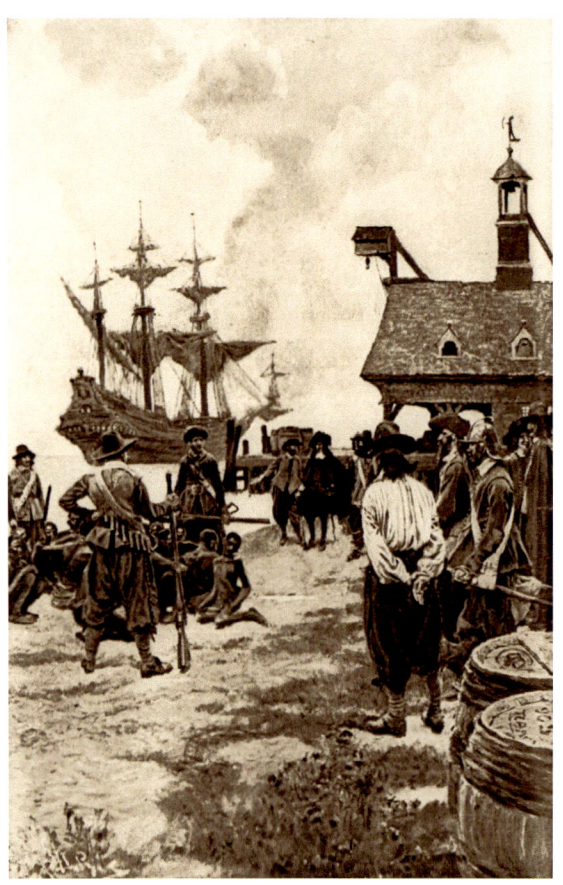

AFRICANS IN THE COLONY (LEFT): The first documented arrival of Africans to the colony of Virginia was recorded by John Rolfe: "About the latter end of August, a Dutch man of Warr of the burden of a 160 tunes arrived at Point-Comfort, the Comandors name Capt[ain John] Jope, his Pilott for the West Indies one Mr. Marmaduke an Englishman. ... He brought not any thing but 20 and odd Negroes, w[hich] the Governo[r] and Cape Merchant bought for victuall[s]. The year was 1619, and as an institution slavery did not yet exist in Virginia. This depiction of the landing of black slaves at Jamestown from a Dutch man-o-war in 1619 first appeared in the January 1901 *Harper's Monthly Magazine*. *Library of Congress.*

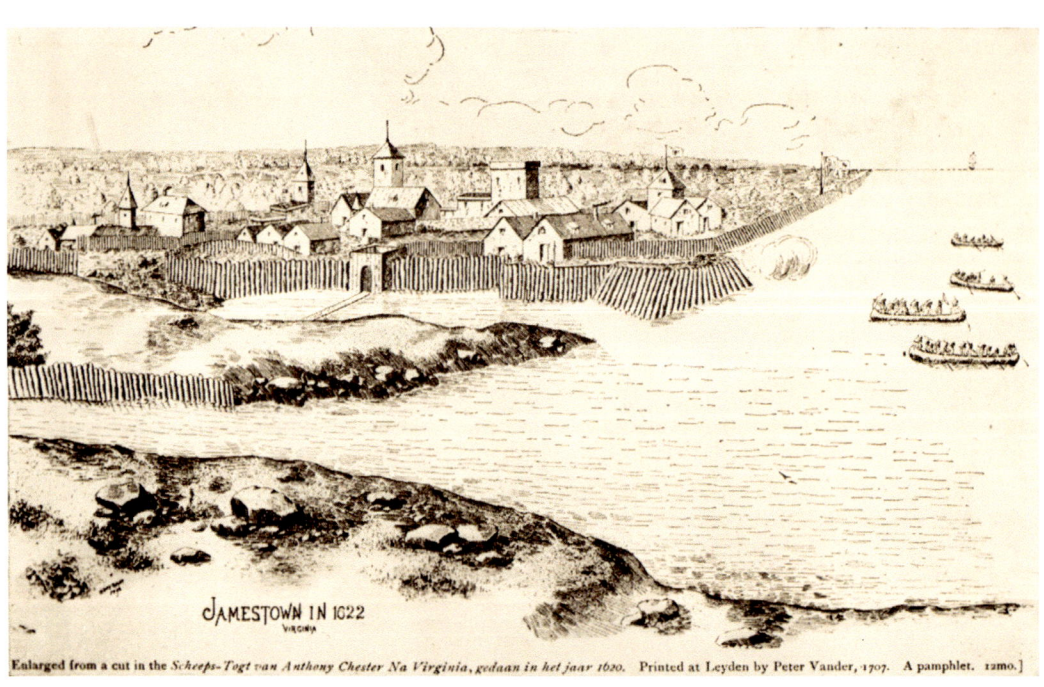

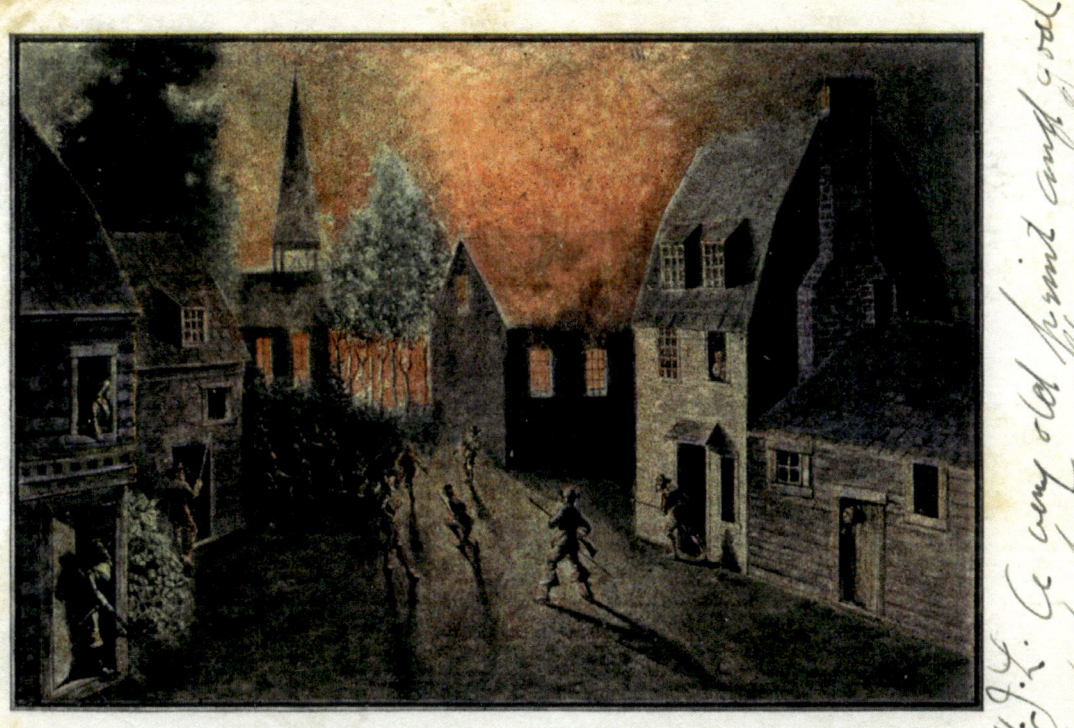

The Burning of Jamestown, Virginia, 1675.

VIRGINIA'S REBELLION: Bacon's Rebellion was probably one of the most confusing yet intriguing chapters in Jamestown's history. For many years, according to National Park Service's official record, historians considered the Virginia Rebellion of 1676 to be the first stirring of revolutionary sentiment in America, which culminated in the American Revolution almost exactly one hundred years later; however, in the past few decades, based on findings from a more distant viewpoint, historians have come to understand Bacon's Rebellion as a power struggle between two stubborn, selfish leaders—Governor Sir William Berkeley and his antagonist and cousin by marriage, Nathaniel Bacon Jr.—rather than a glorious fight against tyranny. In the power struggle that ensued, Bacon burned Jamestown to the ground on September 19, 1676 (depicted on this early postcard), and on October 26, a little over a month later, Bacon died of "Bloody Flux" and "Lousey Disease" (body lice); his body, never found, was probably burned by his men. Shortly after Bacon's death, Berkeley regained complete control and hanged the major leaders of the rebellion.

OPPOSITE BELOW:

JAMESTOWN 1622: This is a sketch of Jamestown, Virginia, in 1622 from the log of the *Margaret and John*, Anthony Chester, captain, a vessel that came to the colony in the years 1620, 1621 and 1622, and also in 1623 where it was in distress and remained for some time, and was last anchored off the island again in 1626 and 1627. Chester's log sketch was reproduced on an early divided-back postcard.

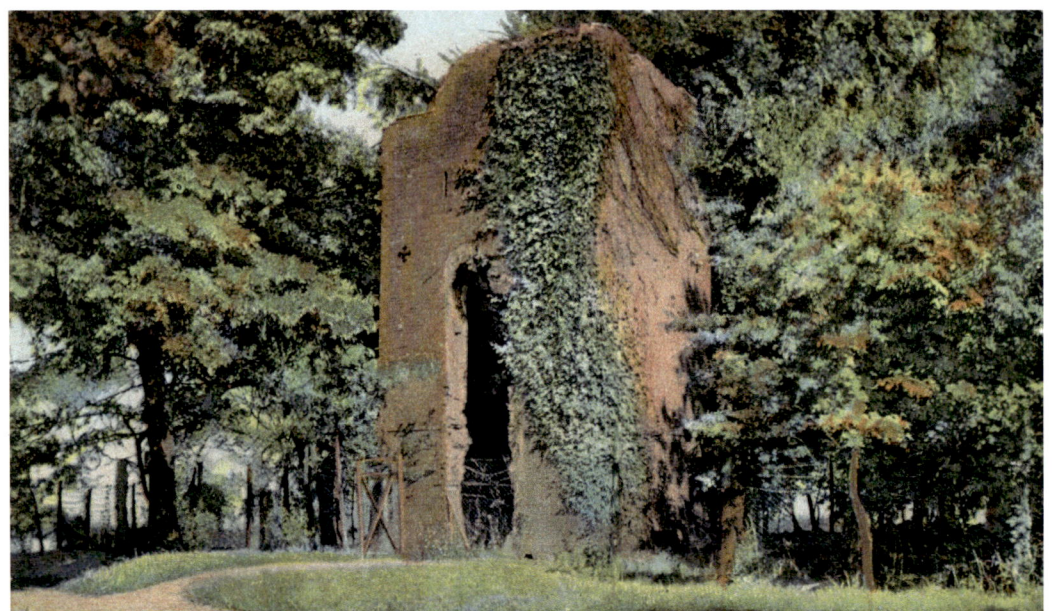

THE BRICK CHURCH (ABOVE): Governor John Harvey reported in January 1639 that he, the Council, the ablest planters, and some sea captains "had contributed to the building of a brick church" at Jamestown to replace the second that had been built there between 1617 and 1619. This fourth church, the ruins and exposed foundations of which are shown on this early postcard (along with remnants of the fifth church that followed it), was slightly larger than the third church and built around it. It was still unfinished in November 1647 when efforts were made to complete it. After it was finished the church tower was added. The tower, documented by Preservation Virginia, is the only seventeenth-century building still standing at Jamestown and it is one of the oldest English-built structures in the United States.

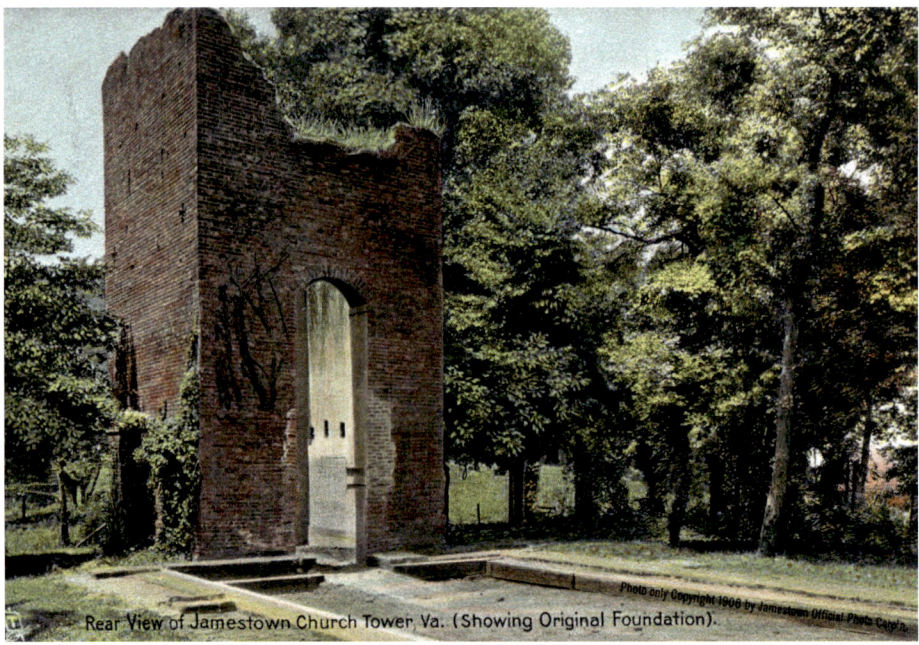

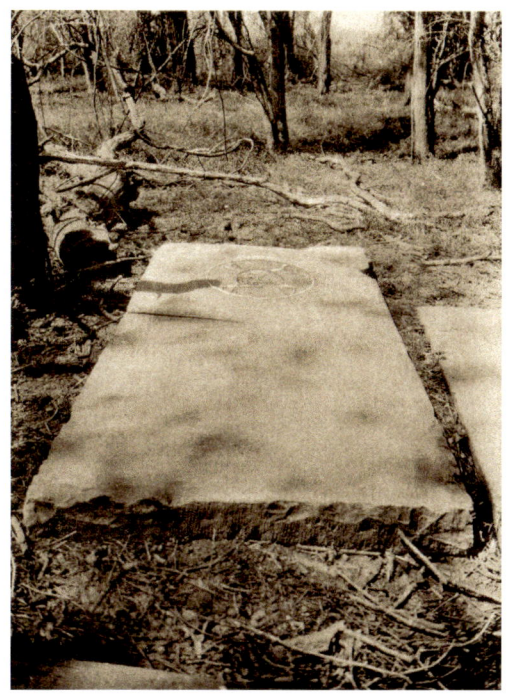

NO PIRATES HERE: The Travis family graveyard is located about 1.5 miles east of the settlement and situated roughly 3.2 miles from the start of Island Loop Road; three tombstones mark seven known and several unknown burials at the site. This prominent family was part of the Jamestown story for two centuries and many of their dead lie buried here. It is of record that Edward Travis II, in 1663, obtained 326 acres in this vicinity near his "dwelling house." Travis' holdings gradually increased until the 1700s; by then, he owned more than half of the entire island. In a grove of trees toward the east end of the island is this private burial ground. Most of the Travis family were buried here between 1700 and 1759. Only two legible tombstones remain. The first is carved with a skull and cross bones, and reads: *Here lyeth (in hopes of a glorious Resurrection) the body of JOHN CHAMPION who was borne the 10th day of November in the yeare of our Lord 1660 and departed this life the 16th day of December in the year of our Lord 1700. And likewise JOHN CHAMPION the son of John Champion who was borne the 11th day of Decr. in the yeare of our Lord 1695 and departed this life the 11th day of September in the yeare of our Lord 1700.* Contrary to the notation on this early postcard, there's no truth to a commonly held myth that skulls on memorials and headstones marked the grave of a pirate. Skulls are a *memento mori*, a reminder of our own mortality, also called an *aide-mémoire*.

OPPOSITE BELOW:

CHURCH TOWER: The fourth church burned during Bacon's Rebellion on September 19, 1676. Ten years later a fifth church was functioning, likely using the walls and foundations of the fourth church. The tower was undamaged and intact. This church was used until the 1750s when it was abandoned in favor of a new church built about three miles from Jamestown. Although the tower remained intact, the remaining structure fell into ruins by the 1790s, when the bricks were repurposed to build the present graveyard wall. The ravages of time and the elements took what remained of the church, with the exception of most of its tower, which still stands today. What remained of the church property was preserved after the Association for the Preservation of Virginia Antiquities (APVA), now called Preservation Virginia, acquired 22.5 acres in 1893. The National Park Service acquired the remaining 1,500 acres in 1934. The ruins of the church are shown on this pre-1907 postcard.

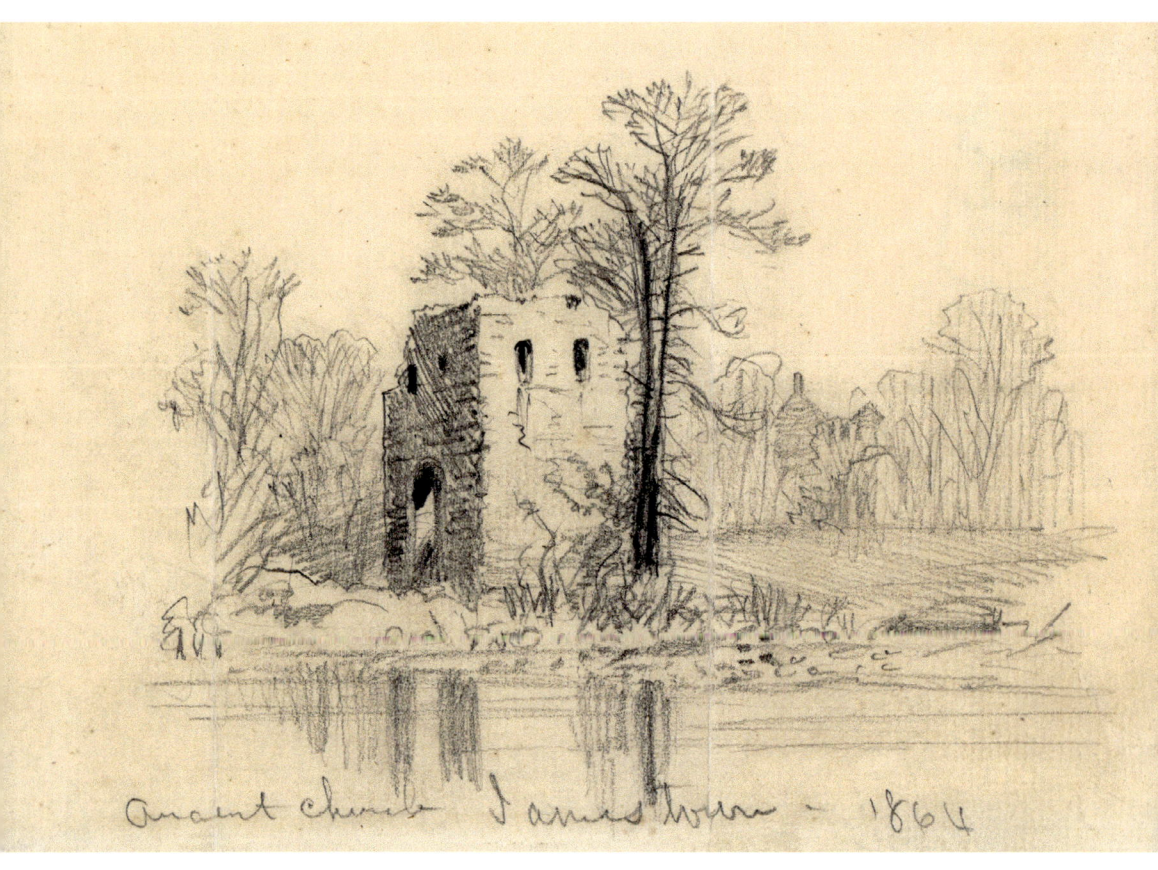

CIVIL WAR SKETCH: Alfred Rudolph Waud, the artist who documented much of the American Civil War for *Harper's Weekly*, among other publications, drew this picture of the Jamestown church ruins in 1864. *Library of Congress.*

1   Wolfe, Brendan. "First Anglo-Powhatan War (1609–1614)," *Encyclopedia Virginia*. Virginia Foundation for the Humanities, 24 June 2014. http://www.encyclopediavirginia.org/First_Anglo-Powhatan_War_1609-1614

Section 2
Jamestown Rediscovered

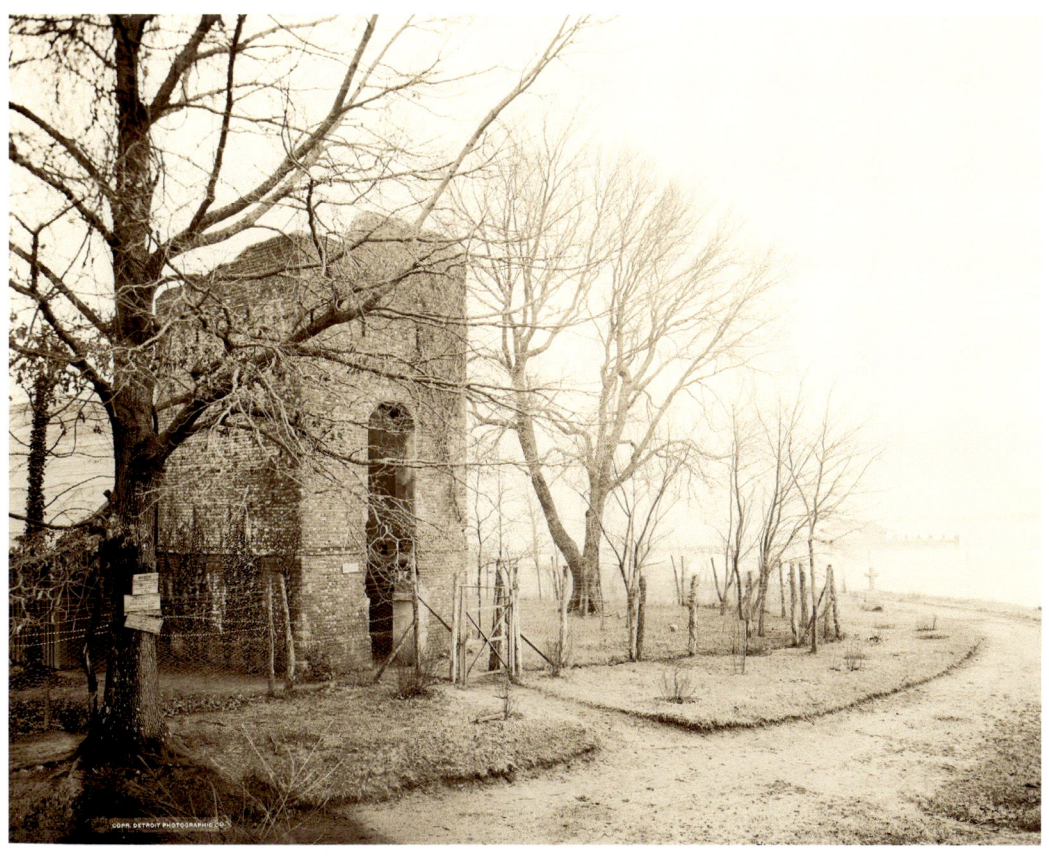

REMAINS ON THE JAMES: William Henry Jackson also took this photograph of the ruins of the fourth church tower looking toward the James River. The granite cross erected by the General Convention of Protestant Episcopal Church to Jamestown on October 15, 1898, is visible to the right. *Library of Congress.*

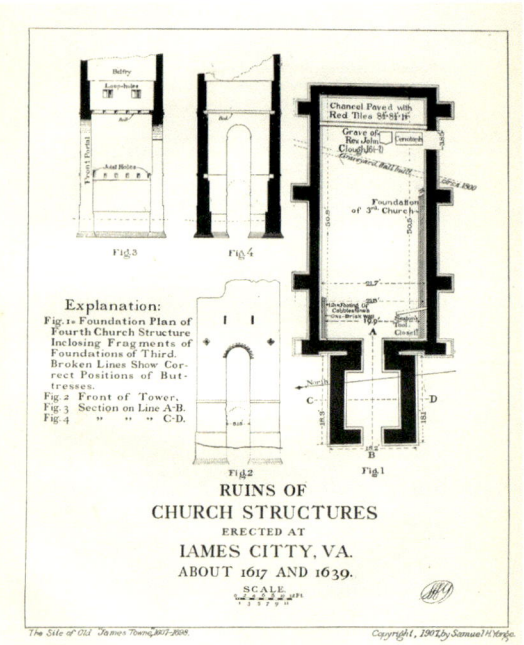

YONGE'S DRAWING: "As the same site was used for the three church buildings erected after 1617," wrote Samuel H. Yonge, in his tercentenary edition of *The Site of Old 'James Towne' 1607–1698* and from which this drawing first appeared, "the churchyard, which was by custom the principal burial ground, most probably never changed, and was probably used even before that year. The finding of a human skeleton, while excavating the foundations, crossed by a wall of the brick church near its southeastern corner, shows that there was a burial ground at its site before the first brick church was built (1639–1647), and possibly even before the building of the timber church about 1618, which covered almost all of the ground occupied by its successor."

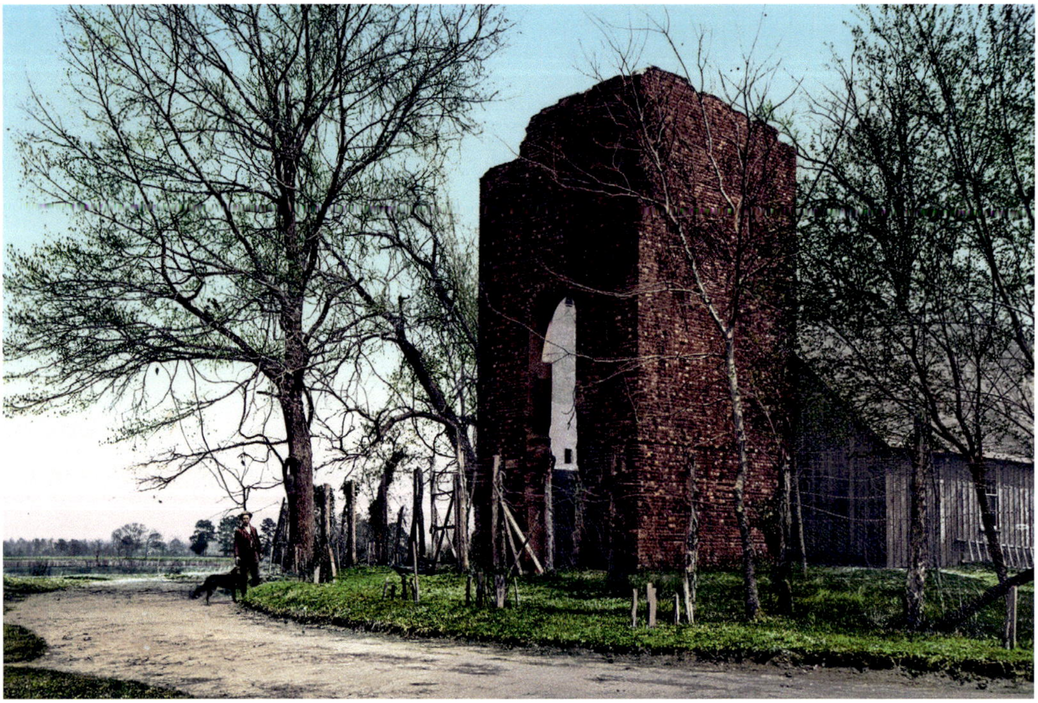

PRESERVATION BEGINS: Before the National Society of Colonial Dames of America added a brick church structure to the ruins of the fourth church tower and outside foundations of prior iterations of the church on the site, it looked like this: a wooden structure stood behind the ruins, fenced off and posted by the Association for the Preservation of Virginia Antiquities. This photochrom was published by the Detroit Photographic Company in 1902 from a William Henry Jackson photograph. *Library of Congress*.

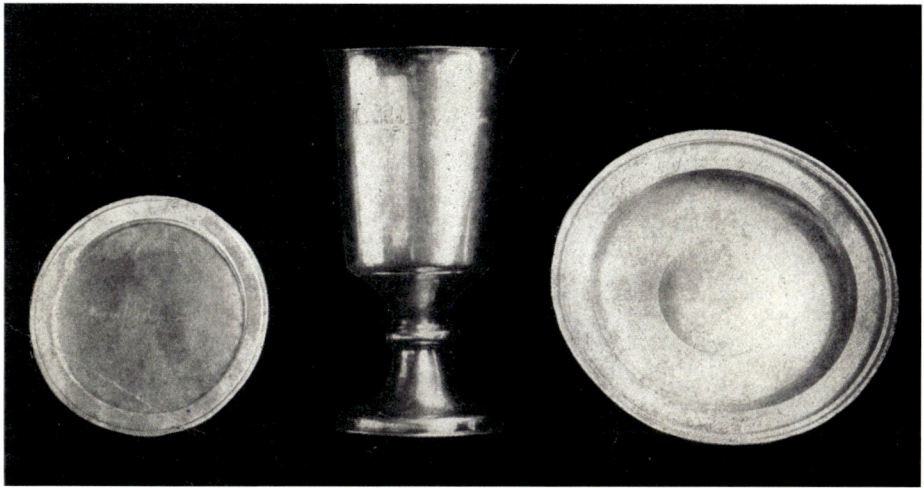

HOLY SERVICE: The Jamestown communion service (shown here) was in the possession of Williamsburg's Bruton Parish Church when the picture was taken in 1906. An inscription on the chalice (center) reads: "Mixe not holy thinges with profane." The chalice also bears the date 1661. The communion service was used by Bruton Parish Church after colonists abandoned Jamestown until such a time that it was placed in curatorial care.

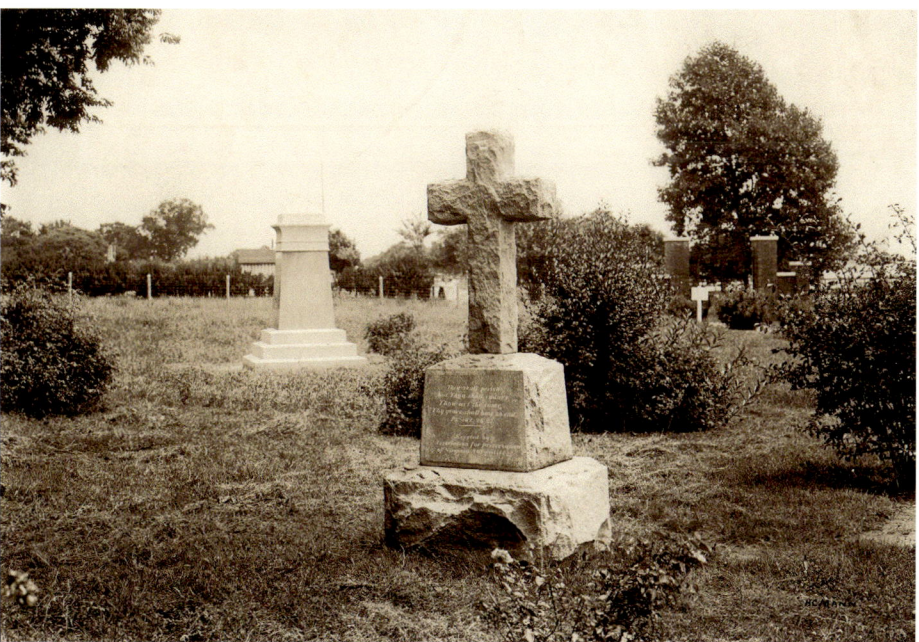

SACRED VISIT: The Pious Pilgrimage Monument commemorates the October 15, 1898 visit of 300 Episcopal bishops and clergymen from a Washington, D.C. convention to the then deserted and desolate Jamestown Island. The monument was photographed by Harry C. Mann circa 1909 as part of a series of historic pictures he took of Virginia's most significant historic sites. The monument base contains lines of scripture from Psalm 102, lines 26 and 27: "They shall perish/ but Thou shalt endure; /Thou art the same/ Thy years shall have no end." Below these lines, it reads "Association for the Preservation of Virginia Antiquities."

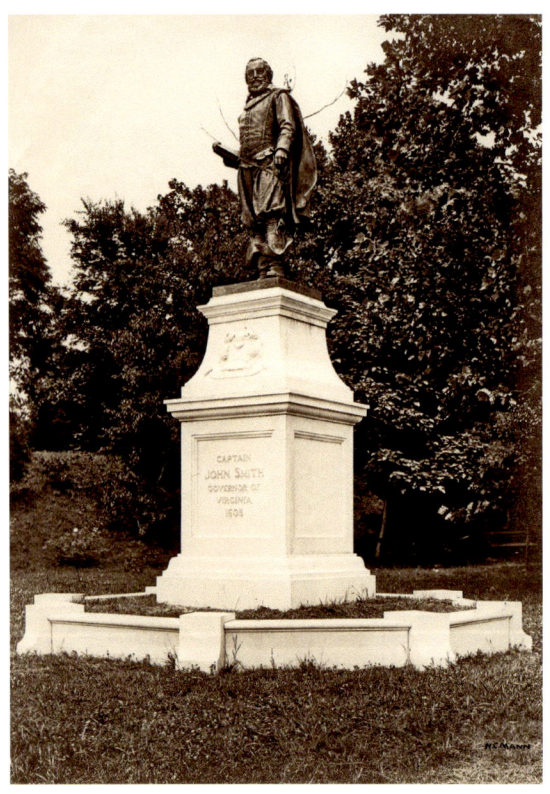

TO LIVE IS TO CONQUER: According to Jamestown Rediscovery, Norfolk native William Couper designed the heroic portrayal of Captain John Smith, who served as leader of the colony for a year but inspired enough envy that he both entered and left the Virginia colony under arrest. With a granite base, the statue measures 20 feet tall. The inscription on the base reads: "John Smith, Governor of Virginia, 1608" and features Smith's adopted coat of arms and motto, *vincere est vivere* ("to live is to conquer"). The statue was a gift from Joseph Bryan and his wife, Isobel Lamont Stewart Bryan, early supporters of the Association for the Preservation of Virginia Antiquities (now Preservation Virginia). The statue was unveiled May 13, 1909, by Joseph Bryan III, grandson of original donor. Harry C. Mann took this picture shortly after the statue's unveiling.

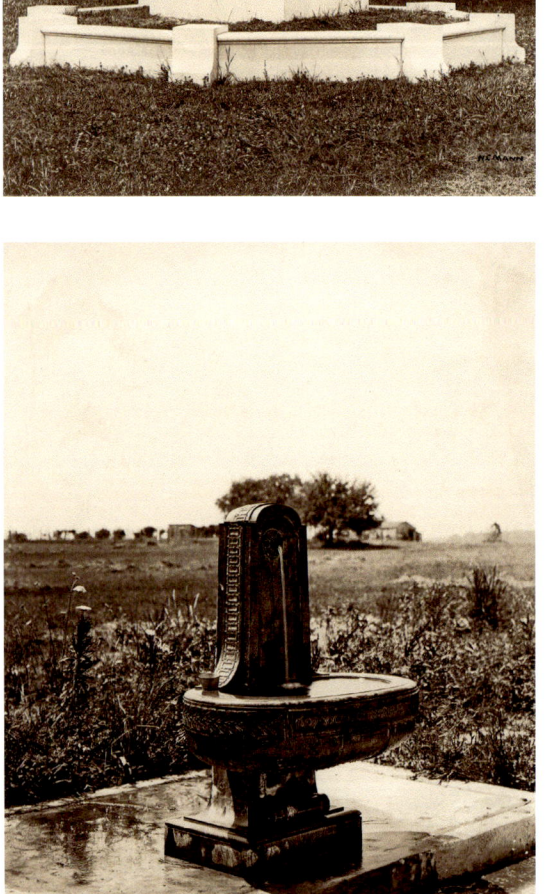

THE HORSE TROUGH: In 1907, as part of the 300th anniversary of Jamestown, the first permanent English settlement in America, the General Society commissioned prominent architect Harold Van Buren Magonigle to design a bronze horse trough for Jamestown. For the 1907 tricentennial, visitors to Jamestown came by steamboat or horse, and the horse trough provided needed water for horses. The horse trough is prominently inscribed "1607 SOCIETY OF COLONIAL WARS 1907" across the front of its bowl. By the time the 400th anniversary of Jamestown occurred, the horse trough was badly in need of restoration, and it was desirable to relocate it to a more prominent location. The restoration and relocation were completed in June 2009. The restored horse trough presently sits just outside the Yeardley House offices of the Jamestown Rediscovery Project, next to a path to the new Archaearium. It is no longer connected to a water supply due to archaeological restrictions and conservation concerns, but remains a handsome historical monument. Harry C. Mann took this picture of the trough in 1909 while it remained in its original location.

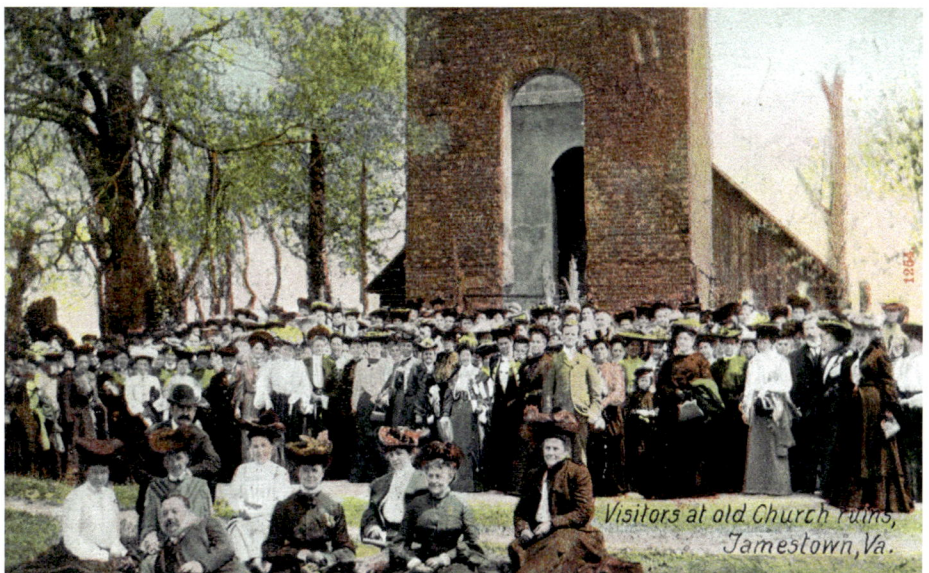

THE COLONIAL DAMES: The National Society of Colonial Dames of America were photographed in front of the ruins of the fourth church tower prior to completion of the brick memorial church in 1906. This early rare view of this visitation was published as a postcard. The Society erected a memorial church building next to the fourth church tower and just outside the foundations of the earlier churches; it was dedicated on May 13, 1907. This is the structure that visitors to Jamestown view today. The cobblestone foundations of the 1617 (third) church, together with the brick foundations of the 1639 (fourth) church, may be viewed under glass within the walls of the present church.

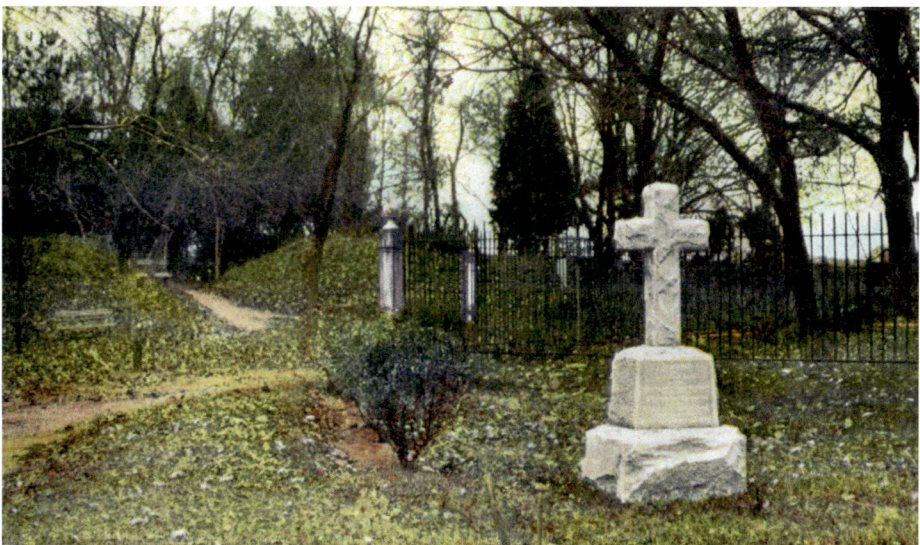

FAITH AND FORTS: The vine covered arbor shown on this early divided back postcard marked the entrance to colonial and Confederate period fortifications at Jamestown. The granite memorial cross in the foreground was erected in memory of the visit of the General Convention of Protestant Episcopal Church to Jamestown on October 15, 1898. The bishops and deputies in attendance traveled from all over the United States to be present for the event.

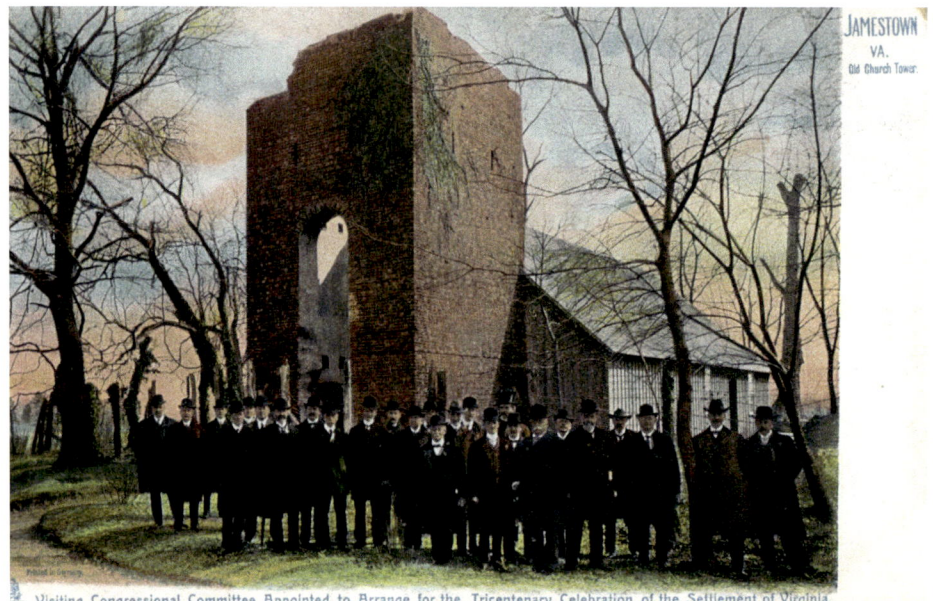

PLANNING THE TERCENTENARY: A congressional committee appointed by President Theodore Roosevelt's administration was sent to Jamestown ahead of the planned 1907 tercentenary celebration of the first English settlement in the New World. At Jamestown, special dedicatory ceremonies were subsequently held marking the National Society of the Colonial Dames of America's donation of the newly finished Jamestown Memorial Church to the Association for the Preservation of Virginia Antiquities as well as the completion of the Tercentenary Monument, erected by the government. The picture was taken by Harry C. Mann.

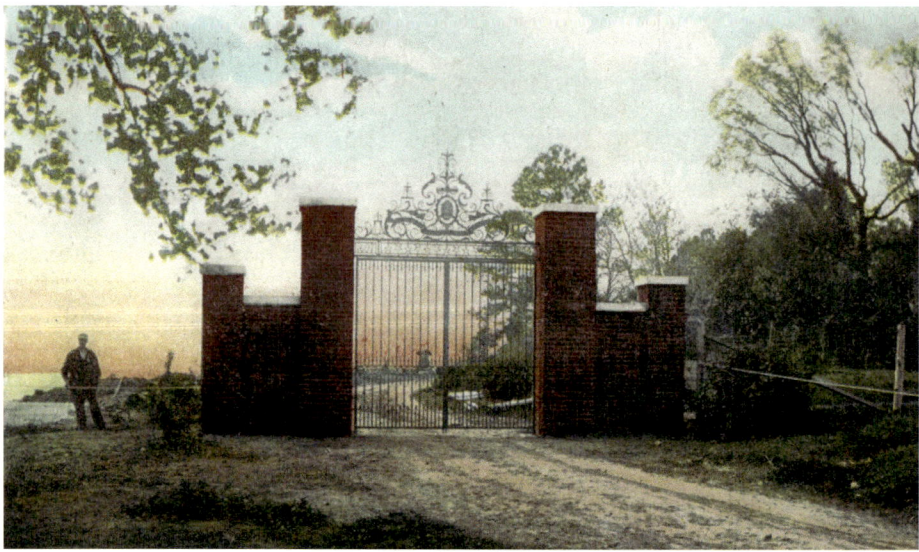

JAMESTOWN ENTRANCE: Colonial gates to the eastern entrance of the Association for the Preservation of Virginia Antiquities' (APVA) grounds at Jamestown, shown on this period postcard, were presented on May 9, 1907, by the National Society of Colonial Dames of America to the association and restored in the twenty-first century by Colonial Dames Chapter XXIII-Virginia.

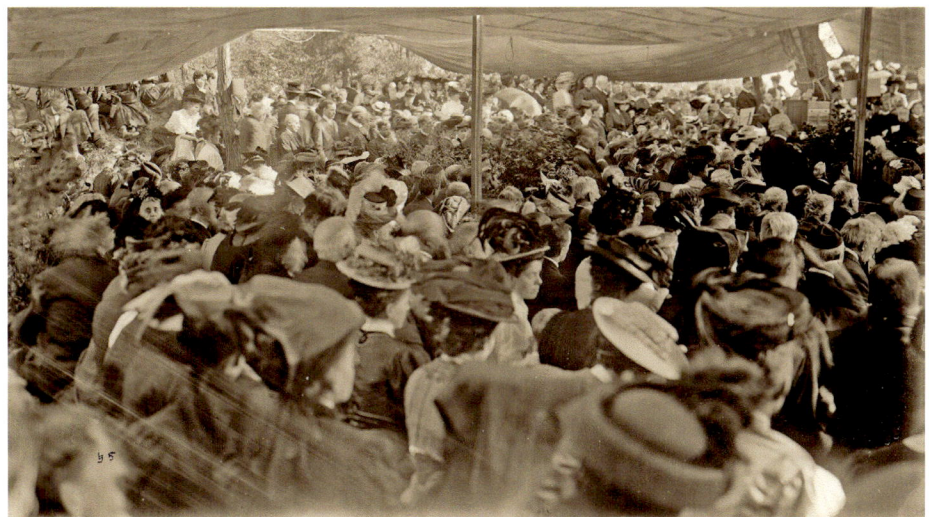

CEREMONIES ON THE ISLAND: This Harris and Ewing photograph was taken at Jamestown during tercentenary ceremonies held on the island to dedicate the General Assembly Monument on July 31, 1907. The James River is barely visible in the background. Most of the crowd is dressed for warm weather and those closest the speaker and musicians are protected from the sun by a large tarp. The monument was a gift of the Norfolk chapter of APVA. *Library of Congress.*

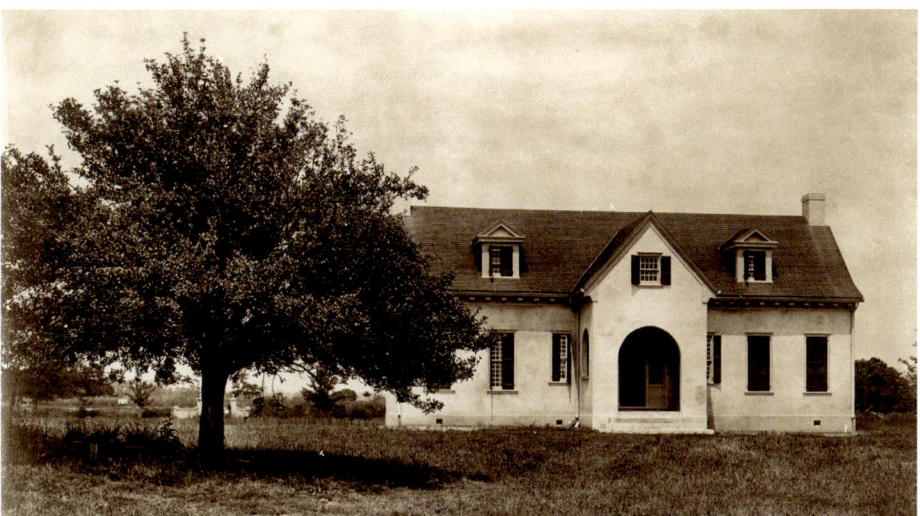

YEARDLEY HOUSE: The house shown in this Harry C. Mann photograph was built as a director's residence in 1907 and given to the Association for the Preservation of Virginia Antiquities (APVA) by the National Society Daughters of the American Revolution (NSDAR); it is named for Sir George Yeardley, remembered best as a prominent plantation owner and three time colonial governor of the British Colony of Virginia. A survivor of the Virginia Company of London's ill-fated Third Supply Mission, and whose flagship *Sea Venture* was shipwrecked on Bermuda for 10 months between 1609 and 1610, he remains a significant figure also for presiding over the initial session of the first representative legislative body in Virginia in 1619. With representatives from throughout the settled portion of the colony, the group became known as the House of Burgesses; it has met continuously ever since, and is known in modern times as the Virginia General Assembly.

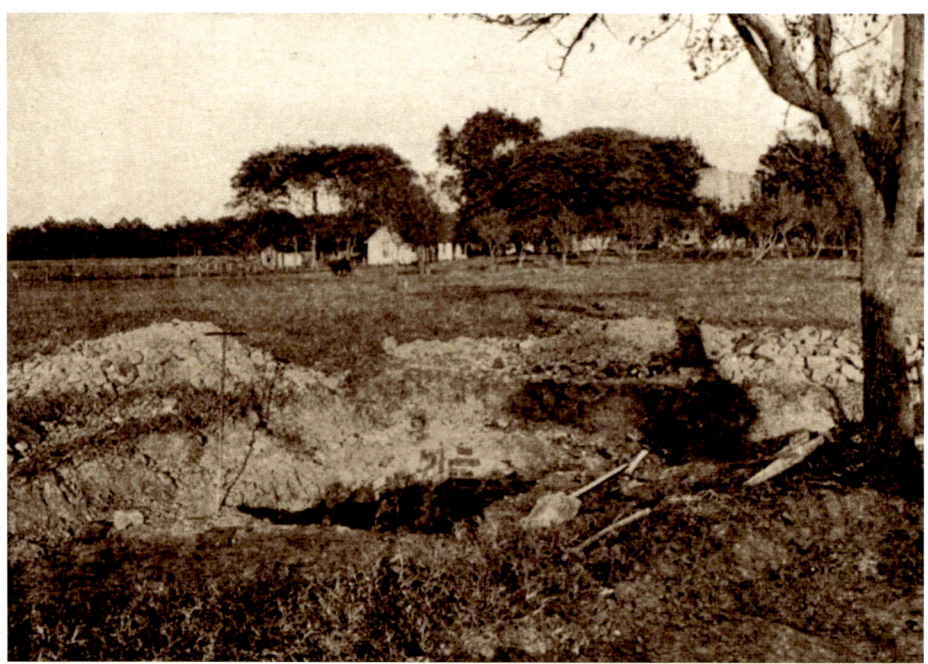

YONGE'S EXCAVATIONS: In 1901, Samuel H. Yonge (1843–1935), a civil engineer with the United States Army Corps of Engineers, spearheaded the design and construction of a seawall/revetment that halted the rapid erosion and loss into the James River of the most historic part of Jamestown Island. His efforts saved large portions of the island including James Fort, making possible continued significant archaeological finds at Jamestown. Yonge located, unearthed, and published many of his findings on the island. The photographs shown here, which date to 1903, are from Yonge's excavations of building foundations he located on the island.

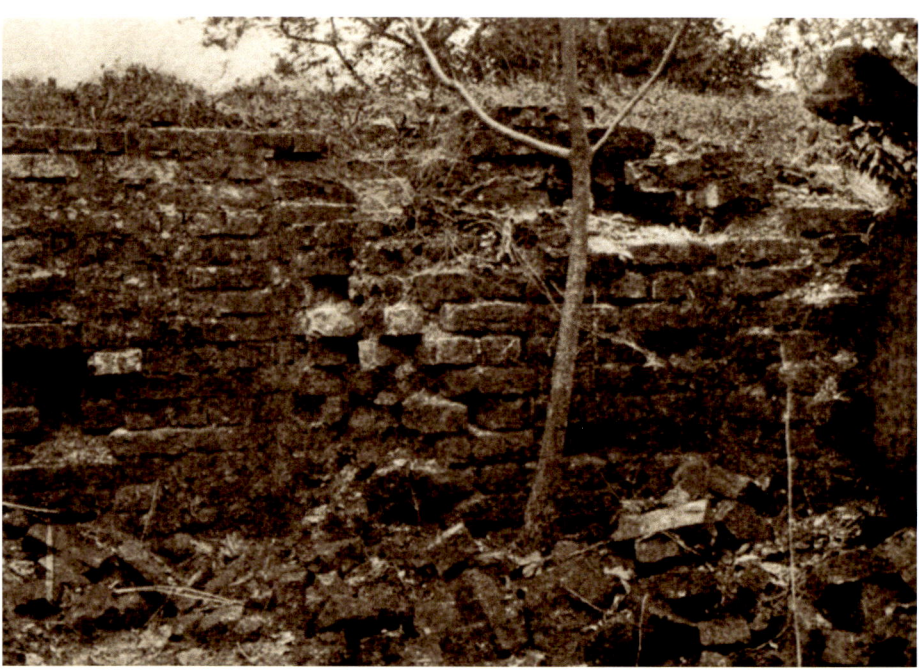

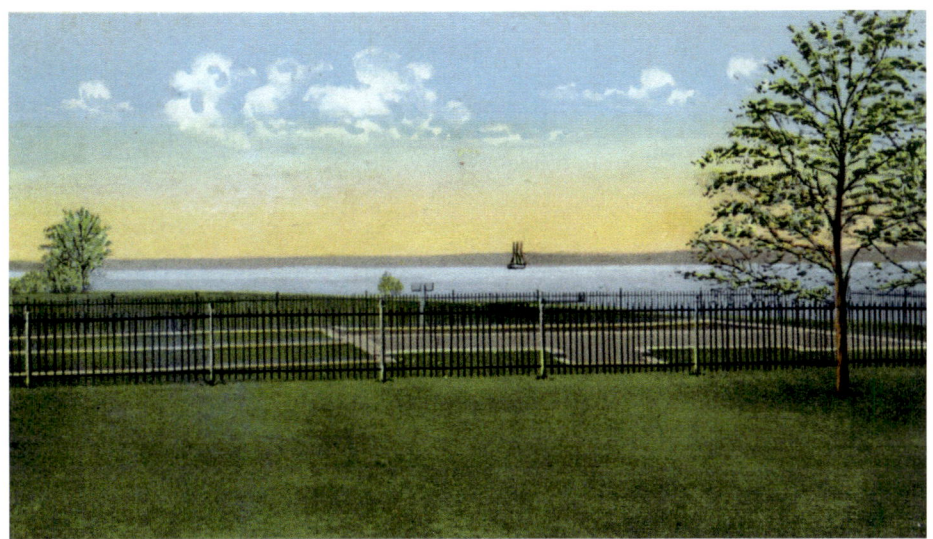

CAPITAL FOUNDATIONS: Yonge's excavations at Jamestown in 1903 revealed the foundation walls of the capital building where the House of Burgesses convened, the governor's mansion, Sir Phillip Ludwell's houses and the "country house." Prior to Yonge's work there, it was assumed that much of the original settlement had eroded into the James River, but his mapping and location of structures of great importance proved more was still present than previously assumed. The plot of this early excavation was enclosed by an iron fence presented to the APVA on May 2, 1925, by the National Society of the Daughters of the American Revolution, and is shown on this white border postcard from that period.

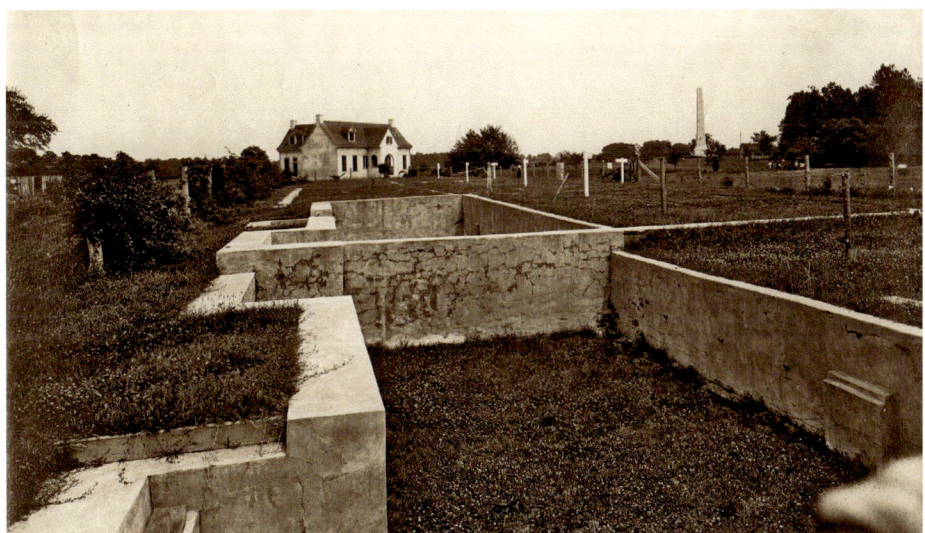

FOUNDATION WALLS: The foundation walls of the House of Burgesses and governor's mansion at Jamestown are shown (foreground) in this Harry C. Mann photograph, taken circa 1909. The National Society of Daughters of the American Revolution (NSDAR) house (previously shown) and government monument are in the background. The partnership between APVA and the National Park Service resulted in an important early archaeological excavation on the island. The foundations of Virginia's first statehouse, as well as the foundations of the third and fourth statehouses, were eventually believed uncovered.

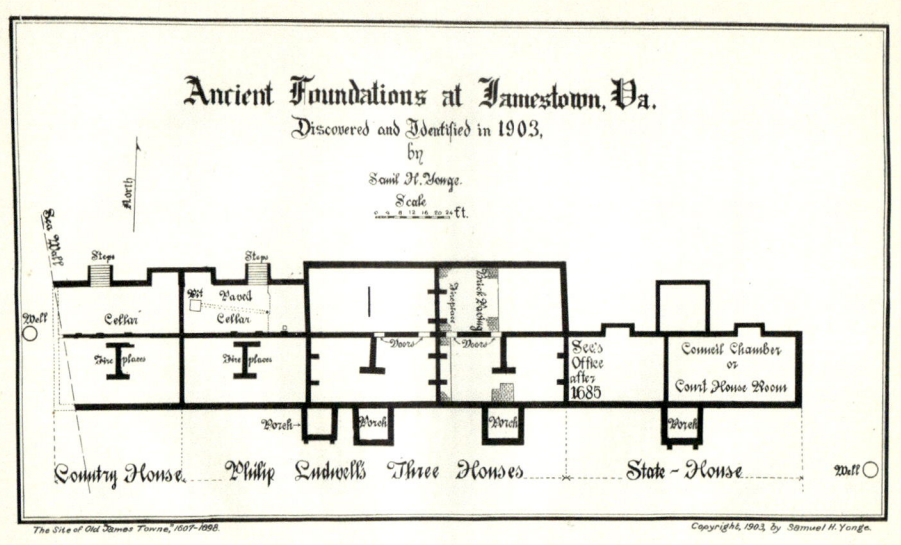

DOCUMENTING JAMESTOWN: According to Samuel Yonge's tercentenary edition of *The Site of Old 'James Towne' 1607–1698* and from which this drawing also first appeared, "The site of the fourth state house was unknown until early in 1903, when,…it was located by [Yonge]. At the eastern end of the first story was an apartment used as the council chamber and for courts house purposes. In the second story was the Assembly room of the House of Burgesses, 'a long room.' At the western end of the statehouse Yonge discovered the adjoining foundation of Philip Ludwell's easternmost house, one of three. All foundations, to include the "country house," were 240 feet long by roughly 24 to 46 feet wide, and had been built on a ridge that put them two-and-a-half to three-and-a-half feet above tide.

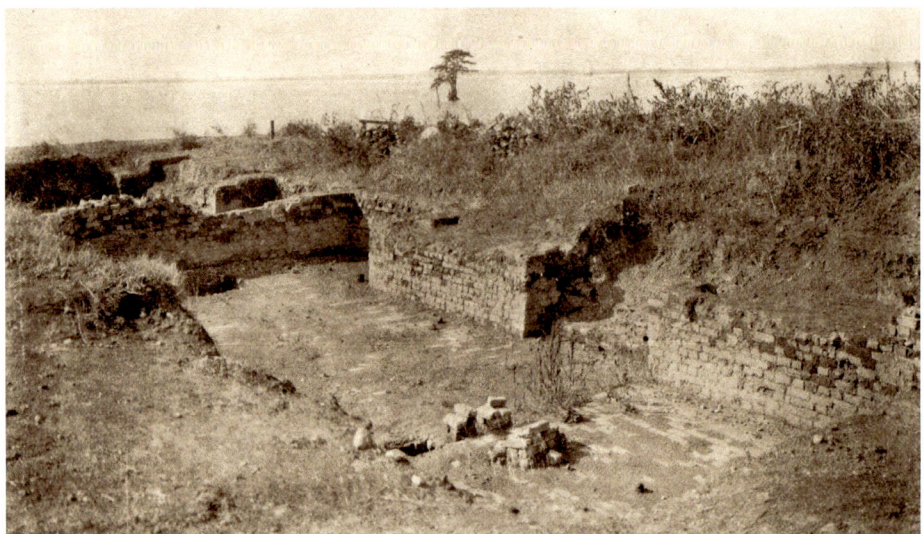

STATEHOUSE UNCOVERED: This is a section of the statehouse foundation uncovered by Samuel H. Yonge in 1903. In the foreground is shown the cellar of Philip Ludwell's easternmost house, and between it and the James River is that of the "Country House." The famous "Lone Cypress" is in the background. The photograph first appeared in Yonge's tercentenary edition of *The Site of Old 'James Towne' 1607–1698*.

GOVERNMENT MONUMENT: The tall monument that looks like the Washington Monument in the nation's capital was placed on Jamestown Island by the United States government in 1907 for the 300th anniversary of the settlement. The Tercentenary Monument cost $50,000, stands 103 feet tall, and is made of New Hampshire granite. The steps at the base were covered with dirt when the first visitors center was built in 1957, but now the platform provides many visitors a shaded resting spot on hot summer days. Harry C. Mann took this photograph shortly after the monument's completion.

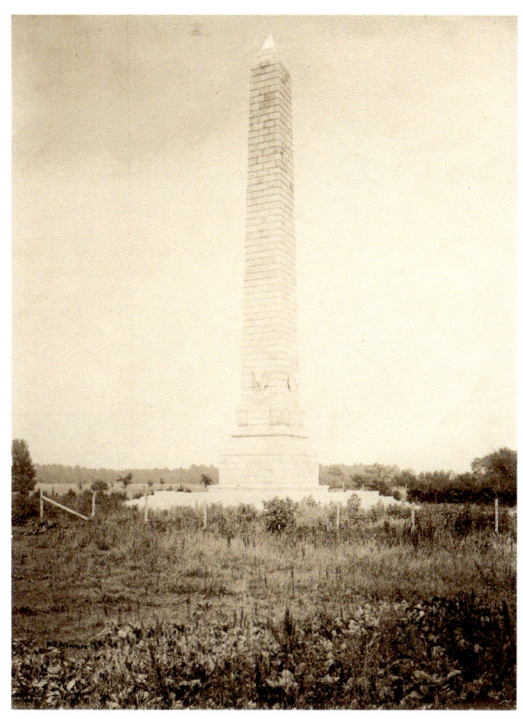

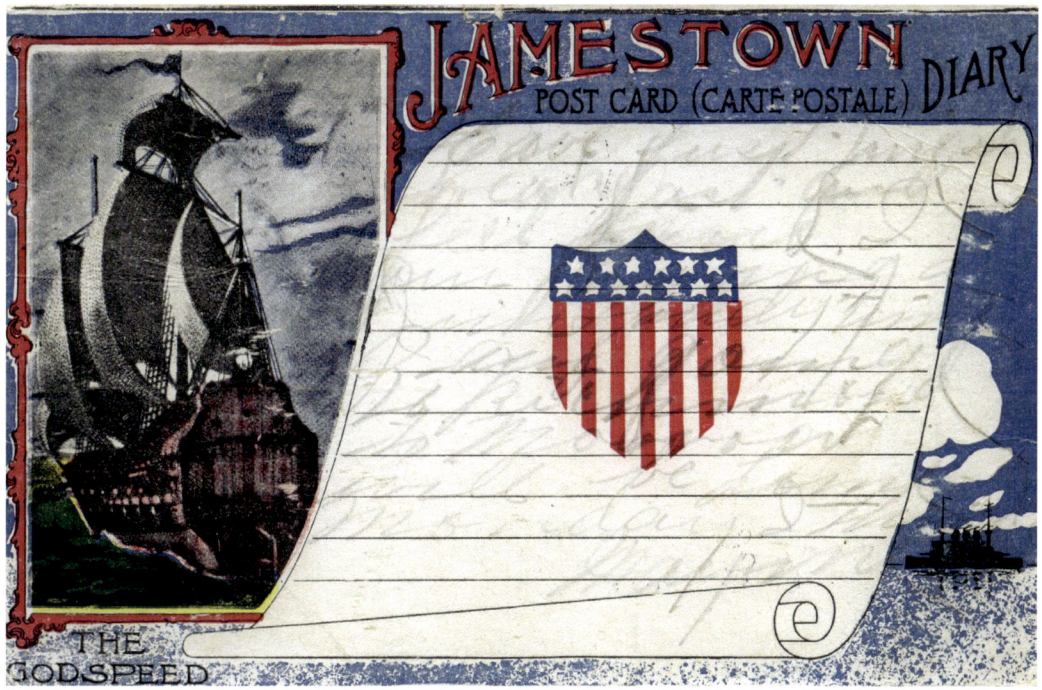

GODSPEED DIARY: This is a 1907 divided back diary postcard depicting the *Godspeed* and also honoring the 300th anniversary of the Jamestown settlement, the focal point of the Jamestown Exposition held at Hampton Roads that started on April 26 of that year. The card was published by A. Allen Fairchild, of Norfolk, Virginia.

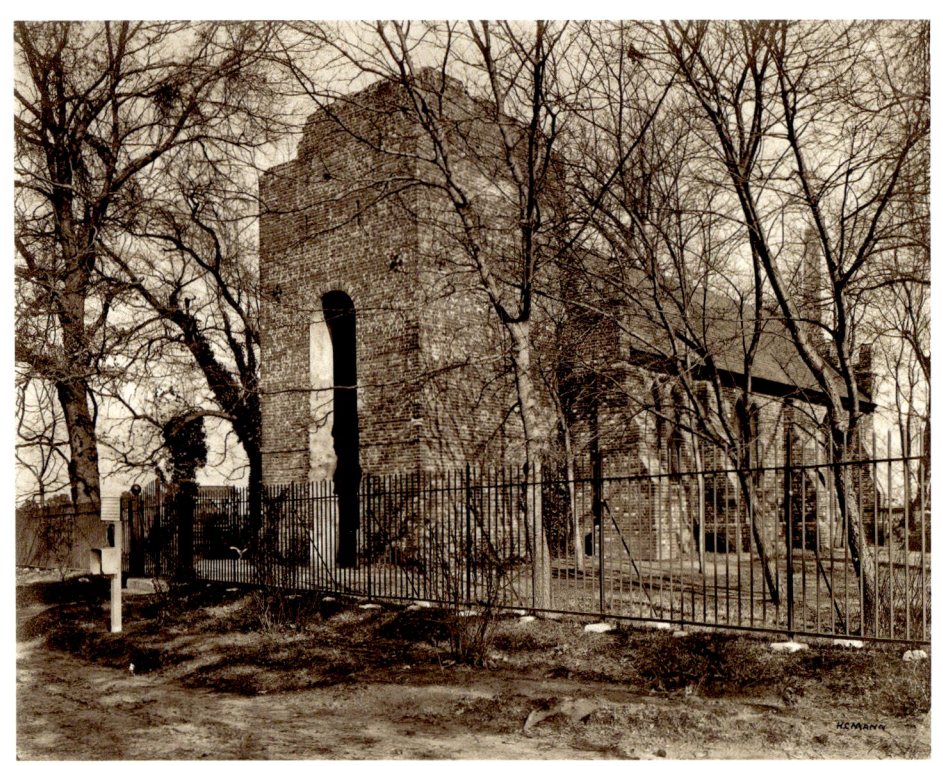

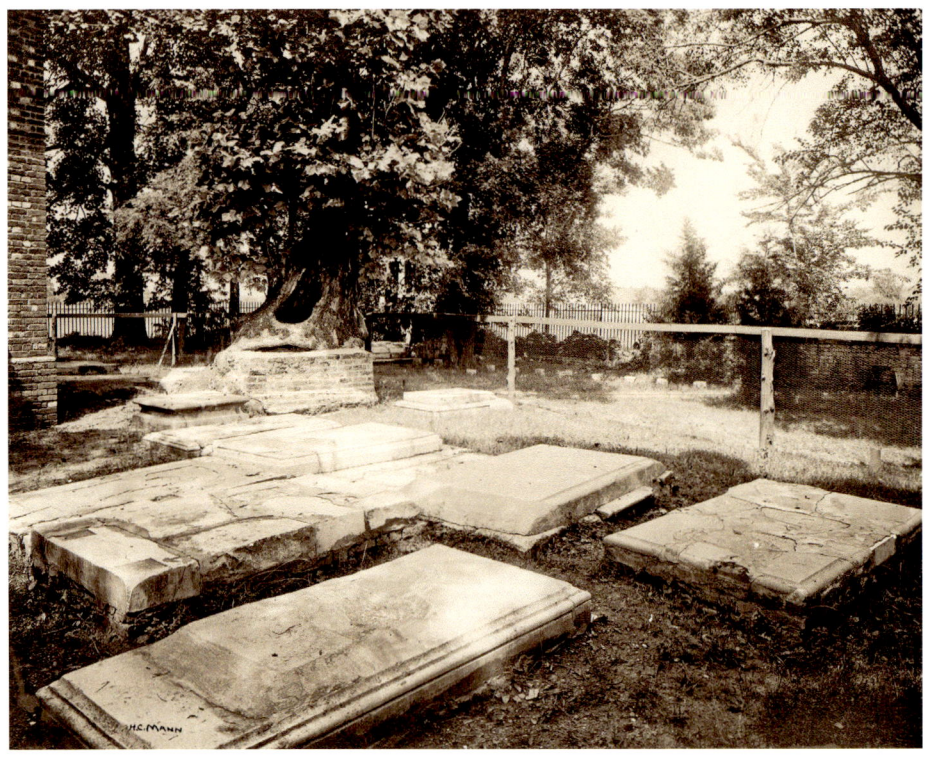

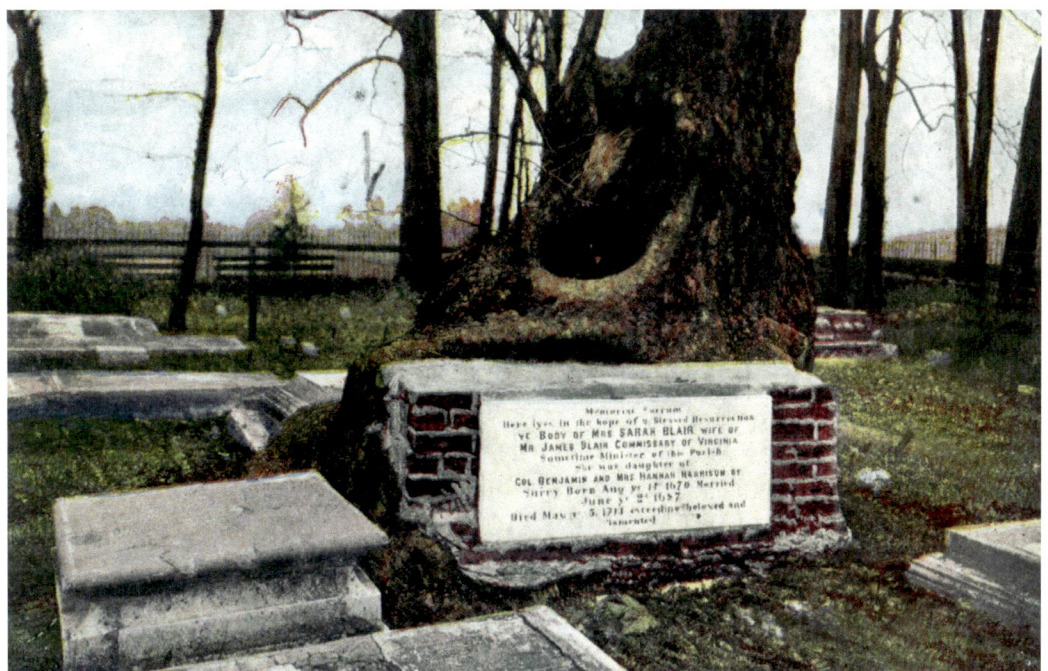

TOMBS TELL A STORY: Caught in the side of a great sycamore is a part of the tomb of Sarah Harrison Blair, wife of Dr. James Blair, founder of the College of William and Mary. On the other side of the tree is the base of Dr. Blair's tomb. Other tombs are those of the Ludwell family, ancestors of Richard Henry Lee and Francis Lightfoot Lee, signers of the Declaration of Independence, Lady Frances Berkeley, wife of colonial governor of Virginia William Berkeley, and of William Sherwood whose epitaph, as his will directs, states that he was a great sinner. The inscription on the side of the Blair grave was restored in 1913.

OPPOSITE PAGE:

MEMORIAL CHURCH (ABOVE): Harry C. Mann photographed the memorial church with the newly completed Tercentenary Monument in the background in 1907. A footpath extended from the monument terrace to the church area, crossing the trace of what settlers called the "Greate Road" and that also passed close to the site of a seventeenth-century brick kiln just inside the entrance to the APVA grounds.

JAMESTOWN GRAVEYARD (BELOW): Harry C. Mann took this photograph of the graveyard adjacent to the newly built memorial church in 1907.

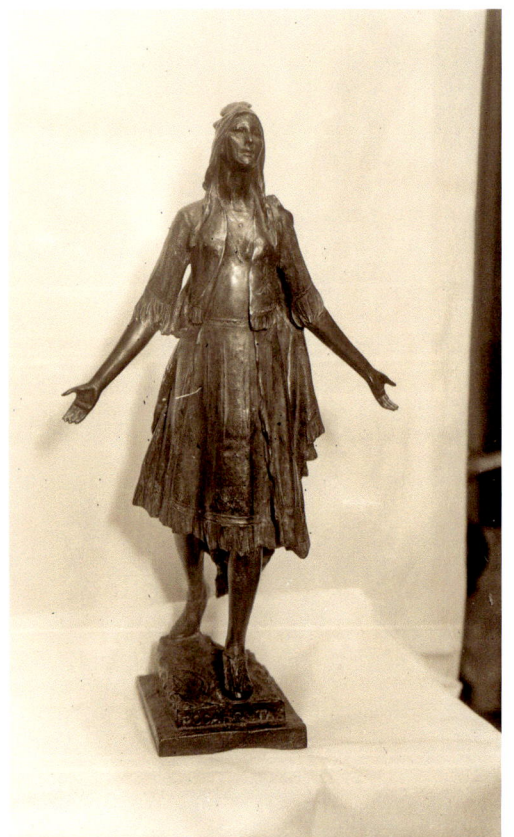 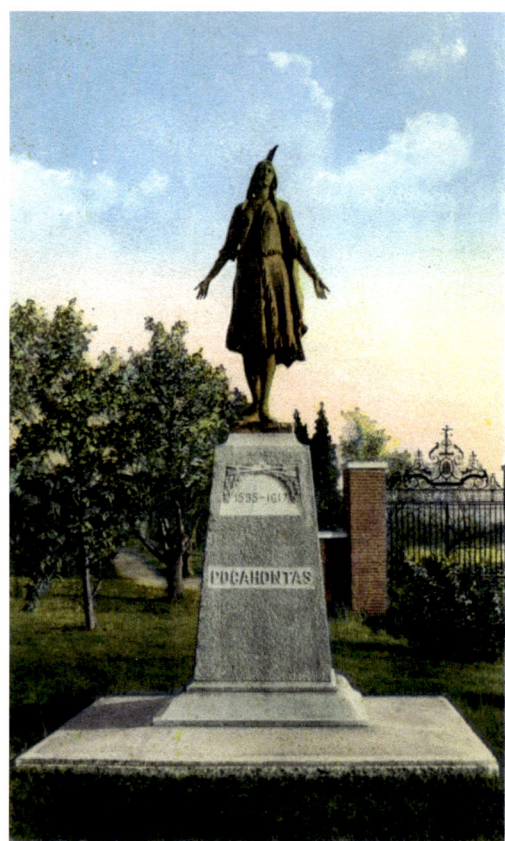

PARTRIDGE'S POCAHONTAS (LEFT): Sculptor William Ordway Partridge worked on a statue of Pocahontas for the tercentennial events held in 1907, but funding ran out and it was not until the federal government donated $5,000 in 1913 that the bronze statue was finished. This is a picture of Partridge's model for the larger-than-life statue that would eventually be dedicated in June 1922. *Library of Congress.*

POCAHONTAS ON A PEDESTAL (RIGHT): Partridge's Pocahontas statue, shown here on this early white-border postcard, was originally 18 feet high with the pedestal and erected just south of the memorial church by the Pocahontas Memorial Association and presented to the APVA on June 3, 1922.

OPPOSITE BELOW:

HUNT SHRINE: The National Society of Colonial Dames of America erected this shrine to the Reverend Robert Hunt (1568–1608), the first Anglican minister of the Virginia colony, in June 1922 to commemorate the earliest celebration of the Holy Communion in the first permanent English settlement in America. The shrine was designed by Ralph Adams Cram; it frames a bas-relief depicting the 1607 service with two 16-foot-high brick pillars supporting a sandstone arch. When first installed in 1922, shown on this period postcard, the shrine was position with its back to the James River but in 1960 the shrine was turned to face the river from the northern earthwork of the Civil War's Fort Pocahontas. This position takes advantage of a small amphitheater setting.

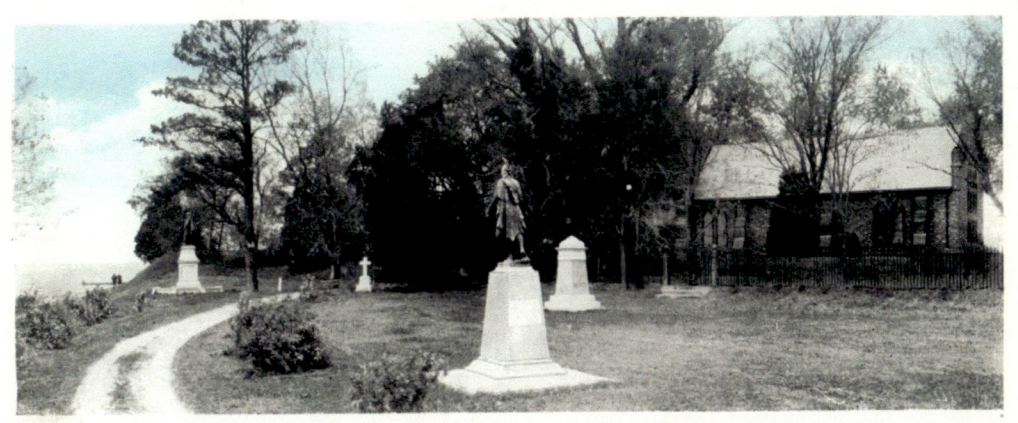

JAMESTOWN ISLAND, VA.

The site of the first permanent English settlement in America May 13, 1607. It is undoubtedly the most interesting of all historic places in the United States. Here was the seat of government in Virginia from 1607 to 1698. Here the Princess Pocahontas was baptized in the Christian faith and married to John Rolfe. The center monument is that of Princess Pocahontas.

61221-C

Iconic Statuary (above): This postcard, dating to 1925, shows the rear of the memorial church as well as the iconic statuary of Jamestown Island, including (left to right) the statue of Captain John Smith, the 1898 granite memorial cross, the statue of Pocahontas, and the General Assembly Monument.

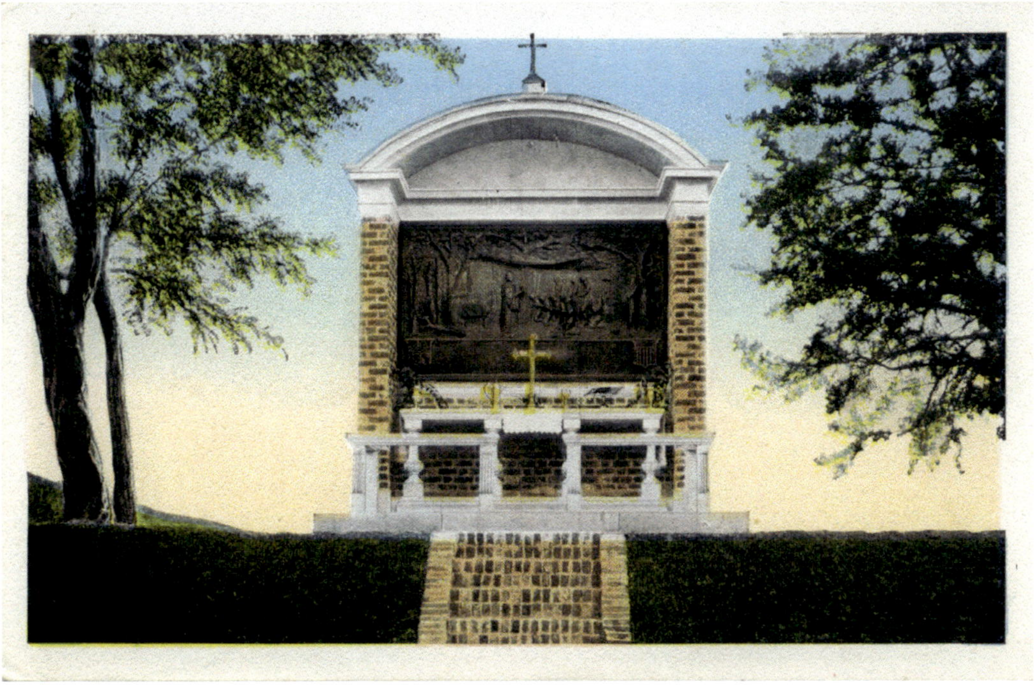

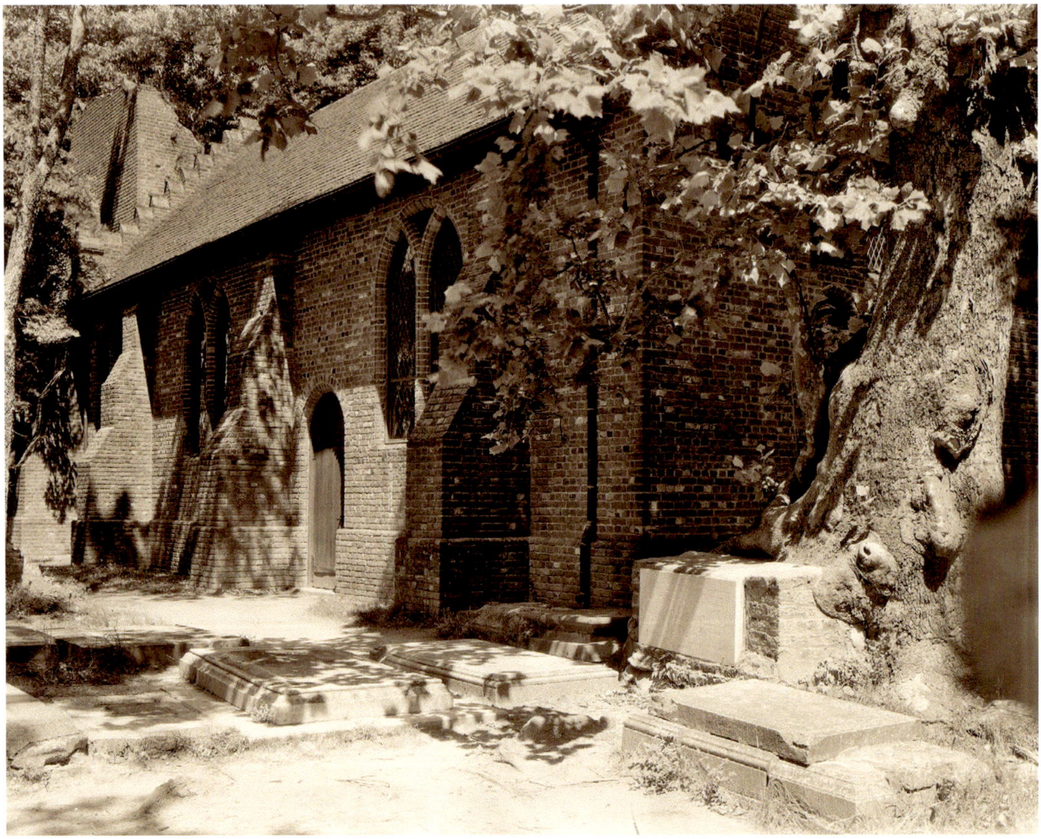

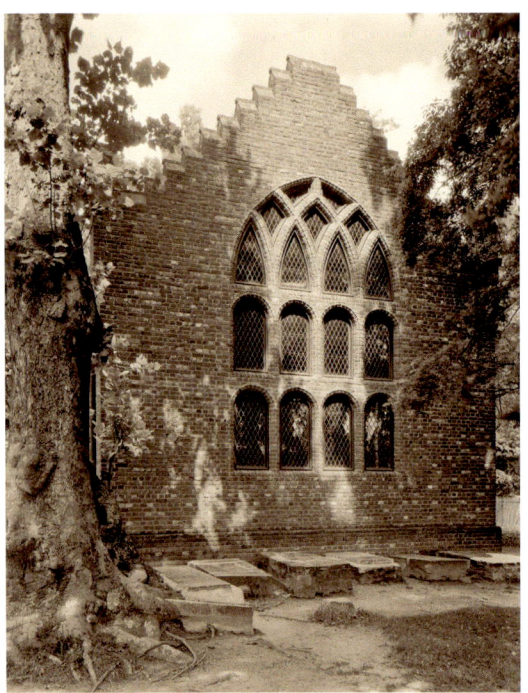

JOHNSTON PHOTOGRAPHS JAMESTOWN:

Frances Benjamin Johnston took these two photographs of the Jamestown memorial church addition, erected in 1906 behind the remnants of the old tower that belonged to the fourth church dating to 1639. The tower is slightly over 18 feet square and the walls are three feet thick at the base. Originally the tower was about 46 feet high, ten feet higher than the ruins that remain, and was crowned with a wooden roof and belfry; it had two upper floors as can be seen from the large beam notches on the inside. Six small openings at the top permitted light to enter and the sound of a bell to carry across the river and town. The memorial church addition preserves views of the foundations of earlier iterations of the church as well as the tower interior. Johnston's pictures date to 1930. *Library of Congress.*

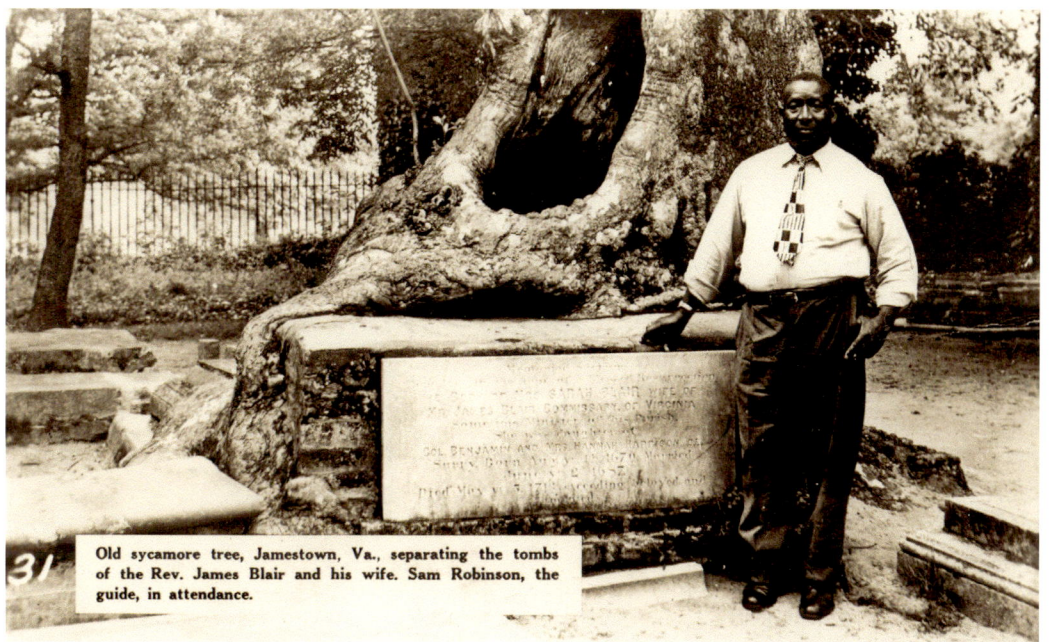

Old sycamore tree, Jamestown, Va., separating the tombs of the Rev. James Blair and his wife. Sam Robinson, the guide, in attendance.

SAMUEL ROBINSON: Longtime Jamestown churchyard guide and caretaker Samuel Robinson is shown in this picture, likely taken about 1940. Robinson's career started in 1934 after he came up with a colorful repertoire of stories that extolled the rich history and folklore of those buried there. He is famous for having entertained Queen Elizabeth II and Prince Philip during their visit in 1957 with his recitation of "The Mother-in-Law Tree," the story of the sycamore tree shown here that, as it grew, pushed apart the graves of Reverend James Blair and his wife, Sarah Harrison Blair, whose mother disapproved of their marriage. Robinson died on November 7, 1965.

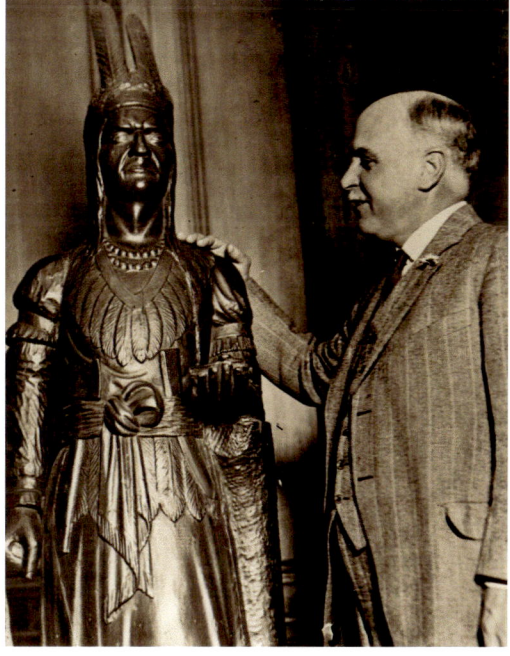

JAMESTOWN'S ALLURE: Whether it was Jamestown's historic significance or the romanticized folklore that captured the public's interest and imagination, the nation's fascination with this sacred site traveled far beyond the attention drawn to it by the tercentenary celebration of 1907 that included events not only on the island but the international exposition at Hampton Roads, Virginia, the same year. Jamestown was remembered and commemorated for many years to come. Even San Francisco's mayor and later the twenty-seventh governor of California, James Rolph Jr., shown here in this April 15, 1923 Pacific and Atlantic photograph, kept this statue of Wahunsenacawh, better known at Powhatan, father of Pocahontas, in his office because he claimed Powhatan as an ancestor.

The Landing

LANDINGS REENACTED: Children from Lynchburg, Virginia (or the vicinity thereof) were photographed reenacting scenes from Jamestown's establishment, marking events that they had learned in their history books; a series of 12 photographs were taken (all around Lynchburg c. 1920), including this one in which they portray the first landing at Cape Henry (now part of Virginia Beach, Virginia). In the picture below, the landing at Jamestown that came later is depicted by staff of the Colonial National Historical Park circa 1935 as part of a visitor program on the island.

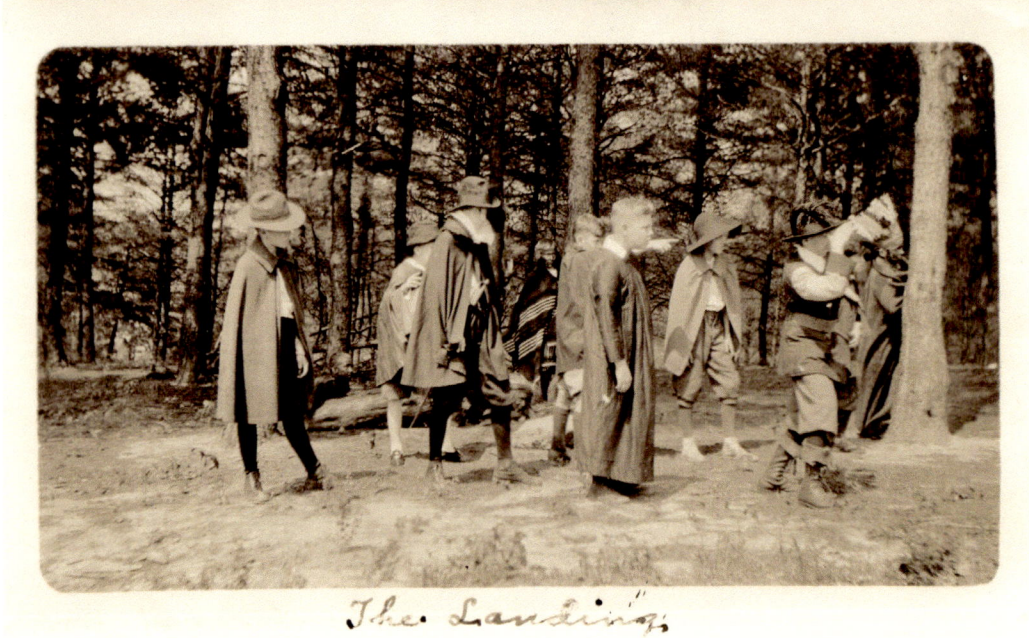

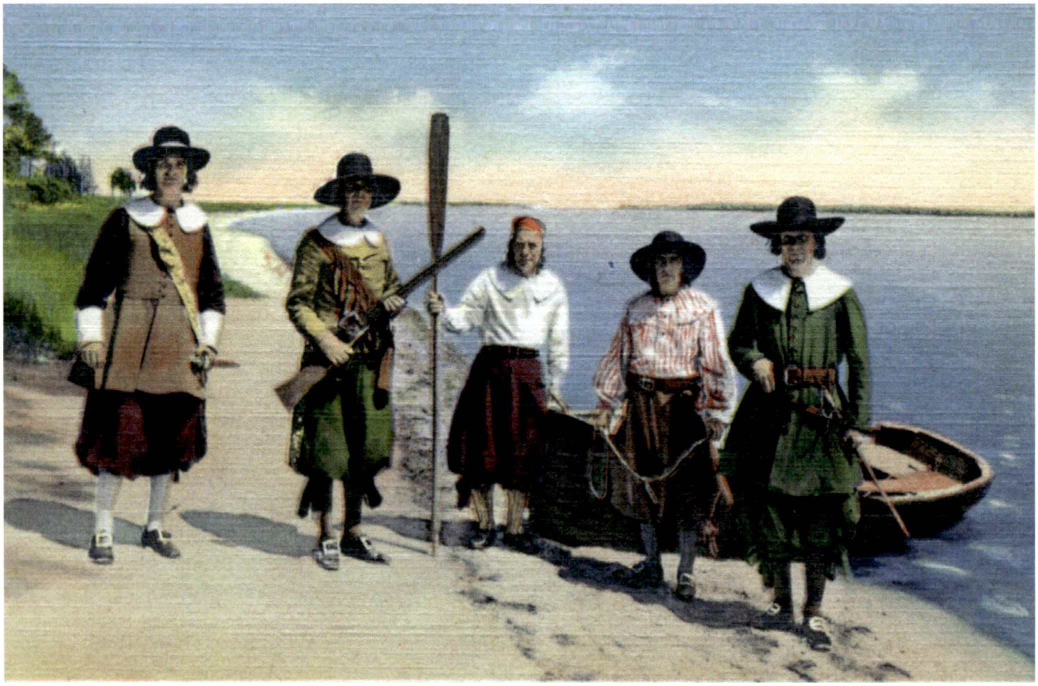

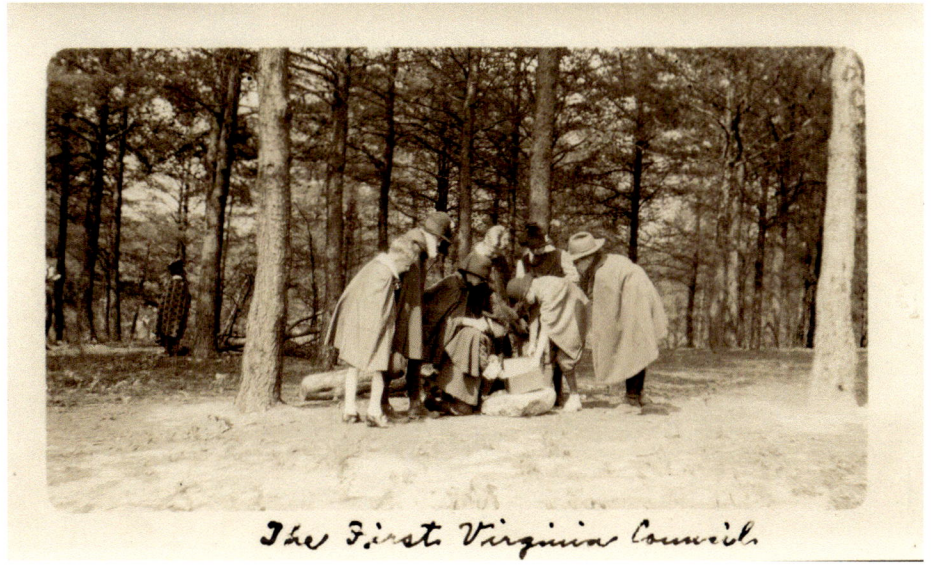

The First Virginia Council

SCHOOLCHILDREN REENACT THE FIRST COUNCIL: Lynchburg (or vicinity) schoolchildren depict the first council's opening of the chest containing sealed orders that would establish governance of the fledgling Virginia colony. The orders named Captain John Smith as a member of the governing council, even though he had been arrested for mutiny during the voyage and was incarcerated aboard one of the ships. Though he had been scheduled to be hanged upon arrival, Smith was freed by Captain Christopher Newport after the opening of the orders. The same orders also directed the expedition to seek an inland site for their settlement, which would afford protection from enemy ships.

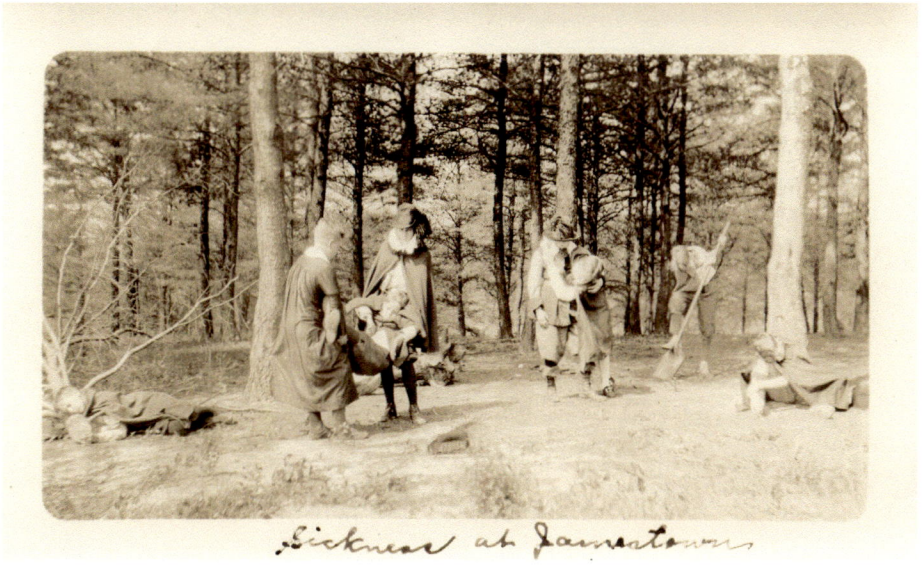

Sickness at Jamestown

SICKNESS AT JAMESTOWN: This is a reenactment of the sickness at Jamestown by Lynchburg (or vicinity) schoolchildren. Shortly after Captain Christopher Newport returned to England on June 22, 1607, for supplies, the colonists began to die of a variety of diseases, from swellings, fluxes, fevers, by famine, and sometimes by wars with the Powhatan Indians who surrounded them.

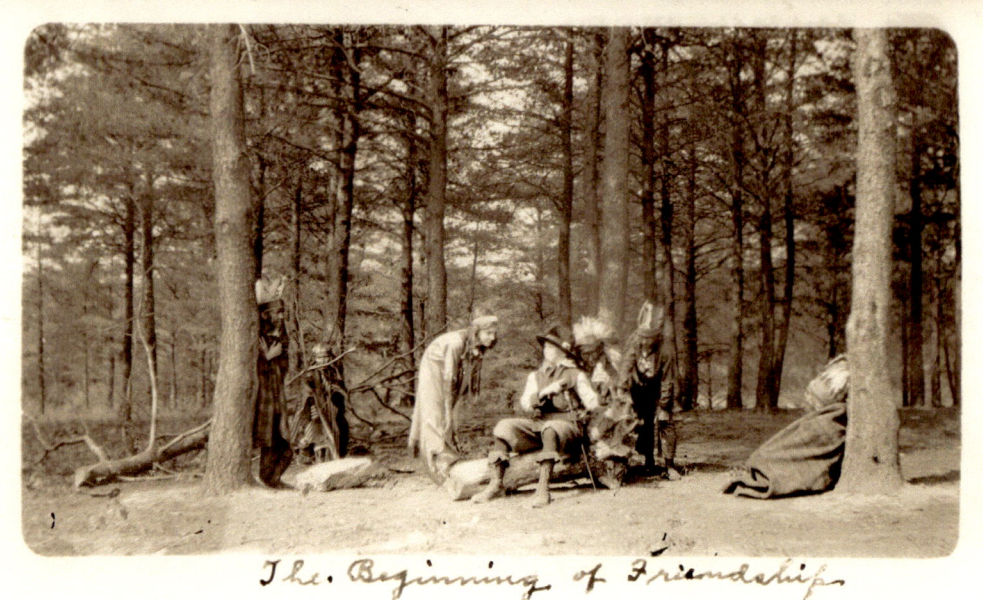

BEGINNING OF FRIENDSHIP: Reenactment of the "beginning of friendship" recalls the warming of the relationship between Chief Powhatan, portrayed here with Pocahontas extending a helping hand, as he began to send the starving English gifts of food. In those early years, before the end of 1609, when the relationship soured, Powhatan saved the colony, which would have likely failed due to starvation and the diseases that followed poor diet and health.

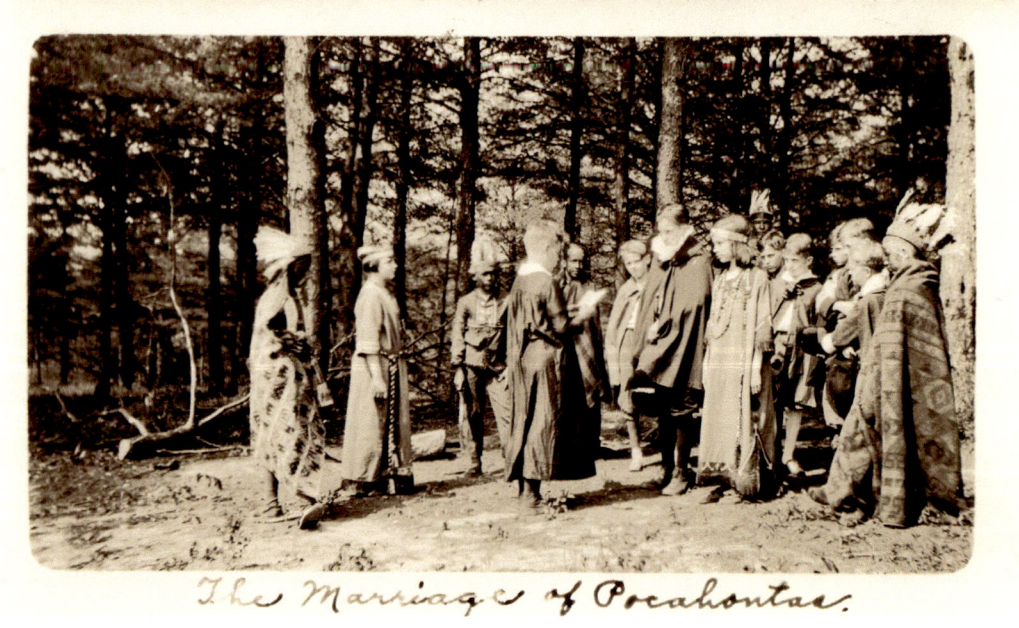

REENACTING THE POCAHONTAS WEDDING: One of the most reenacted historical moments from the nascent Jamestown colony is the marriage of Pocahontas in April 1614 to tobacco planter John Rolfe, depicted here by Lynchburg area schoolchildren.

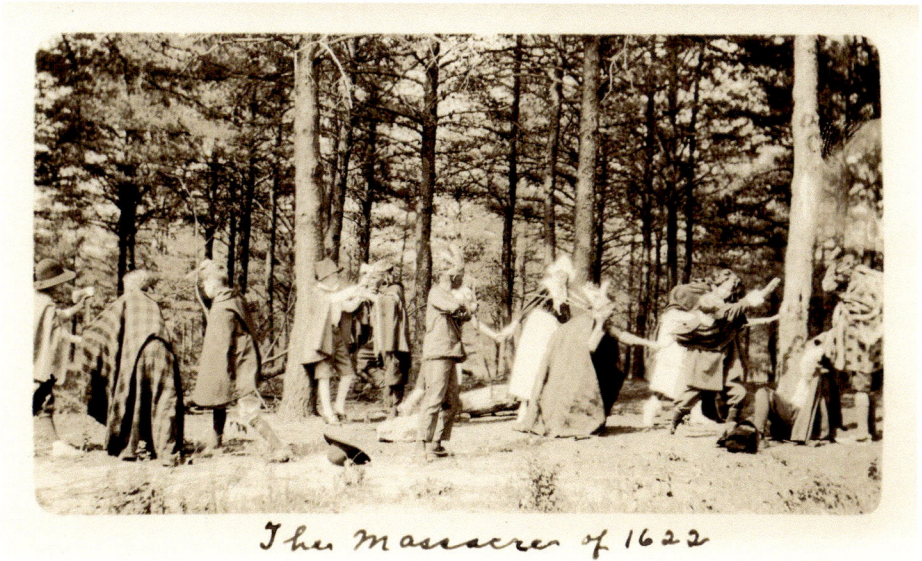

The massacre of 1622

JAMESTOWN HISTORY COMES ALIVE: In March 1622 the Powhatan paramount chief, by then Opechancanough, planned a coordinated attack against the English settlements, tired of the settlers' encroachment on Powhatan lands. Jamestown escaped being attacked, due to a warning from a Powhatan boy living with the English. During the attack 350 to 400 of the 1,200 settlers were killed. The massacre of 1622 was reenacted by Lynchburg area schoolchildren about 1920.

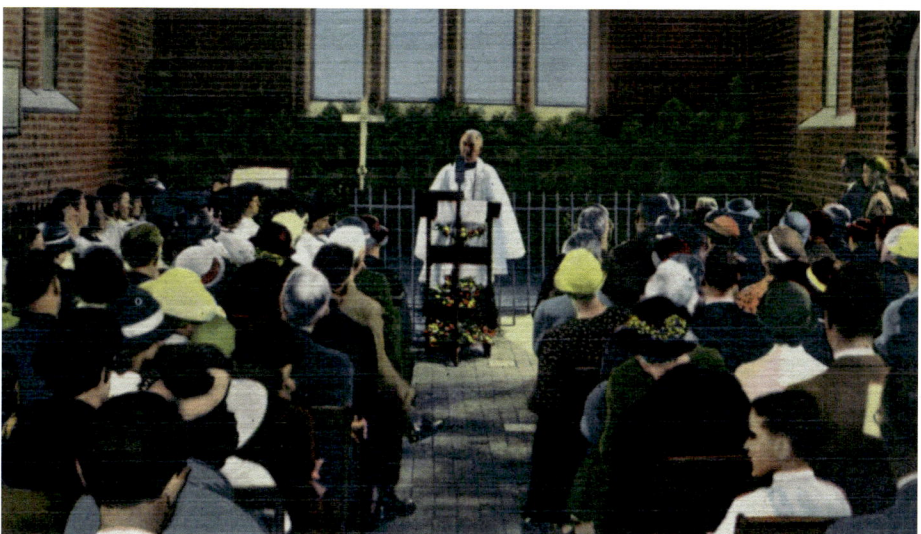

REMEMBERING DR. GOODWIN: The Reverend Dr. William Archer Rutherfoord Goodwin (1869-1939), the father of the Colonial Williamsburg restoration, is shown here conducting services commemorating the arrival of the first permanent English settlers in 1607 inside the memorial church; the photograph from which this linen postcard was printed dates to about 1930. In 1929, Goodwin, long-time rector of Bruton Parish Church, historian, preservationist and author, recommended that Williamsburg, Jamestown and Yorktown be connected by a parkway and also made into a national park. On July 3, 1930, the park with plans for a parkway were authorized by Congress as part of the national park system.

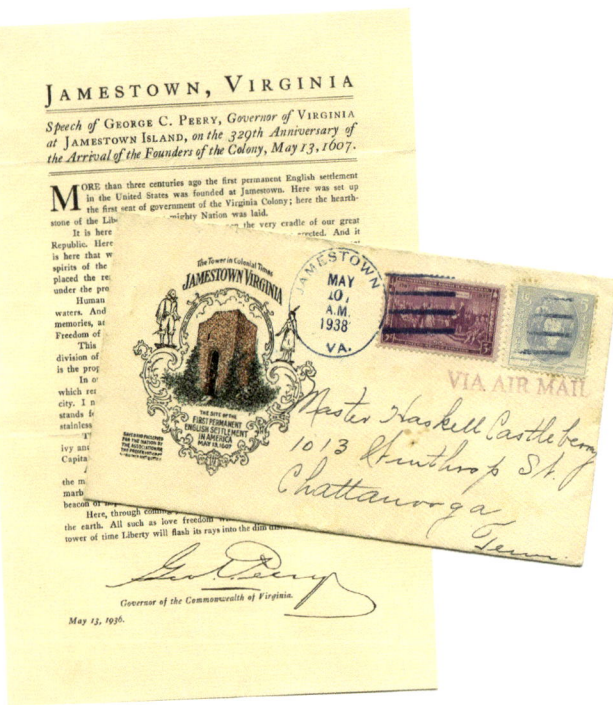

SHRINE OF NATIONAL INTEREST: The copy of the May 13, 1936 speech delivered by Virginia governor George C. Peery at Jamestown Island on the occasion of the 329th anniversary of the arrival of the founders of the colony, shown here, was shared by the philatelic community as an insert in a postal cachet cover such as the one here, postmarked May 10, 1938—a later date—with artwork and a Jamestown, Virginia cancellation. "This shrine of national and world interest," wrote Peery, "belongs to no individual division of this great country. Jamestown Island with its inspiring traditions is the property of a whole people. It is sacred to Liberty and to the Nation."

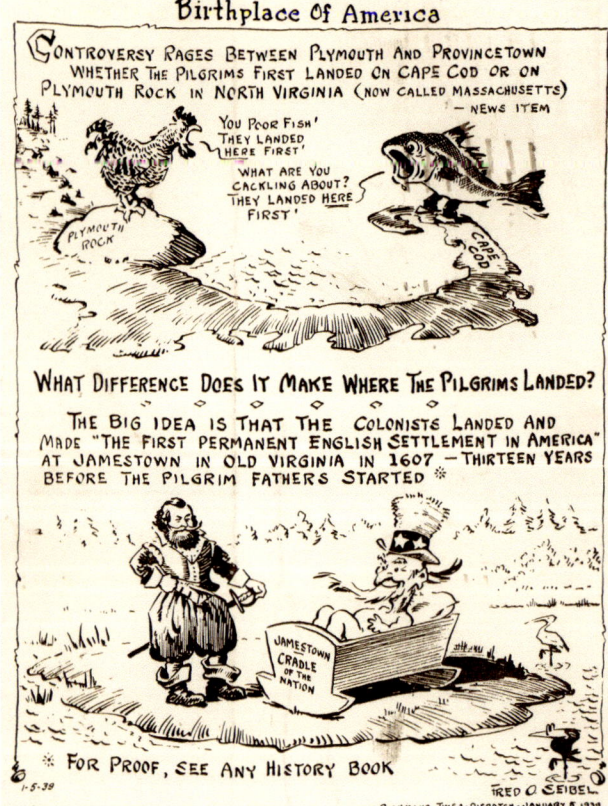

UNCLE SAM IN THE CRADLE: "The big idea," says the caricature of Captain John Smith, to Uncle Sam in the cradle, "is that the colonists landed and made the first permanent English settlement in America at Jamestown in old Virginia in 1607—thirteen years before the Pilgrim fathers started." At the end of Fred O. Seibel's political cartoon, he wrote "For proof, see any history book." Seibel's cartoon ran in the January 5, 1939 *Richmond Times-Dispatch* and was shortly thereafter made into a postcard (shown here).

Section 3

Exploring Jamestown Island

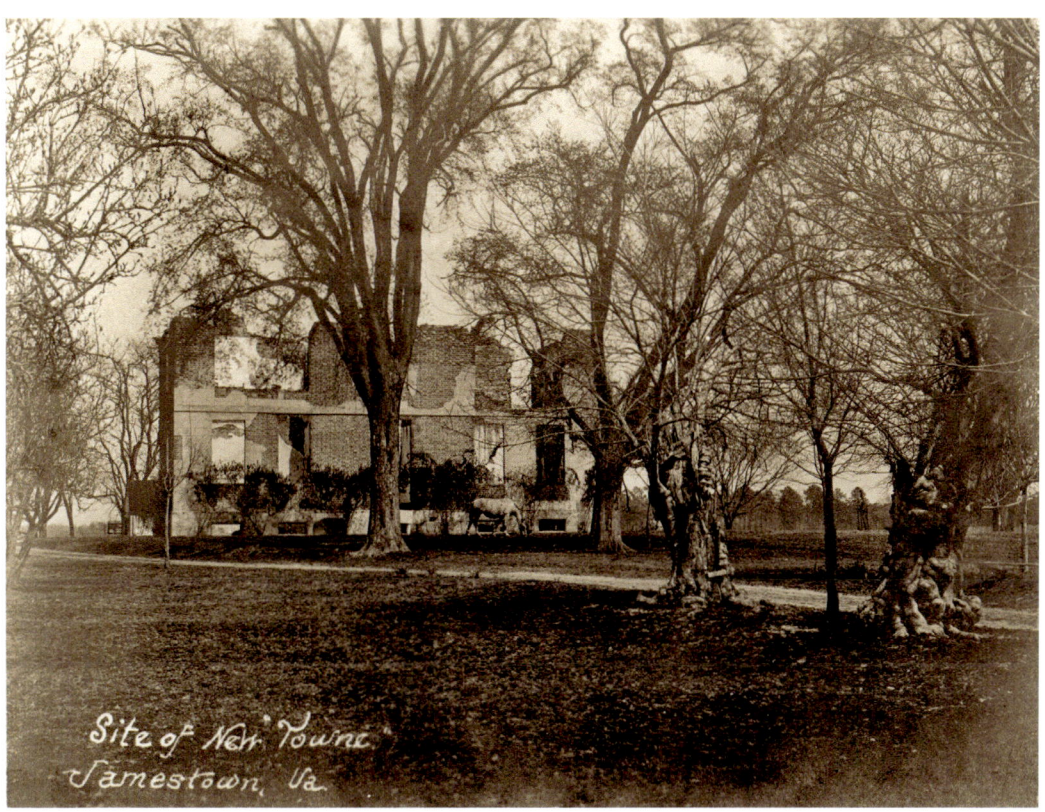

The Amblers at New Towne: The Ambler family dominated the western end of Jamestown Island by the beginning of the nineteenth century, though, of note, how that came to be requires a bit of history; in the latter part of the seventeenth century William Sherwood and Edward Jaquelin were the dominant landholders on the island. With Sherwood's death in 1697, his lands were added to Jaquelin's, and the combined Jaquelin-Sherwood estates would eventually pass to Richard Ambler with his marriage to Elizabeth Jaquelin in 1724. The Ambler family otherwise arrived relatively late to the Virginia colony. Richard Ambler moved to Virginia from England in 1716 and settled in Yorktown; he probably contacted a maternal uncle named Burkadik who immigrated to the colony in 1694. Most likely, Richard inherited his first property from this uncle. In 1724, Richard Ambler drastically improved his status and wealth by marrying Elizabeth Jaquelin, heiress to a large tract of land on Jamestown Island. When this inheritance was turned over to him in 1739, it marked the beginning of the Amblers' domination of the western end of the island through the mid-nineteenth century.

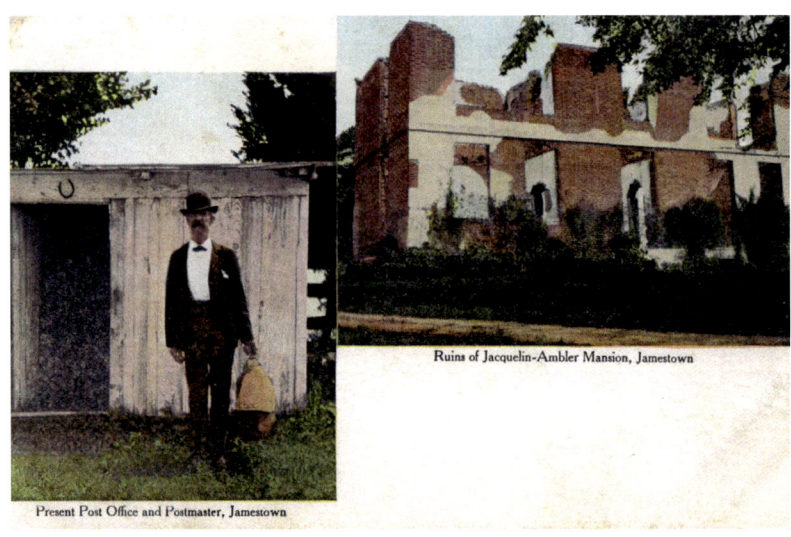

Ruins of Jacquelin-Ambler Mansion, Jamestown

Present Post Office and Postmaster, Jamestown

JAMESTOWN LAND BARONS (ABOVE): The Amblers contributed greatly to the political, economic and social aspects of Virginia society. On April 29, 1724, Richard assumed the respected and important position of collector for the port of the York River. Richard died in 1766, and his will divided his estate among his three sons. To Edward, the oldest, he left his holdings on Yorktown's Main Street. John Ambler inherited most of the Jamestown holdings, including the house (shown as it looked after it burned in 1895, on this private mailing card that dates to the turn of the twentieth century, and that also depicts the island's post office and postmaster), and he also acquired a seat in the House of Burgesses. Jaquelin Ambler inherited various Jamestown and Yorktown properties. John died soon after his father in 1766, and Edward took over John's properties and moved from Yorktown to Jamestown, replacing John in the House of Burgesses and as collector at Yorktown. The Ambler plantation was the center of New Towne, as shown on this early twentieth-century postcard.

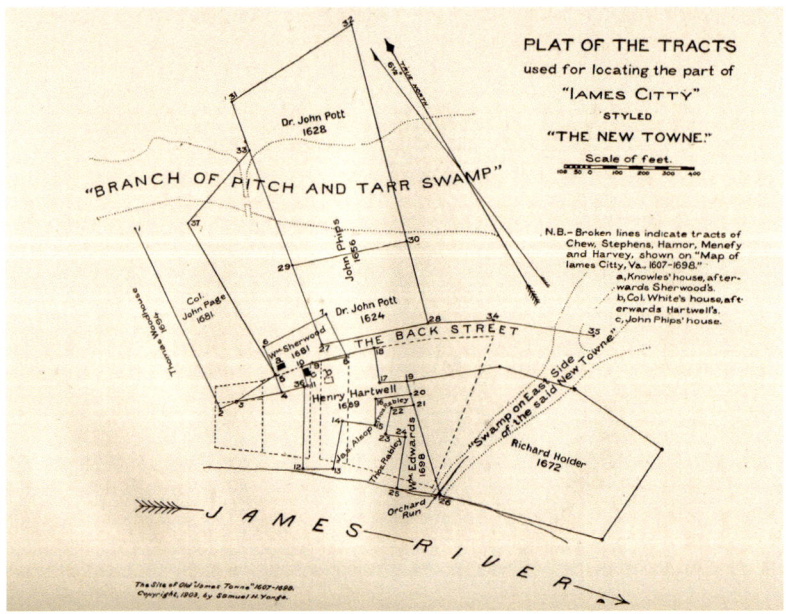

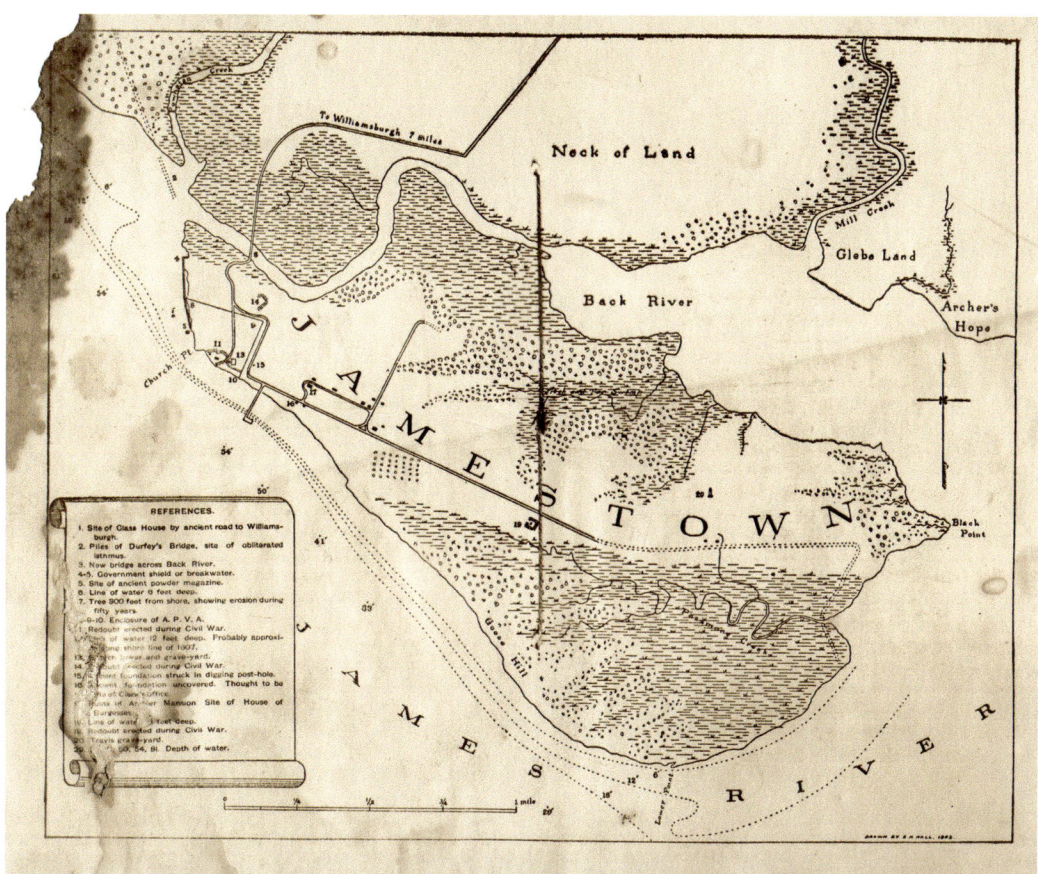

EXPLORING JAMESTOWN ISLAND: This map of Jamestown Island was drawn by E. H. Hall in 1903. The legend for the map is as follows: 1) site of the glasshouse by ancient road to Williamsburgh [sic]; 2) piles of Durfey's Bridge, site of obliterated isthmus; 3) new bridge across Back River; 4, 5) government shield of breakwater; 6) line of water six feet deep; 7) tree 300 feet from shore, showing erosion during 50 years; 8, 9 and 10) enclosure of Association for the Preservation of Virginia Antiquities; 11) redoubt erected during the Civil War; 12) line of water twelve feet deep, probably approximately showing shoreline of 1607; 13) church tower and graveyard; 14) redoubt erected during Civil War; 15) ancient foundation struck in digging posthole; 16) ancient foundation uncovered, thought to be the site of the clerk's office; 17) ruins of Ambler mansion and site of the House of Burgesses; 18) line of water [illegible] feet deep; 19) redoubt erected during the Civil War, and 20) Travis graveyard.

OPPOSITE BELOW:

THE NEW TOWNE: Jamestown quickly began expanding beyond the boundaries of the three-sided fort first built on the banks of the James River in 1607. In the 1620s, surveyor William Claiborne mapped out the area to the east of the fort. This land was quickly occupied and used for a variety of purposes by Jamestown inhabitants and visitors—this was New Towne, a busy part of Virginia's first capital—shown on this graphic from Samuel Yonge's tercentenary edition of *The Site of Old 'James Towne' 1607–1698*. The town gradually consolidated into single landholders such as the Ambler family, whose plantation house stood in the center of the town.

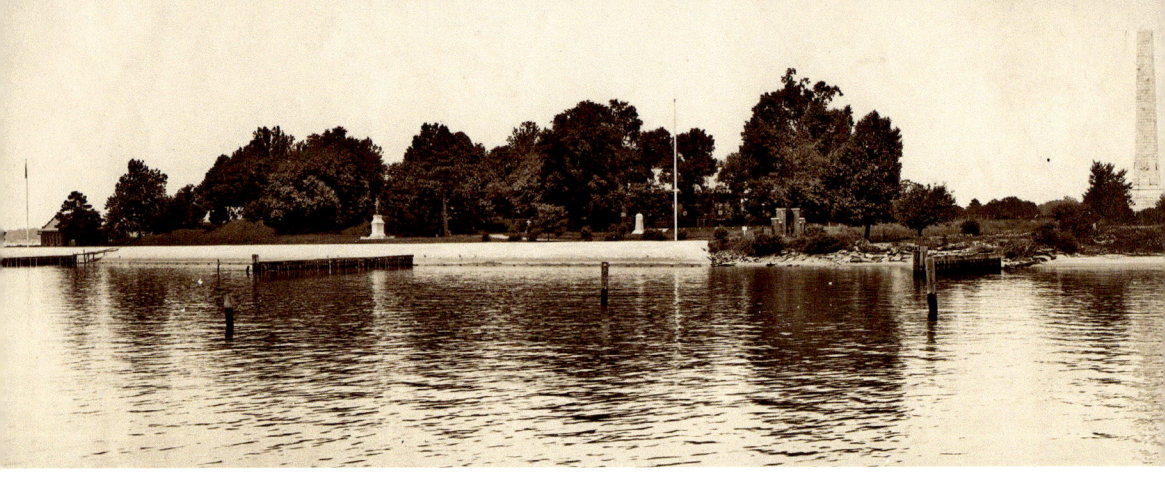

ON THE WATERFRONT: This panoramic Harry C. Mann photograph of the Jamestown shoreline was taken circa 1909 from the wharf and shows the sweep of the seawall erected by the United States government as well as the island's significant historic monuments up to that period, including the entrance gates donated by the National Society of the Colonial Dames of America's to APVA on April 9, 1907, visible right, just beyond the seawall.

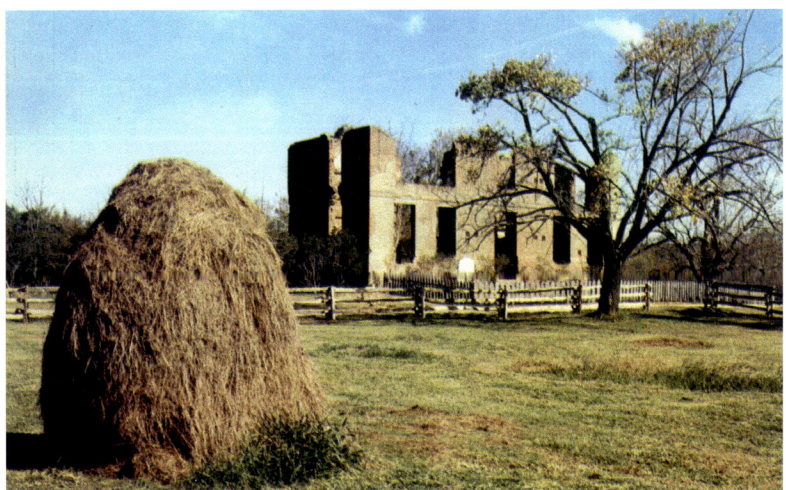

AMBLER AND TRAVIS HOLDINGS: Edward Ambler died in 1768, and his widow, Mary, and their children continued to live on Jamestown Island until the American Revolution. Jaquelin Ambler succeeded his brother Edward as collector. As an committed patriot during the war, Jaquelin would serve on Virginia's Council of State in 1780 and as treasurer of Virginia from 1782 until his death in 1798. As for the house, the ruins of which are shown on this mid-twentieth century postcard, it has a long and difficult history. Built about 1750 along Back Street, 350 yards east of the church, the Amblers preferred to call their homestead a mansion, though it was not built to that scale. The brick house was typical of early Georgian architecture; it had two stories, a central hall and two rooms on each side. The yard consisted of elaborate garden walkways. Unfortunately, the home burned during the Revolutionary War and was restored by Colonel John Ambler. The house burned again during the Civil War and was restored a second time. When the house burned for a third time in 1895 it was not rebuilt. At that time, the property belonged to David Bullock who bought the Ambler and Travis holdings on the island in 1831. Today, the National Park Service administers the remains of the former Ambler estate.

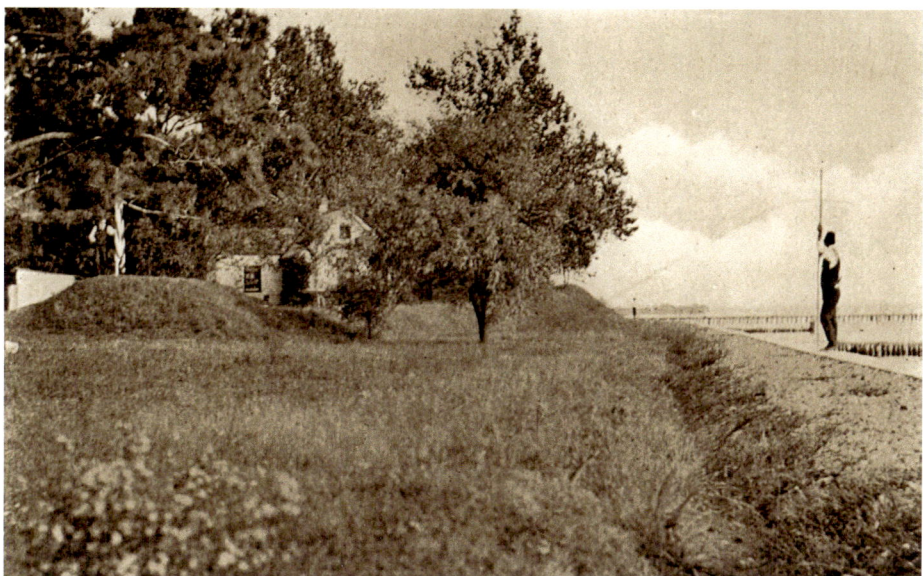

THE THREE CORNERS: The gentleman on the right is looking over what was left of the Jamestown settlement in this illustration that first appeared in Frank and Cortelle Hutchins' May 1910 *Houseboating on a Colonial Waterway*. "For a rough approximation," they wrote [of where the old settlement once was], "all we had to do was to get Mr. Leal, the caretaker, to stand at the most westerly angle of the fort, and his son on the seawall at the lower end of the fort, and Henry on the seawall a hundred yards farther upstream; then, straight lines connecting these three men enclosed all that was left of that first little fortified settlement where Anglo-Saxon America began." While the men stood at the three corners, they took their picture.

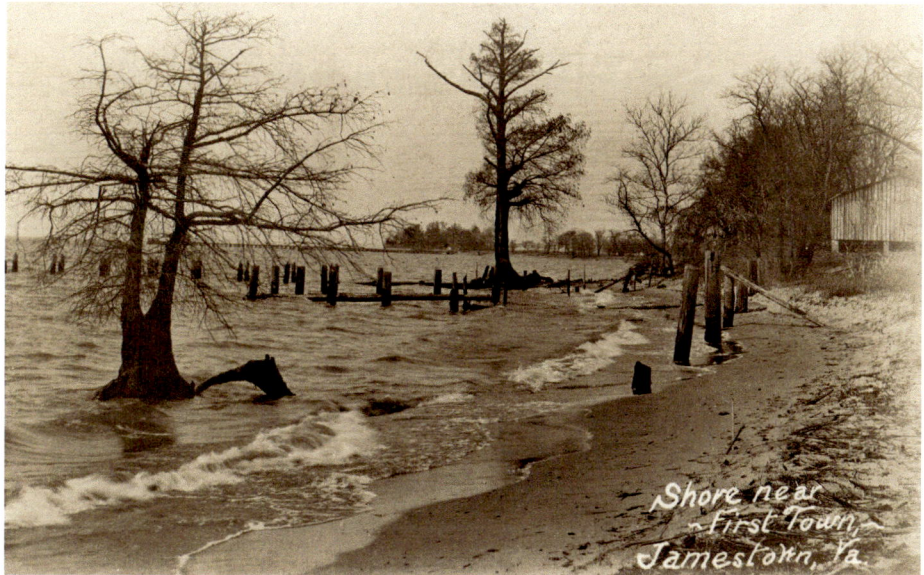

SHORE NEAR FIRST TOWN: This is the shoreline near the first Jamestown settlement at the turn of the twentieth-century. At that time, those who visited the island could sit in the grassy fort undisturbed but for the sound of the water lapping the shore and the twitter of birds.

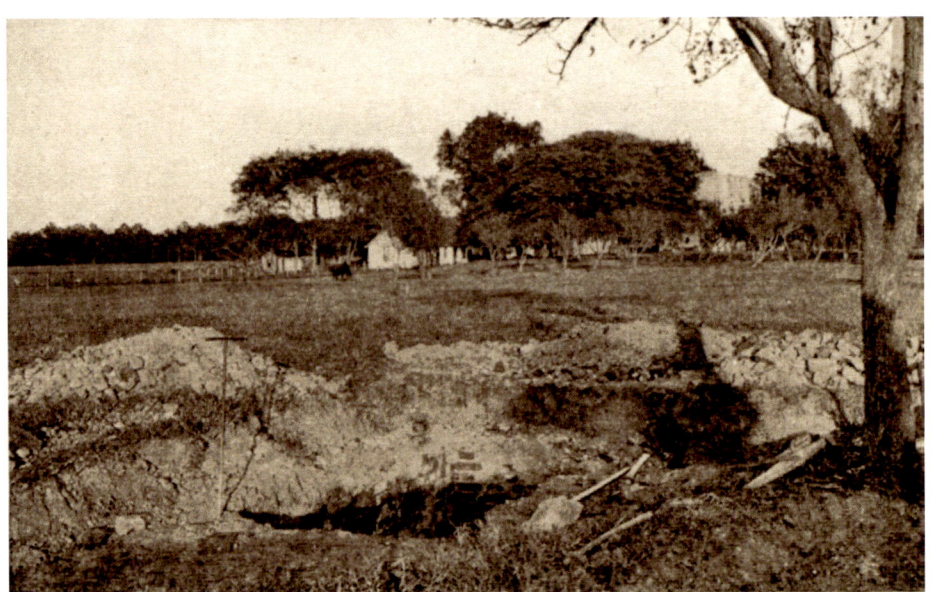

TOURISM DRAW: Samuel Yonge's 1903 excavations were a major tourism draw at Jamestown Island. This photograph, which first appeared in Frank and Cortelle Hutchins' May 1910 *Houseboating on a Colonial Waterway*, is another perspective of Yonge's discoveries at the site of the first statehouse, Philip Ludwell's houses and the "country house." In these foundations were found what appeared to captivated observers to be "an endless number of pieces of broken pottery; and the design of a blue dog chasing a blue fox was evidently a popular one for such ware at James Towne." The Hutchins' would write later that diggers would find "a wrong piece of the blue dog mixed with bits of brass and iron and pottery that brought vividly to mind the scenes and the folk of that vanished village."

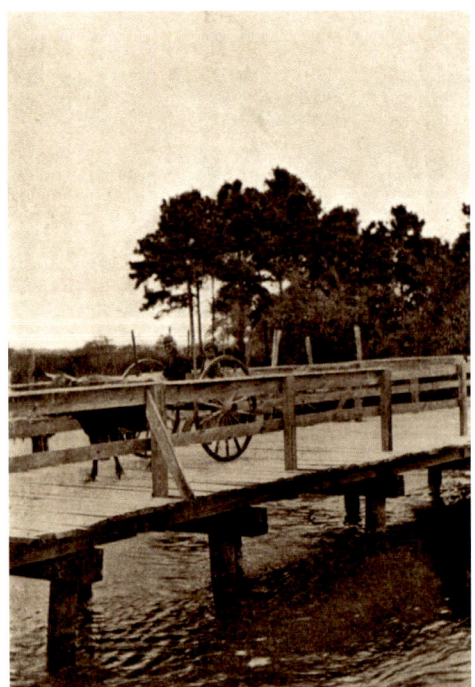

BACK RIVER SCENE: The bridge over the Back River, shown in this illustration from the Hutchins' *Houseboating on a Colonial Waterway*, carried an occasional ox-cart with a load of hay and sometimes a small carryall filled with strangers curious to visit the site of Jamestown. This bridge on and off the island had to be rebuilt, as it had long ago sunk, as they observed, beneath the waters.

WALKING THE ISLAND: After visitors landed a shore boat near the end of the bridge at the little cove that made through a greenery of what the Hutchins' described as fox grape and woodbine, they reached the road shown here and started off into the woodland to reach the old settlement ruins. "It was a pleasant walk among the fragrant pine trees and in the soft light and the lengthening shadows of the waning summer day," they wrote. "Abruptly the grove ended, and thereafter the road led across a succession of marshy hollows and cleared ridges on its way to the other side of the island."

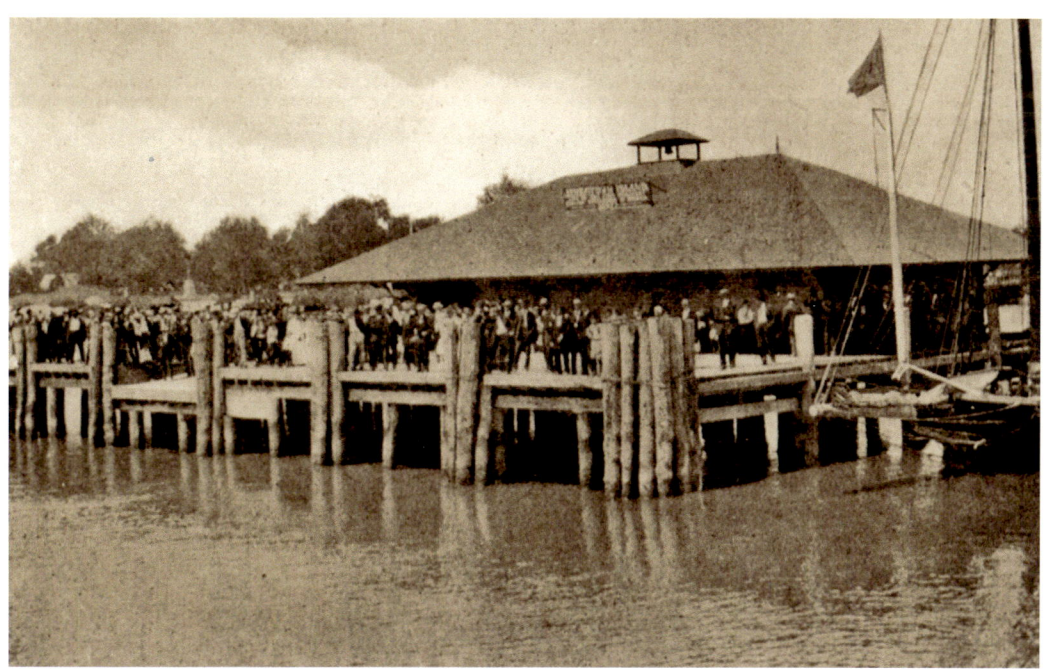

THE PIER: On the James River side of the island, the marshes gave way to a bank of good height edged with a gravel beach. As the Hutchins' houseboat *Gadabout* came closer, buildings were in sight, and there were horses and cattle grazing. "We passed a pier with a warehouse on it, bearing a sign (shown here) which read, 'Jamestown Island, Site of the First Permanent English Settlement in American, 1607." At that point, they could see the ruins of it, namely the old church tower.

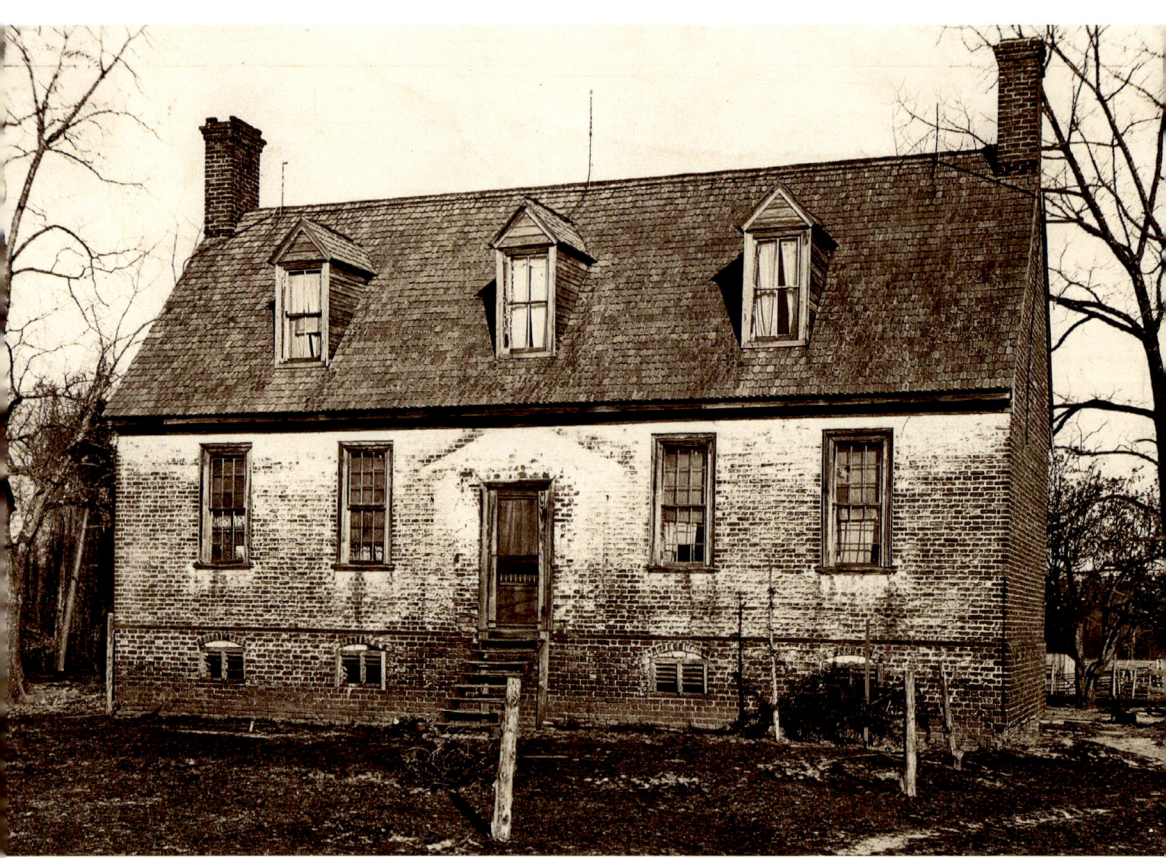

OFF THE ISLAND: According to Preservation Virginia, Smith's Fort Plantation is nestled on the south side of the James River in Surry County, located on the site of Captain John Smith's planned "New Fort," on the land given by Chief Powhatan as a dowry for his daughter Pocahontas upon her marriage to John Rolfe. The eighteenth century manor house (shown as it appeared on November 23, 1928) retains much of its original woodwork and provides examples of early American and English period furnishings from the late 16th through the early 18th centuries. Built sometime between 1751 and 1765, this story-and-a-half Flemish bond brick house was home to Jacob Faulcon and his family. The name "Smith's Fort Plantation" comes from the fact that John Smith began construction of a second fort on this site in 1608. Smith's Fort offered a strategic location for a retreat fort away from the original settlement, but construction was abandoned early due to starving conditions at the first fort and conflicts with the local Native American tribe. A few years later after the successful union of Pocahontas and John Rolfe, the bride's father, Wahunsenacawh, was the paramount chief of Tsenacomoco. Since Preservation Virginia acquired Smith's Fort Plantation from the John D. Rockefeller Foundation in 1933, just five years after this picture was taken, it has been fully restored and boasts a fine collection of colonial English and early American furnishings. The original 1609 fort site is just a short walk or drive away from the plantation. Today, visitors can see the site of the proposed retreat fort, the manor house, and its small garden maintained by the Garden Club of Virginia.

OPPOSITE ABOVE:

ANNUAL SERVICES: A Wide World Photos photographer took this picture of the annual services on Jamestown Island in commemoration of the 321st anniversary of the landing of the first English settlers in the colony, held over several days in May 1928. The picture shown here was taken on May 16, and shows Jamestown settlers' descendants, including Native Americans, standing under the statue of Pocahontas.

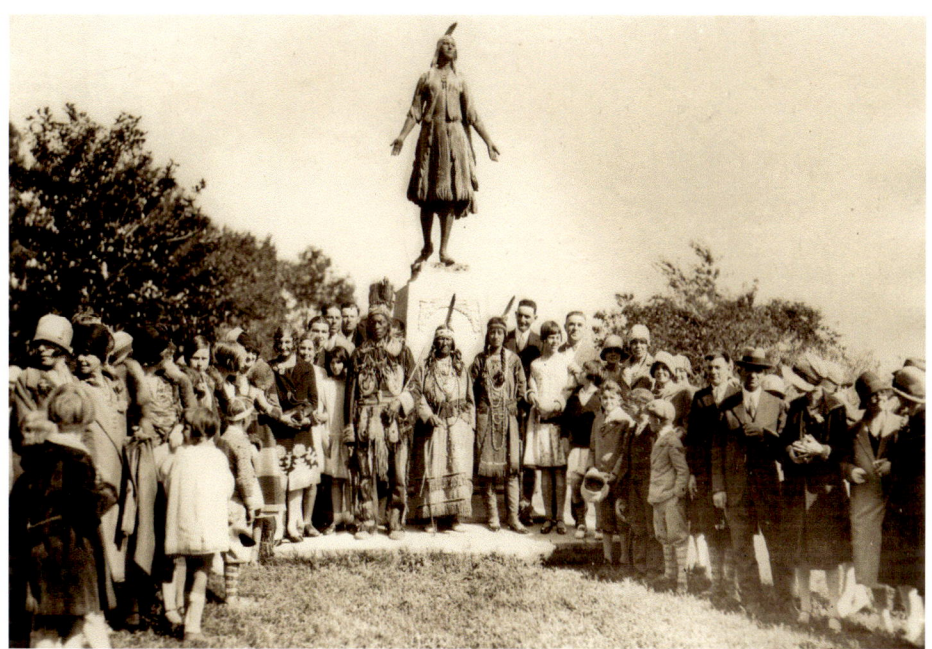

HISTORICAL SITE FOR SALE (BELOW): The caption of this Underwood and Underwood photograph of Jamestown Island read "Historical Site for Sale!—Island Where Pocahontas and Captain John Smith Met Awaits Buyer." The picture shows the scene of the first permanent English colony in America as it looked on July 17, 1930. In 1893 the Jamestown church ruins and twenty-two and a half acres of adjacent land were donated to the APVA (now Preservation Virginia) by the then single owners of Jamestown Island Mr. and Mrs. Edward E. Barney, of Dayton, Ohio. After Edward Barney died, his widow wanted the federal government to buy the rest of the island for $1 million for use as a historical park. Congress approved funding at the time this picture was taken for improving and protecting the grounds and landmarks. The remaining acreage on the island was acquired by the National Park Service (NPS) in 1934 and made part of the Colonial National Historical Park. Today, Jamestown is jointly operated by the NPS and Preservation Virginia.

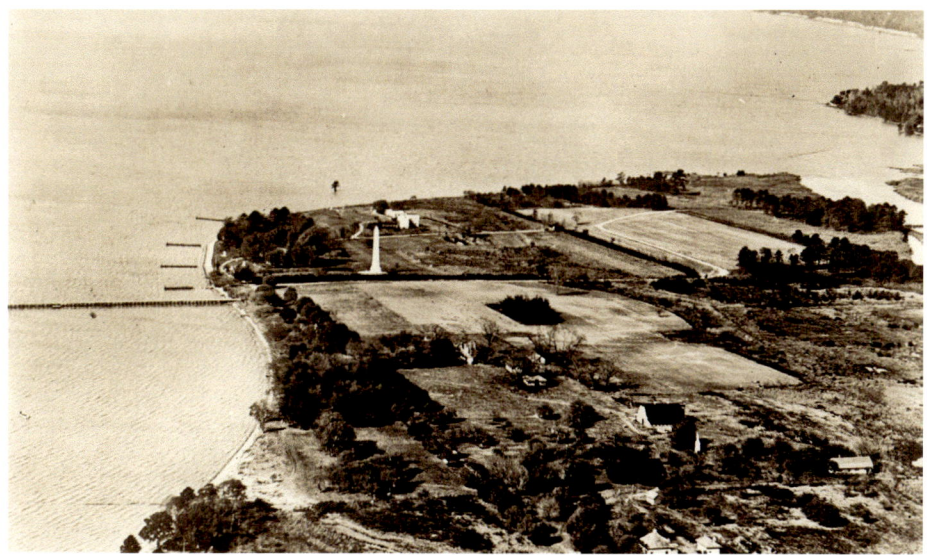

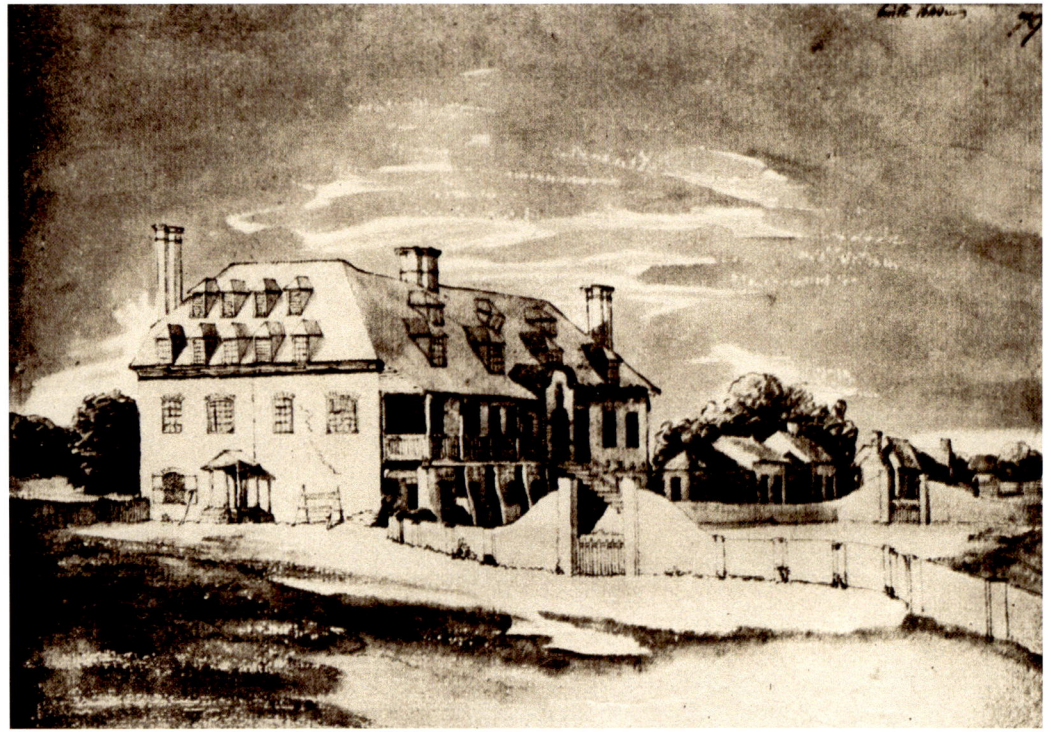

GREEN SPRING: The original manor house at Green Spring was built in 1645, and the iteration of it shown here is circa 1682. The plantation originally encompassed a 2,090-acre experimental farm. Seeking alternative export products to supplement tobacco, which had become the colony's mainstay, Green Spring produced flax, fruits, potash, rice, silk, and spirits, which were shipped to markets in North America, the West Indies, Great Britain, and Holland. This illustration of the Green Spring plantation house is from a 1797 watercolor by Benjamin Henry Latrobe published in the Jamestown Festival official program in 1957.

OPPOSITE ABOVE:

ONLY FOUNDATIONS REMAIN: Built by Sir William Berkeley, only foundations remain of Green Spring Plantation, shown in this Frances Benjamin Johnston photograph dating to 1935. According to the National Park Service, in the spring thousands of daffodils blow in the breeze over level fields a few miles west of Jamestown Island but few would guess that over three centuries ago, the land was the site of a stately governor's mansion and an experimental agricultural center. There is little question that Berkeley began construction of his mansion shortly after he acquired Green Spring; by 1649, his home was built and he was entertaining on a fairly lavish scale. The massive dwelling was seated on a high natural terrace, facing Jamestown. Although the brick house no longer survives, archeological evidence indicates a structure nearly 97 feet long and 25 feet wide, consisting of a row of three rooms and an ell of one room extending another 25 feet on the west end. The 28-inch-thick foundation walls suggest a second story, which a sketch from the late 18th century confirms. All in all, it was a massive and imposing structure. The name Green Spring originated from the natural spring on the site, which continues over 350 years later to produce huge quantities of very beautifully clear, ultra cold water. The Green Spring produced a flow "so very cold that 'twas dangerous drinking the water thereof in Summer-time,' wrote a visitor in the 1680s." *Library of Congress.*

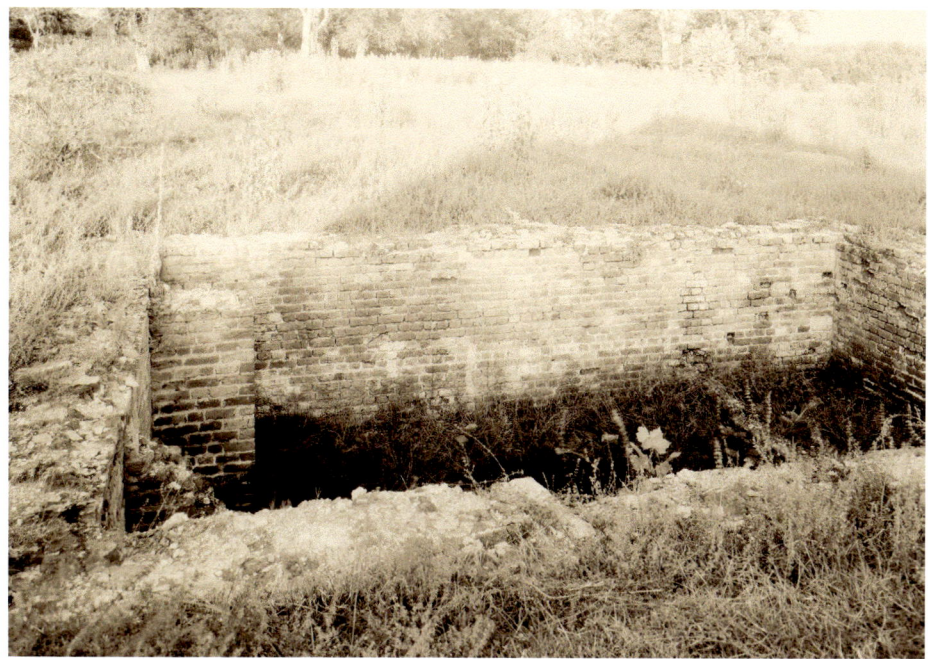

LOST TO REBELLION (BELOW): The site shown here (labeled Unit A, Sub-unit 39) was first excavated in 1934, and the foundations were drawn by Historic American Buildings Survey (HABS) around that time. The archaeological work uncovered a pair of row houses made of brick and likely one-story in height. Each house had a full cellar and later renovations added a shed room on the south side. The location of the chimneys is not clear, but the quality of the artifact assemblage suggests this was a domestic site. Artifacts include a casement window, hardware, and tin-glazed ceramic tiles. Followers of Nathaniel Bacon burned the buildings in 1676. *Library of Congress.*

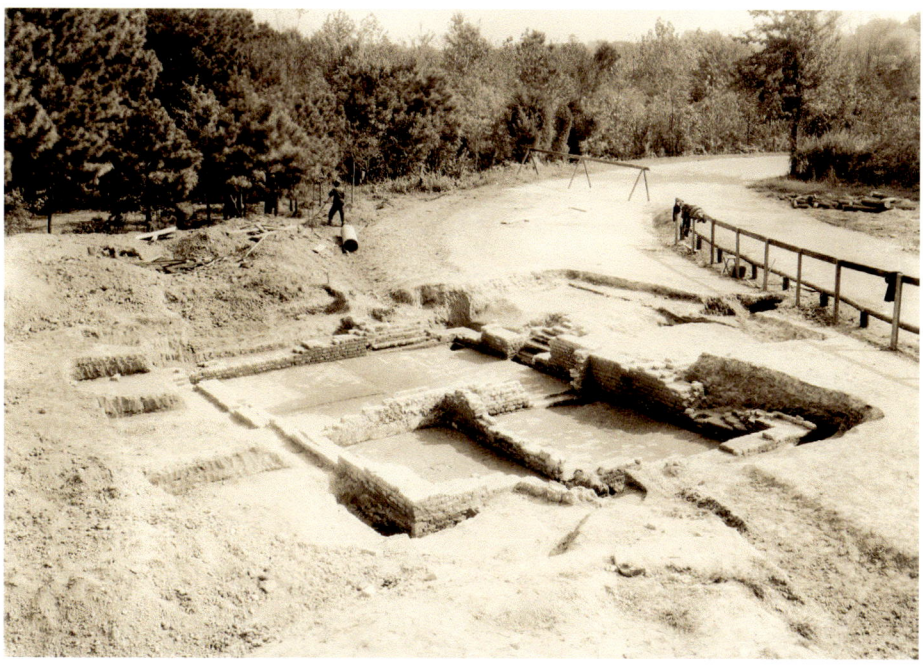

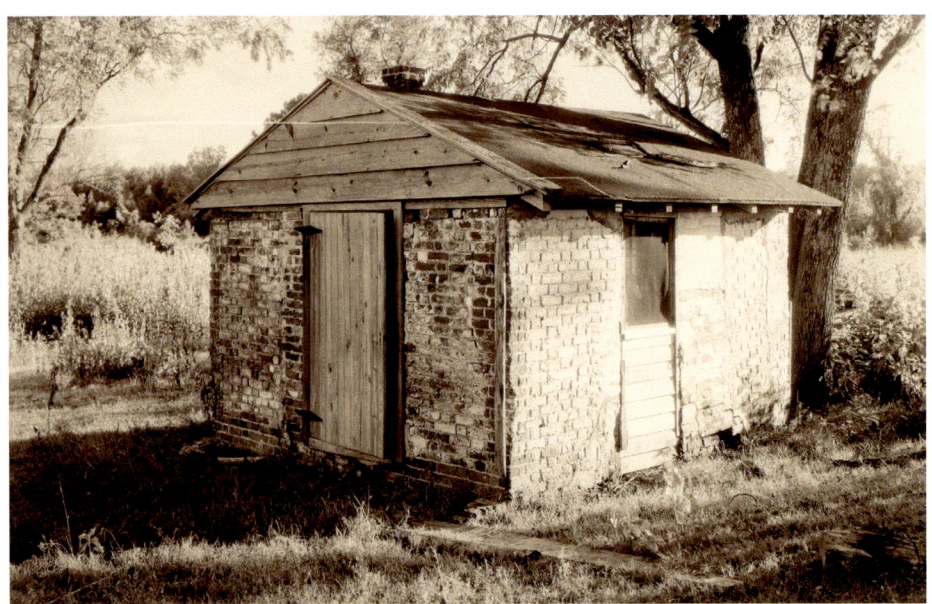

GREEN SPRING OUTBUILDING: This Green Spring Plantation outbuilding was photographed by Frances Benjamin Johnston in 1935 (both views). The plantation witnessed many historic events, including the beginnings of slavery in Virginia, Bacon's Rebellion in 1676, the Battle of Green Spring during the American Revolutionary War in 1781, the emancipation of its slaves in 1803 by the will of William Lee, and the nearby Battle of Williamsburg in 1862 during the Peninsula Campaign of the Civil War. A second mansion on the site was burned during the Civil War. In modern times, about 200 acres of the original plantation are preserved by the National Park Service (NPS) as part of the Colonial National Historical Park, which acquired the property in 1966. The site includes archaeological and architectural remnants of the manor house and ancillary structures such as those shown here. It was listed on the National Register of Historic Places on December 29, 1978. *Library of Congress.*

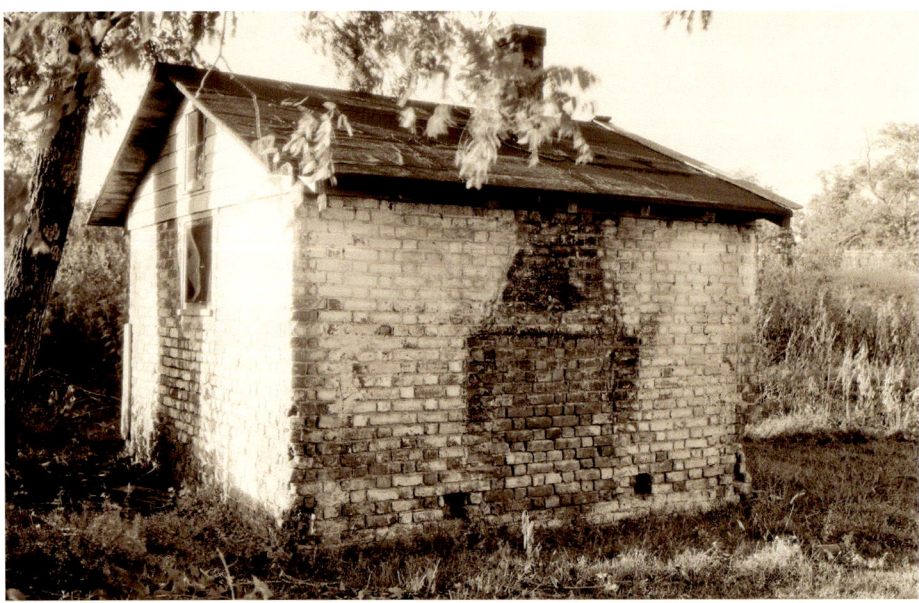

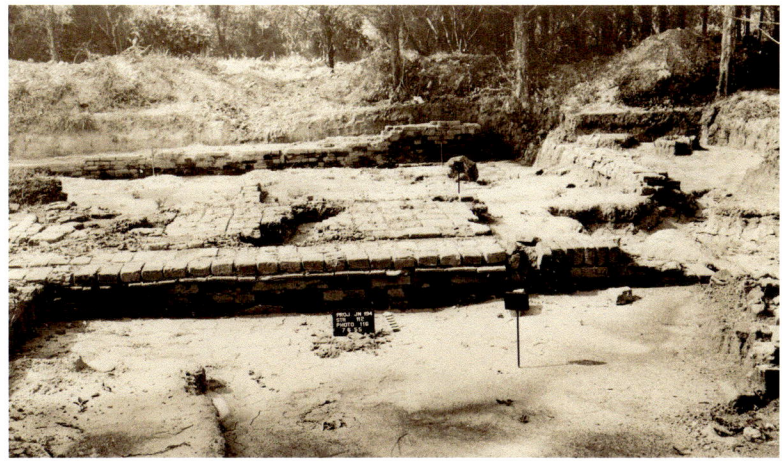

HARVEY'S DWELLING: The dwelling shown here, of which only archeological remains were found, was built by Sir John Harvey in the 1620s and expanded by Harvey (or Governor Sir William Berkeley) around 1640 and is probably the only site with a lifespan matching that of New Towne (1620–98) on Jamestown Island. Initially an earthfast, timber frame building, Harvey or Berkeley improved it and converted the wood building into a larger, brick house measuring 51 feet by 33 feet with three principal rooms and several cellars in a leanto or shed. Likely it was one-story in height; two of the three rooms were heated. This house was damaged in a fire circa 1656. The house was substantially rebuilt in 1665 and was burned on September 19, 1676, during Bacon's Rebellion. *Library of Congress.*

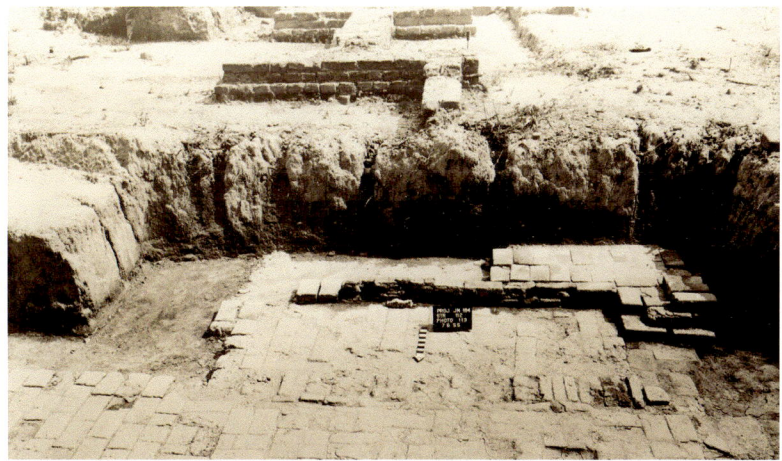

COTTER AND JELKS EXCAVATION: The Harvey (or Berkeley) dwelling was likely rebuilt by 1684 and may have burned again in 1698. The site was excavated by John Cotter and Edward Jelks over a two-year period starting in 1954 and reexamined in 1993. The first house is representative of the framing and building practices used in the Chesapeake that used hole-set or ground-standing posts and interrupted sills supported by brick footings as foundations for clapboard upper frames. Sections of the footings were incorporated into the later south foundation wall and so reveal the posts were set on six foot centers. This corresponds to construction techniques used in the brewhouse and apothecary and at Flowerdew Hundred. Around 1640, of interest, this house was expanded and improved with brick walls. The original north wall was rebuilt for two chimneystacks and the shed added. Evidence of this period includes pipe stems, quarrels, and both domestic and imported ceramic wares. *Library of Congress.*

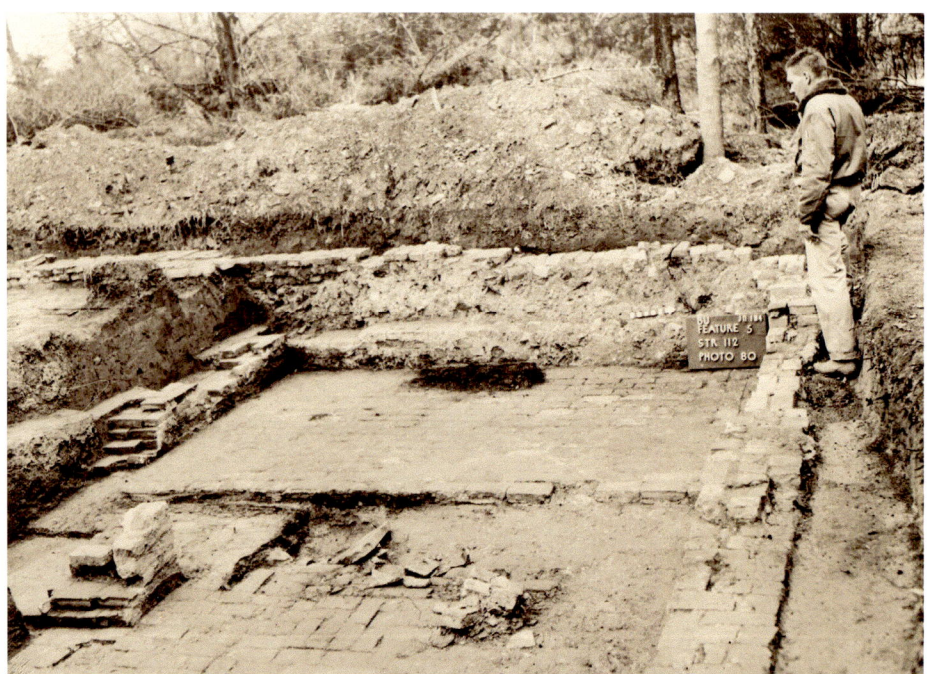

STATEHOUSE BUILDING (ABOVE): The rebuilding of Harvey (or Berkeley) dwelling that followed the 1656 fire was extensive, and some suggest it served as the colony's first statehouse although the evidence now leans toward structure 144 in the Ludwell statehouse complex as having that distinction. Nonetheless, architectural evidence for this building has striking parallels to the Maryland statehouse, including the square tiles used for the floor and the ornamental plasterwork. The building was raised to two stories, and incorporated a porch tower. It was made of brick and had large casement windows with cames and diamond-shaped quarrels. After 1676, it was rebuilt largely as it had been before the fire. *Library of Congress*.

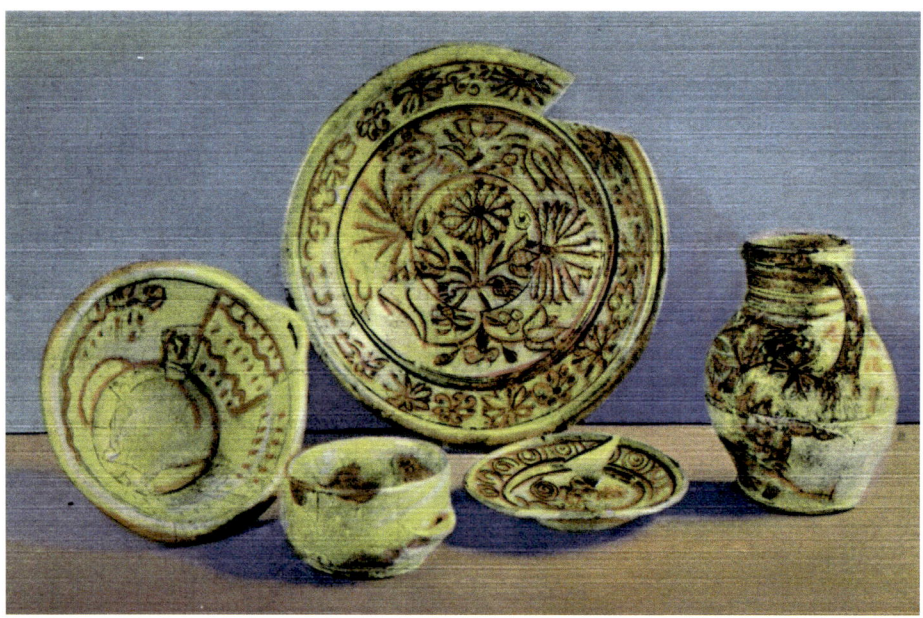

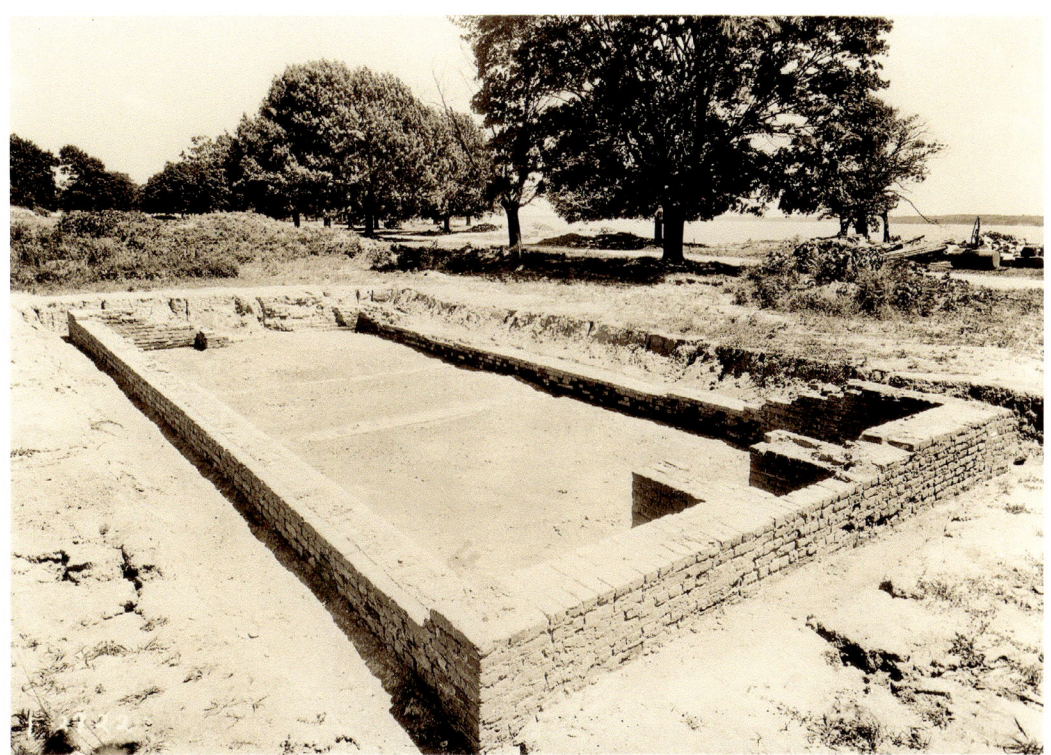

THE TRAVIS HOUSE: The architectural remains shown here were uncovered in 1935 and suggest the gambrel-roofed dwelling built by Edward Champion Travis after 1755. The house stood through 1781 and likely until 1803. The house was built of brick and had a central passage plan with internal end chimneys. It was one-story in height, over a basement. Accompanying the house were several outbuildings, including a kitchen and a dairy or meat house. This house site was excavated by the National Park Service archaeologist John T. Zaharov between September 1 and October 29, 1934, who along with H. Summerfield Day, Alonzo W. Pond and W. J. Winter directed the Civilian Conservation Corps (CCC) excavators, although stratigraphic documentation of this time was lost. *Library of Congress*

OPPOSITE BELOW:

SGRAFFITO SLIPWARE: Sgraffito slipware unearthed at Jamestown is shown on this linen postcard that is circa 1940. The objects in the picture were pieced together from fragments recovered during archeological excavations that took place under the direction of Herbert Summerfield "Pete" Day, who ran the digs at the settlement between 1934 and 1935. According to Day's archeological report dated 1935, the dig recovered English and Italian sgraffito-decorated wares and many other gravel-tempered coarse earthenware utilitarian vessels and seventeenth-century English delftware objects. Soon after excavation, the slipwares were repaired and restored. At least 47 slipware vessels and many more large fragments were cataloged. The slipwares identified by Day were ultimately dated circa 1670 from the coastal region of North Devon in southwest England, most in sgraffito-style.

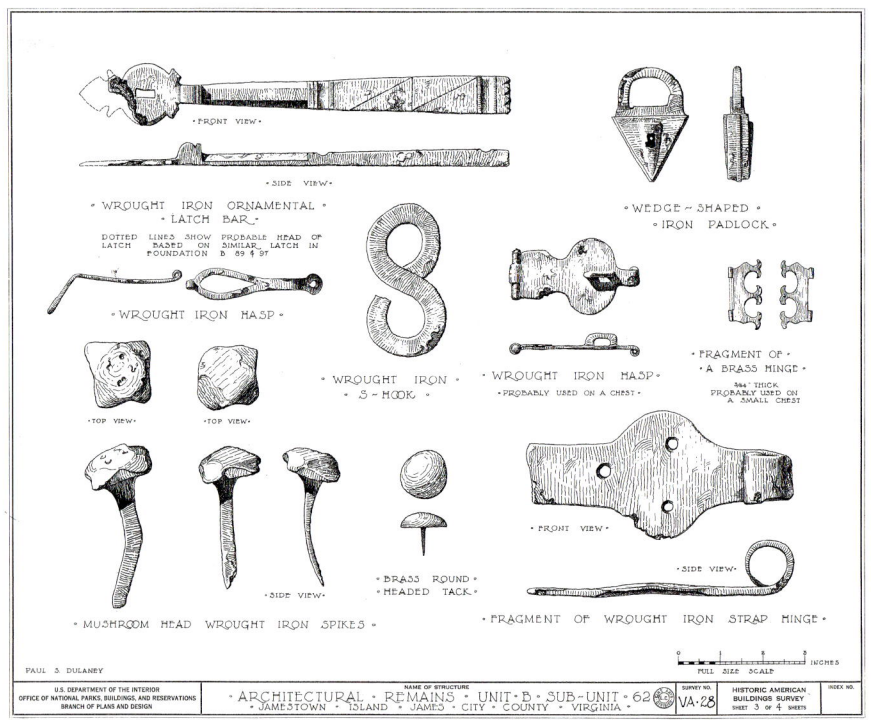

HARDWARE FINDS: The most interesting fragment of hardware recovered from the Edward Champion Travis dwelling was an ornamental latch bar of wrought iron, almost identical with one recovered from the foundation of the first brick statehouse in Virginia (and shown in this HABS line drawing, top left, and the photograph, top right). The latch shown here is slightly shorter than the one found in the statehouse site. The wedge or v-shaped padlock shown here (drawing and photograph), though smaller, is very similar to one found near the APVA enclosure. *Library of Congress*.

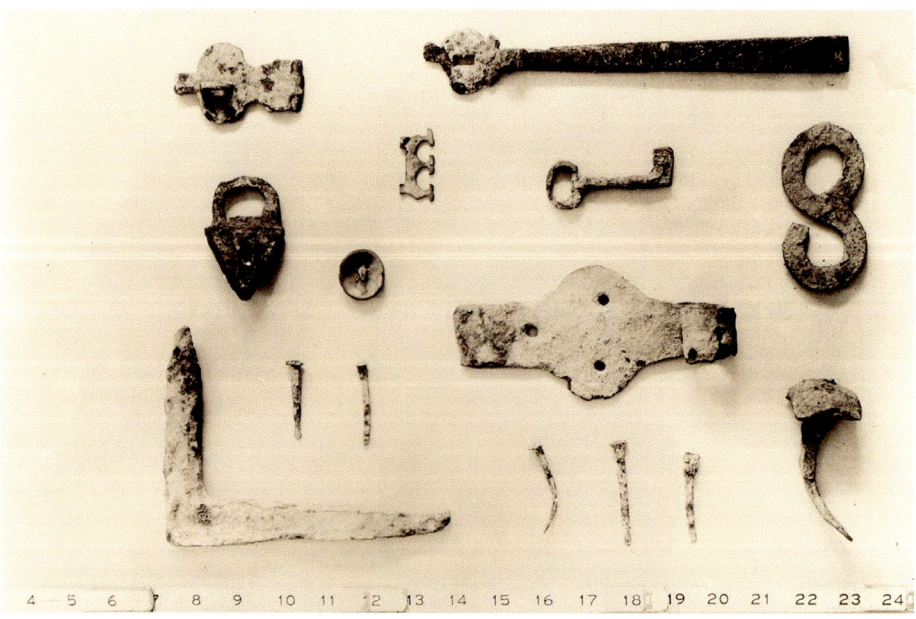

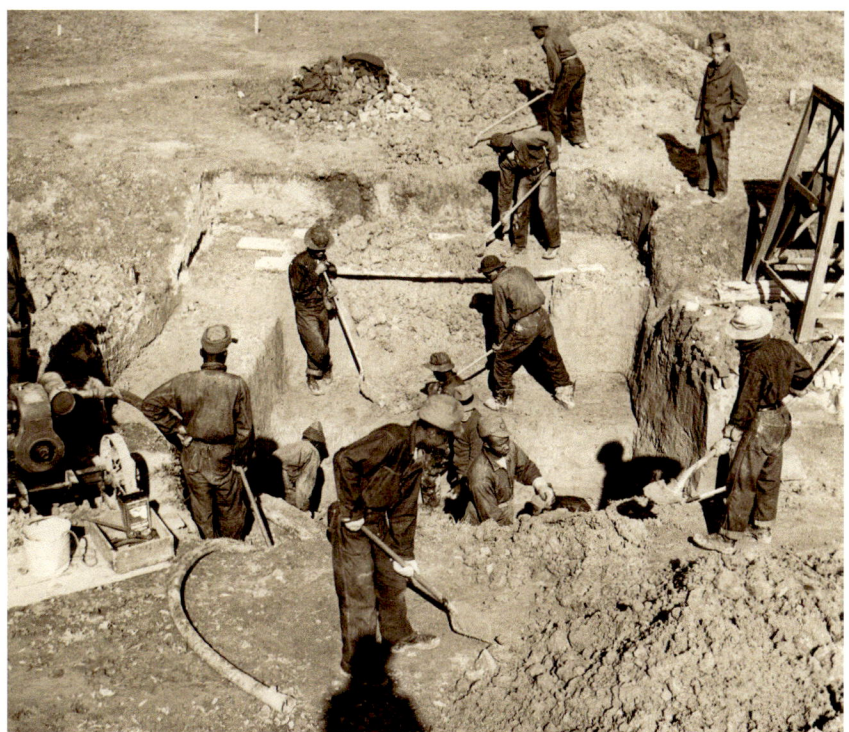

CCC Digs: Excavation of Jamestown had been going on for over four years using Civilian Conservation Corps (CCC) labor when this picture was taken by an Associated Press photographer on November 11, 1938.

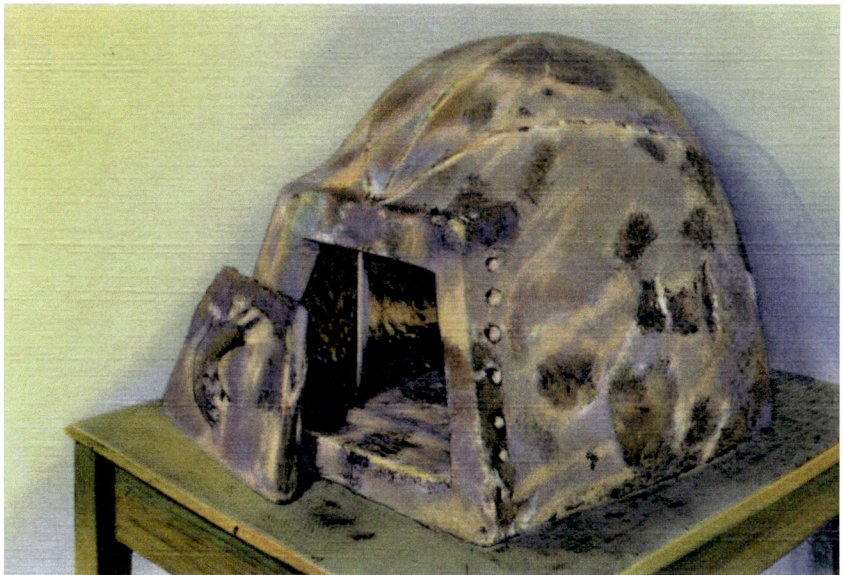

Restored Find: This fire-clay baking oven, restored from fragments recovered during early archaeological work performed at Jamestown was on display at the National Park Service museum when this early divided-back postcard was issued.

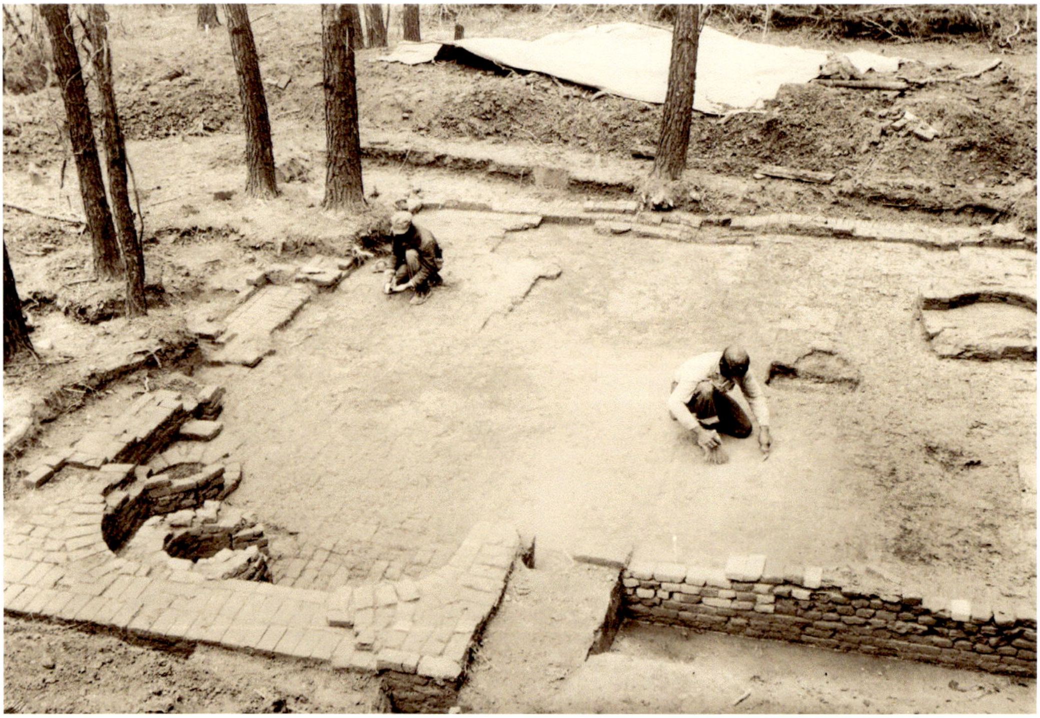

THE BREWHOUSE AND APOTHECARY (ABOVE): Evidence suggests that this structure served as a brewhouse and apothecary between circa 1623 when it was constructed until circa 1650 when it was destroyed. The work building was constructed by either Sir Francis Wyatt or Sir John Harvey. *Library of Congress.*

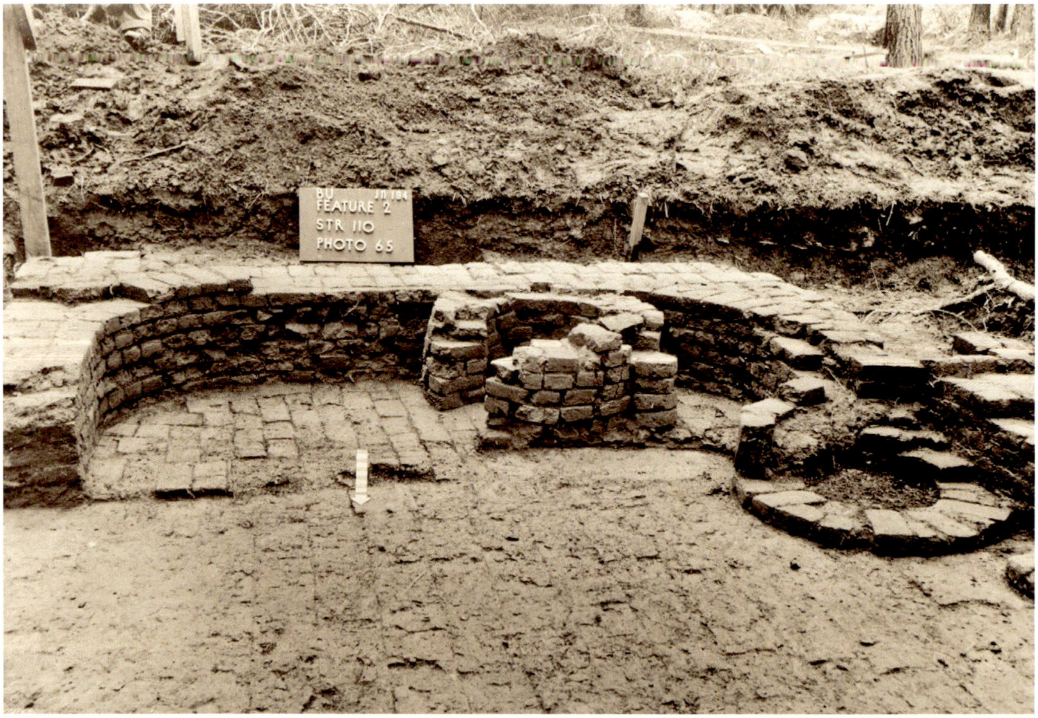

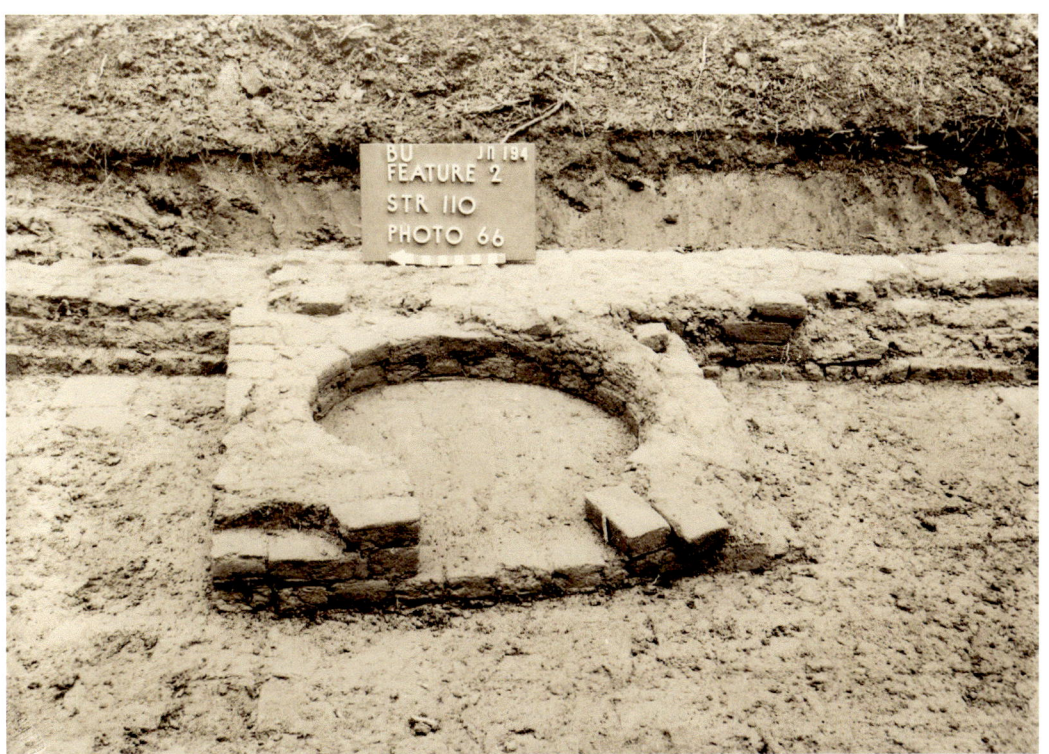

BEER WAS KING: Built with one boiler and a large fireplace, the interior of the brewhouse and apothecary was not partitioned and the floor was paved. Two other boilers were added. The site was excavated in 1954/55 and reexamined in 1993. Alcohol consumption was a way of life for the colonists. Beer, cider and other rather weak fermented beverages were consumed from the earliest days of Virginia history. *Library of Congress.*

OPPOSITE BELOW:

UNCOVERING THE BREWHOUSE: The brewhouse and apothecary was two bays, 22 feet 6 inches by 24 feet 6 inches, likely with a clapboard frame and M roof covered in flat tiles, and resting on a raised hole-set or ground-standing foundation with brick footings and interrupted sills. The six brick footings housed an upright timber for the upper frame; these are suggested on the HABS drawings and more clearly described in the field notes of the archaeologists, John Cotter and Edward Jelks, who excavated it in 1954/55. *Library of Congress.*

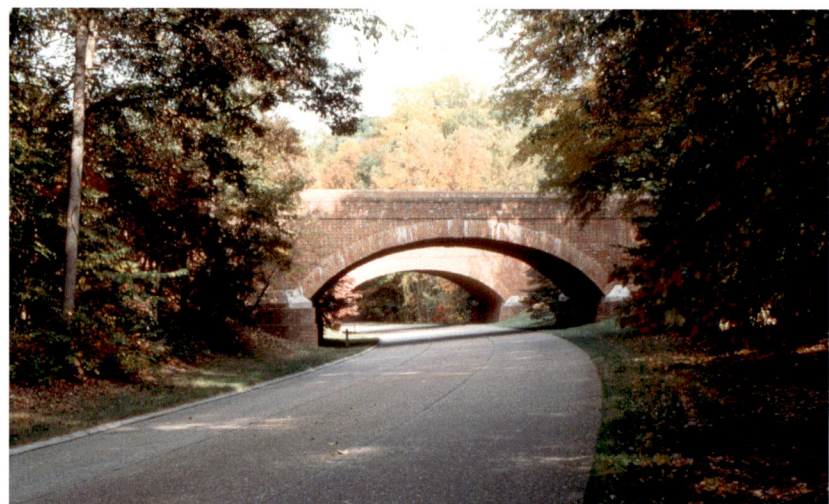

COLONIAL PARKWAY: The Colonial Parkway is a 23-mile scenic drive connecting the historic sites of Historic Jamestown, Colonial Williamsburg, and the Yorktown Battlefield. Free of any modern commercial development, the parkway was designed to provide continuity to the visitor experience of motoring through nearly 400 years of American colonial history. Traversing a diverse environment, the parkway provides visitors with dramatic open vistas of the James and York rivers and tidal estuaries as well as shady passageways through pine and hardwood forests. This contemporary photograph was taken by the National Park Service, Colonial National Historical Park. *National Archives.*

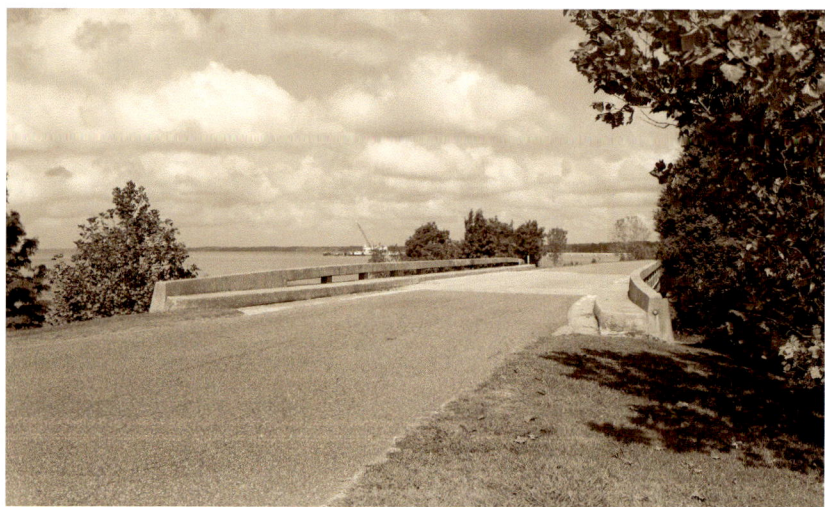

THE ISTHMUS BRIDGE: The establishment of the Colonial Parkway, beginning in 1931, made the historic sites at Jamestown, Williamsburg, and Yorktown more accessible to the ever expanding motor public. The parkway's designers, through the use of a curved three-lane road with an exposed aggregate surface, intended this highway to serve not only as a means for visitors to enjoy the park but also to limit the speed and numbers of vehicles on the road itself. The parkway's bridges and tunnel (under Williamsburg), all relatively small and sparsely ornamented, reflect the desire of the planners for these structures to complement the natural environment of the Colonial National Historical Park. Jack E. Boucher took this picture of the isthmus bridge to Jamestown Island (the view is from the southeast on the road). Note the ferry pier in the background. *Library of Congress.*

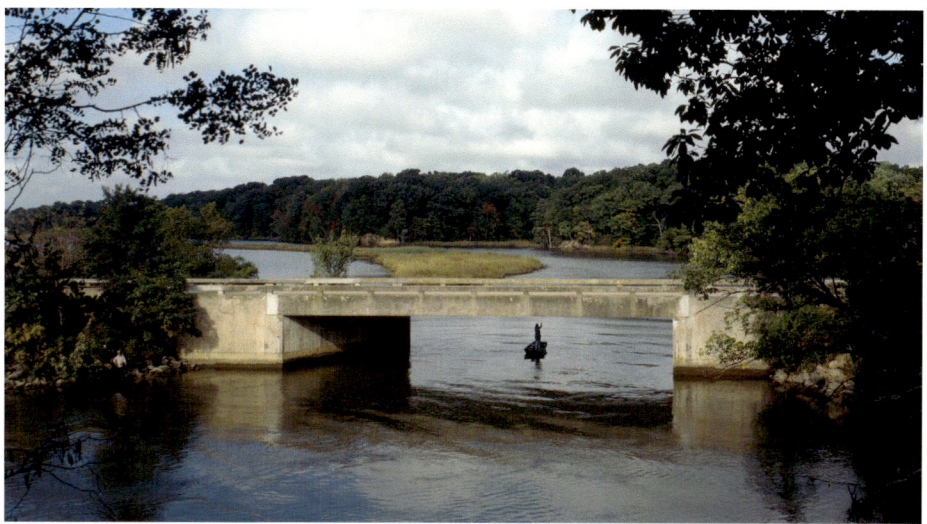

COLLEGE CREEK BRIDGE: During the spring of 1955, contracts were awarded for the construction of bridges over College, Mill and Powhatan creeks and a bridge along the recreated isthmus linking Glasshouse Point to Jamestown Island; twenty years later the bridge at College Creek was reinforced and refurbished. Bridges over small bodies of water, such as the structures at College and Felgates creeks and Jones Pond, have modern reinforced concrete linear spans with low post-and-lintel concrete railings that imitate the design of the wood guardrails found throughout the Colonial Parkway. These white concrete bridges have no ornamentation; their low railings do not interfere with the motorist's view of the creeks and rivers. This September 1995 view of the College Creek Bridge was taken by Jack Boucher. *Library of Congress.*

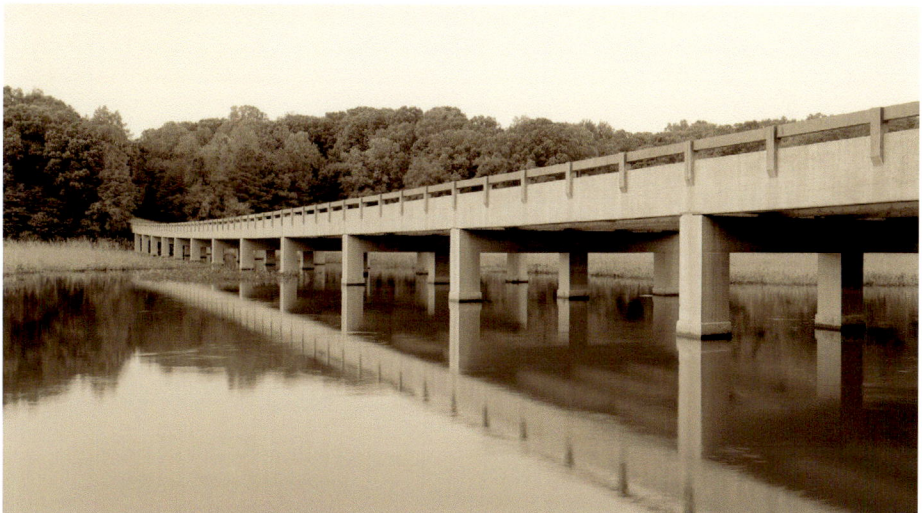

HALFWAY CREEK BRIDGE: The Halfway Creek Bridge is the longest structure located along the Colonial Parkway, measuring 850 feet. The reinforced concrete slab bridge was completed in December 1942, and marked the first extension of the parkway south of Williamsburg toward Jamestown Island. Since the roadway was not completed to Jamestown until the 1950s, Halfway Creek Bridge was an isolated structure with no approach road for thirteen years. This picture of the Halfway Creek Bridge, partial view from the southwest, was taken by Jack Boucher in September 1995. *Library of Congress.*

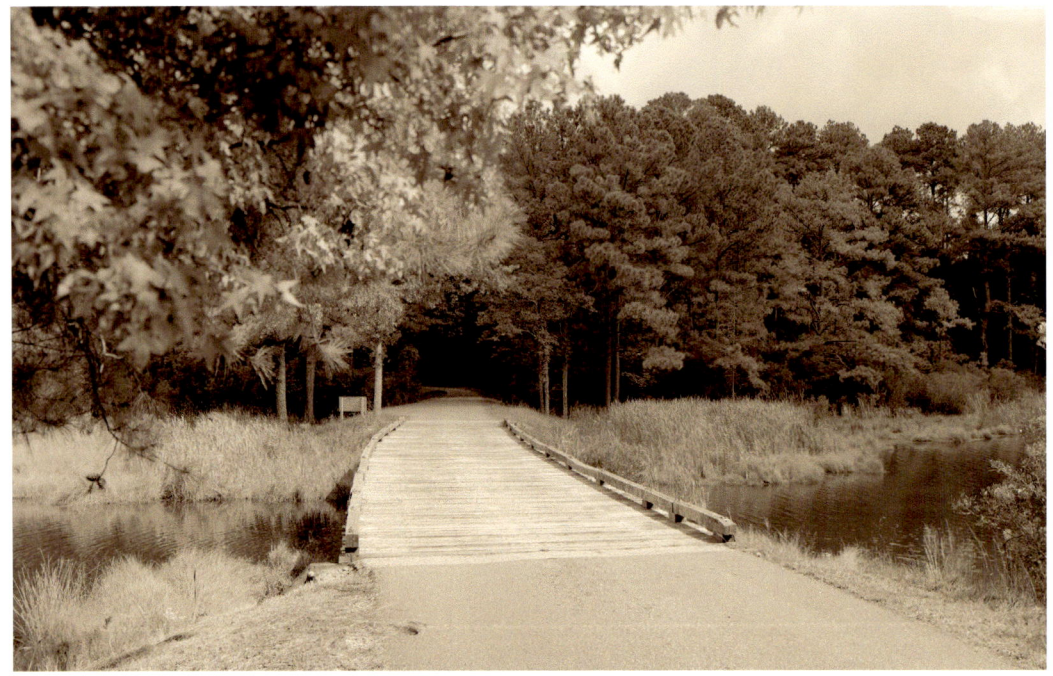

THE WILDERNESS ROAD: Considered a "wilderness road," the full circuit is designed to provide visitors a sense of the primitive isolation of the seventeenth-century frontier. Shown here is a southwest view of the first wooden bridge, photographed by Jack Boucher in September 1995. *Library of Congress*.

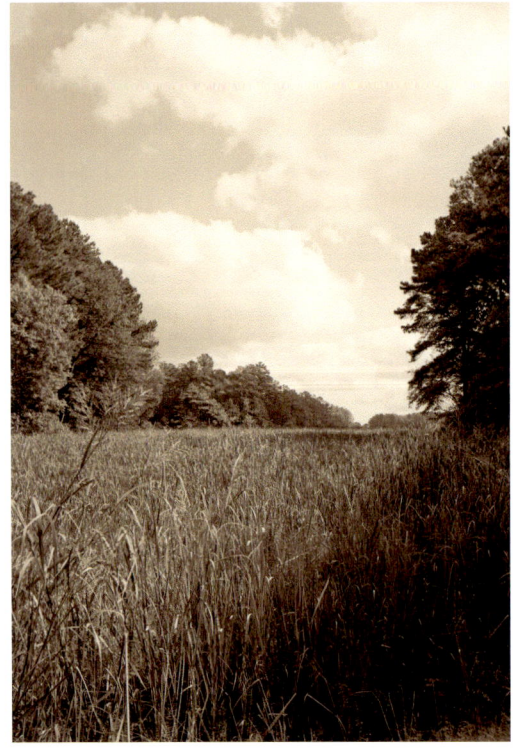

THE ISLAND LOOP ROAD: This is the view east along the Jamestown Island loop road, also photographed by Jack Boucher in September 1995. *Library of Congress*.

Section 4

Preserving the Past for the Present

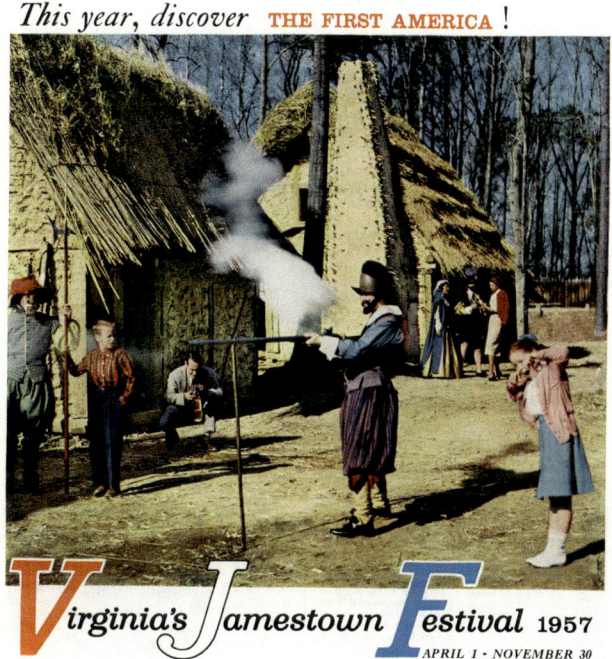

THE SEMISEPTCENTENNIAL: The Jamestown semiseptcentennial—the 350th— celebration was held from April 1 to November 30, 1957. This advertisement was produced by the Virginia Department of Conservation and Development to encourage visitation to "The First America." This celebration united the National Park Service (NPS), the Commonwealth of Virginia and the Colonial Williamsburg Corporation for a special preservation effort, including finalized plans for enhanced visitor facilities, and better protection and greater appreciation of Jamestown, Williamsburg and Yorktown.

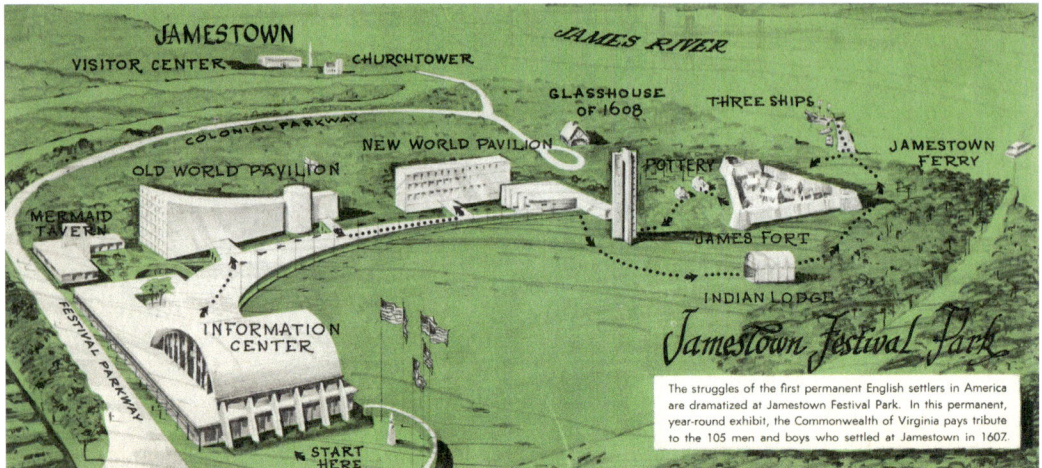

JAMESTOWN FESTIVAL PARK: To improve the historical atmosphere, State Highway 31 and the ferry wharf were moved west of Jamestown, and the scenic Colonial Parkway, linking the historic triangle, was completed. The staging area for the celebration, known as the Jamestown Festival Park, was located near Jamestown and today remains the site of the visitor and education center. Along with the National Park Service site, it hosted special activities during the celebration. At the NPS site, the reconstructed glasshouse, the memorial cross and the visitor center were completed and dedicated. This celebration continued from April 1 to November 30 with over a million participants, notably dignitaries and politicians, including the British ambassador, Queen Elizabeth II and Prince Philip, and Vice President Richard Nixon. This 1957 postcard shows the layout of the festival park.

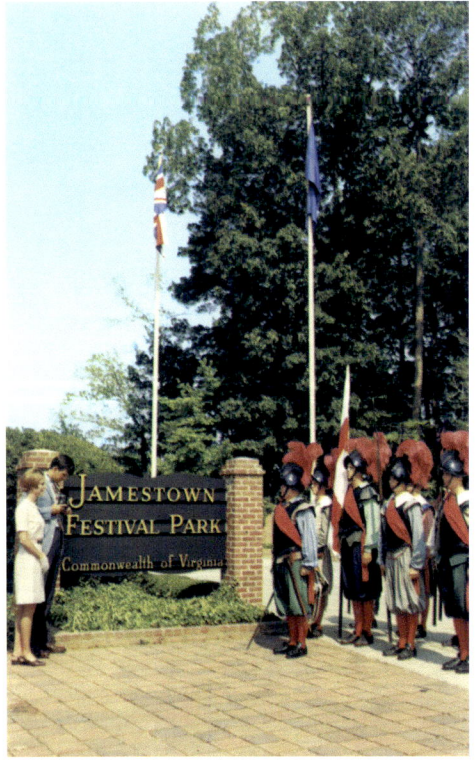

FLAG RAISING CEREMONIES: Flags of the nations surround the entrance to the commonwealth's year-round exhibit area at Jamestown Festival Park in 1957. Guides clad in the uniforms of Jamestown's early halberdiers were tasked to perform daily flag-raising ceremonies each summer.

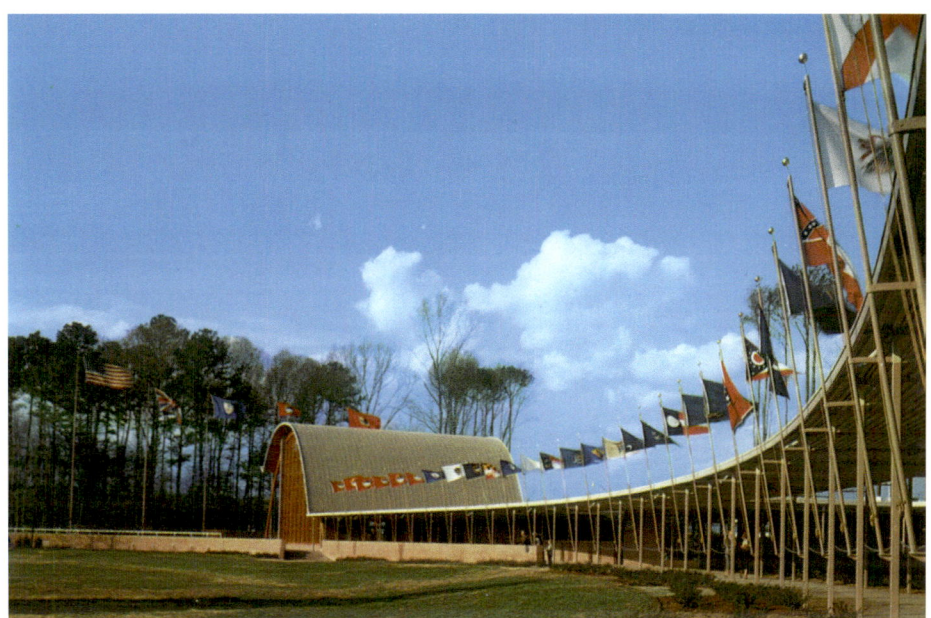

THE CURVED ARCADE: Flags of the states of the union (shown on this 1957 postcard of the Jamestown Festival Park) were displayed along the curved arcade that linked the festival buildings. Beginning with Virginia's, they followed the order in which the colonies were settled and the states admitted to the Union.

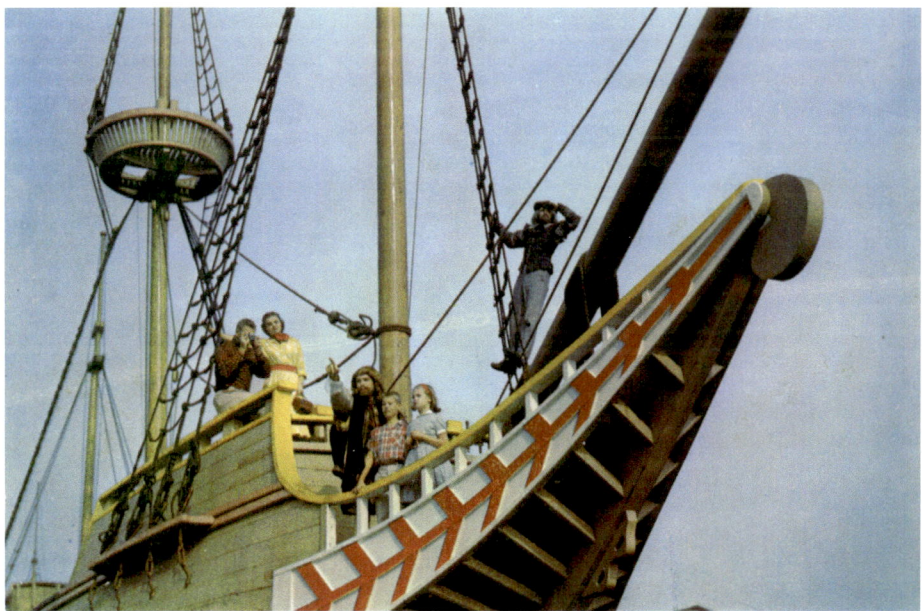

SUSAN CONSTANT: The bow of the flagship *Susan Constant*, one of three replica vessels that brought the first English colonists to the Jamestown settlement, is shown on this postcard, issued in the same period of the Jamestown 350th celebration. Replicas of the *Susan Constant* and her sisters, the *Discovery* and *Godspeed*, remain docked today in the James River at Jamestown Settlement, formerly Jamestown Festival Park, adjacent to the Jamestown National Historic site.

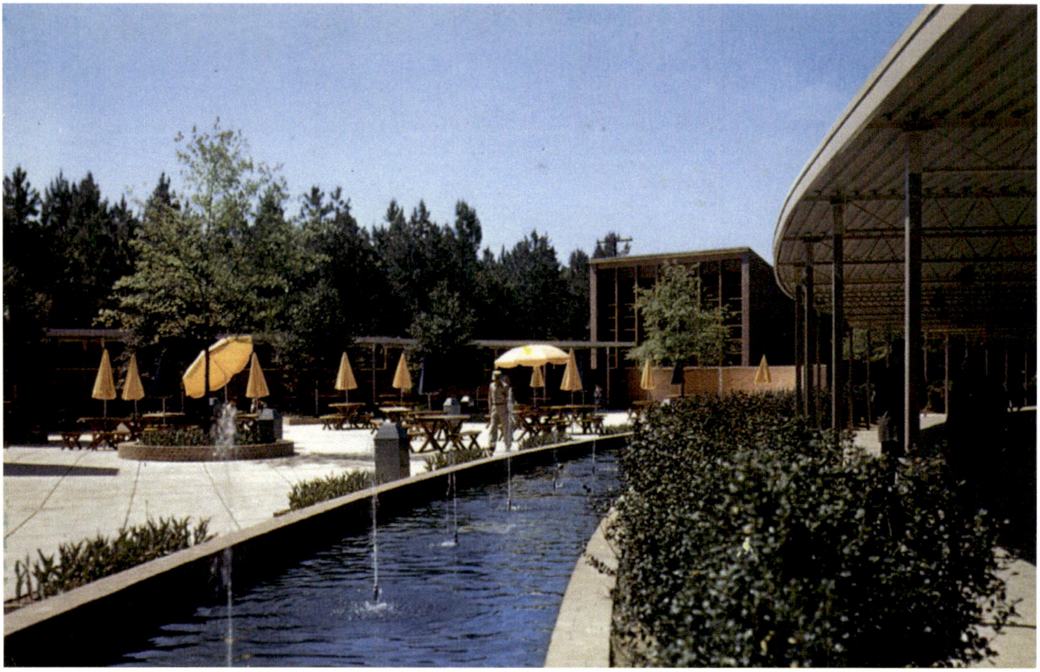

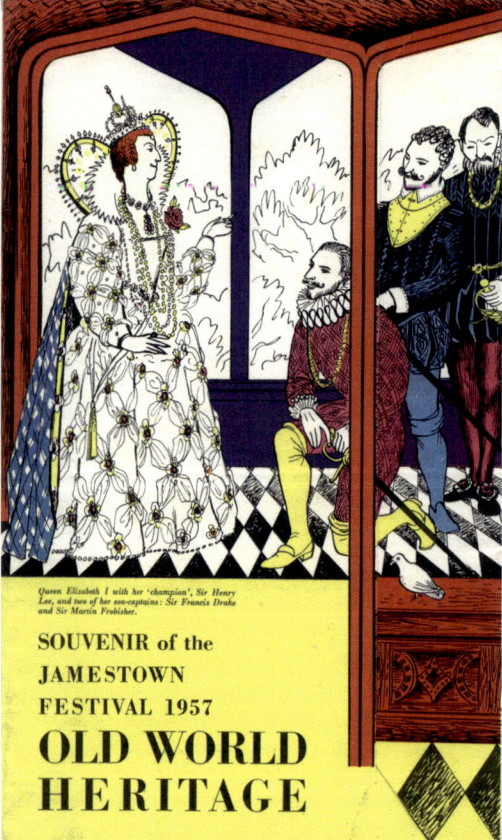

OLD WORLD HERITAGE: The Old World Pavilion pictured on this 1957 postcard contained an "Old World Heritage" exhibit presented by the British government, which also printed a special program (shown here).

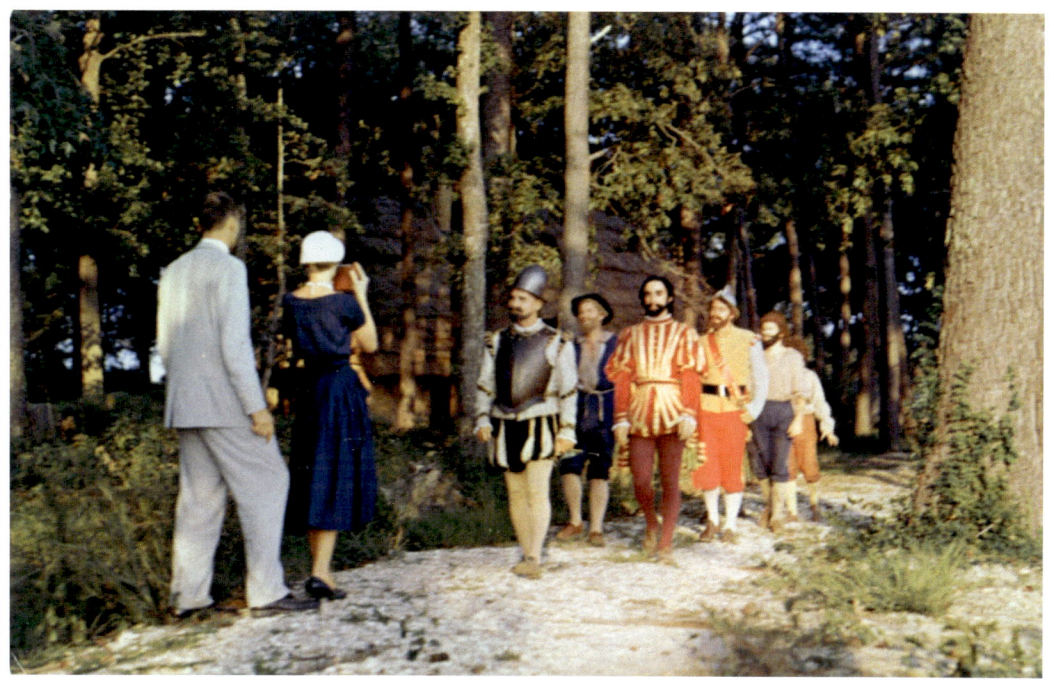

THE GREATE ROAD: The scene of visitors taking pictures of re-enactors on the "great road" near the glasshouse site on Glasshouse Point in the Colonial National Historical Park takes us back to the period of the 350th anniversary celebration. The "Greate Road" was the principal way to and from Jamestown Island in the early period of settlement.

WAX FIGURES AND ARTIFACTS: A wax model of Sir Francis Drake and the actual silver-gilt cup presented to Drake by Queen Elizabeth I to commemorate his circumnavigation of the world between 1577 and 1580, one of Jamestown's Old World Pavilion's many blendings of real and reconstructed items, was on display for the settlement's 350th anniversary. The British government installed a large exhibit inside the pavilion that told the story of Jamestown's beginnings and the history of British colonization that followed. The cup shown here forms a globe topped with an armillery sphere and an early navigational instrument; it is engraved with a map of the world and breaks open at the center, the line of the Equator. The cup belongs to Drake's resident town of Plymouth, in England's Devon, historically known as Devonshire. The photograph was taken on August 16, 1957, by the British government.

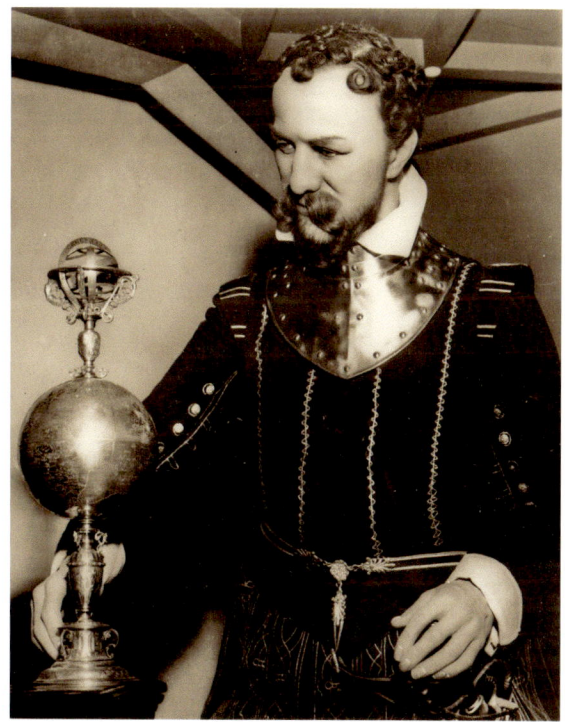

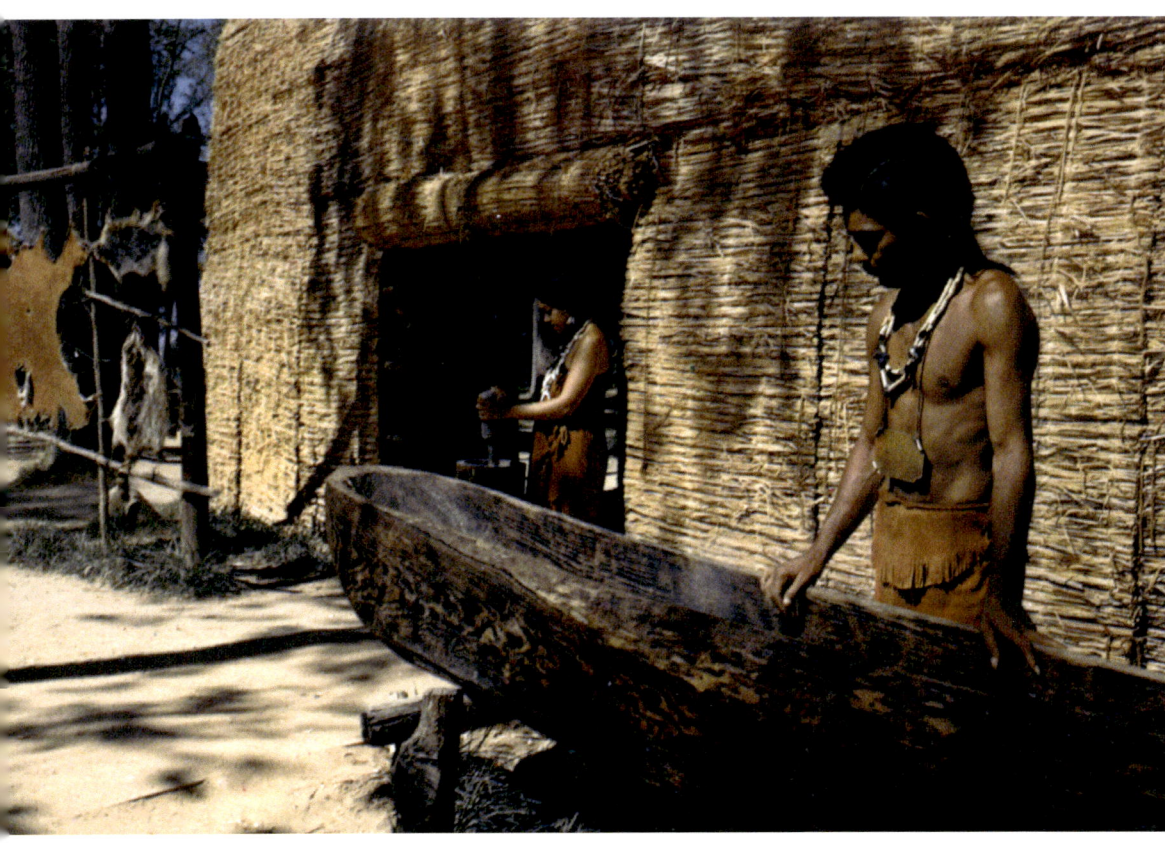

THE DUGOUT: For more than three centuries, the log—also called a dugout—canoe was essential to life on the Chesapeake Bay, the United States' largest estuary, for travel, harvest and trade. Fashioned from single trees by Powhatan Indians, the log canoe was the dominant watercraft at the time English colonists arrived at Jamestown in 1607. The bald cypress was the preferred tree from which the Powhatan men built their dugouts. The adaptability of this open, shallow vessel for navigating and fishing along the Chesapeake waterways led to the canoe being used by European colonists who built their own version of it with metal tools and boatbuilding technology that they imported from their native England. Indian log canoe making was part of the Powhatan village exhibit at Jamestown Festival Park in 1957 and is shown on this period postcard.

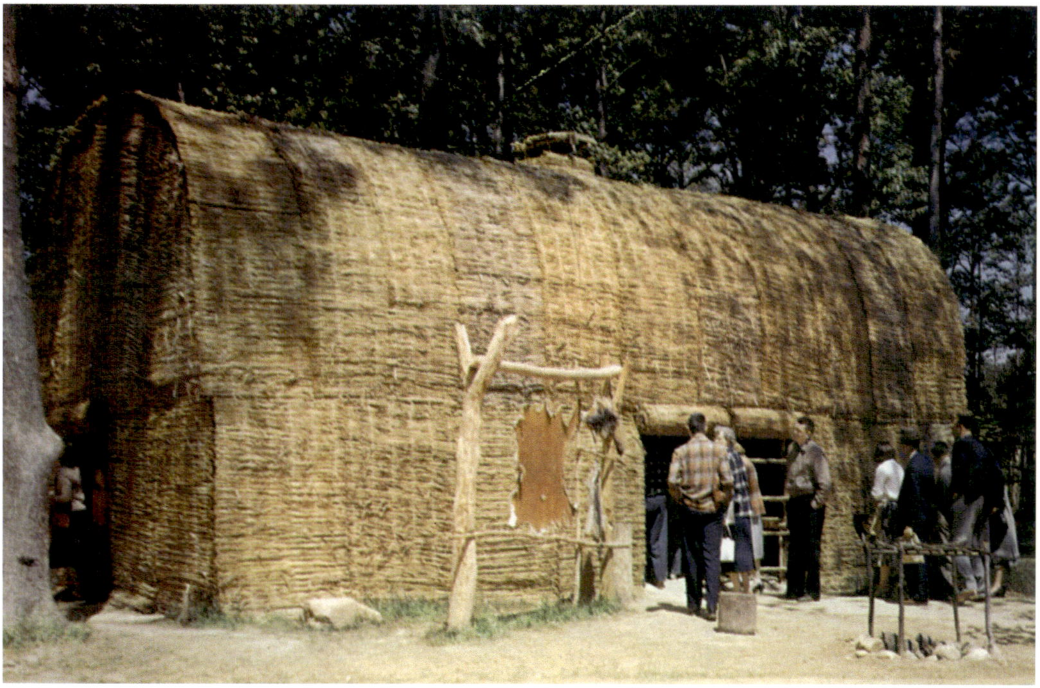

POWHATAN VILLAGE: The recreated Powhatan Indian village is based on archaeological findings at a site once inhabited by Paspahegh Indians, the Powhatan tribal group closest to Jamestown, and descriptions recorded by English colonists. In anticipation of the 1957 celebration, a replica of Powhatan's lodge—a long house—was built within the historic area and is shown on these exterior and interior photographs reproduced on period postcards.

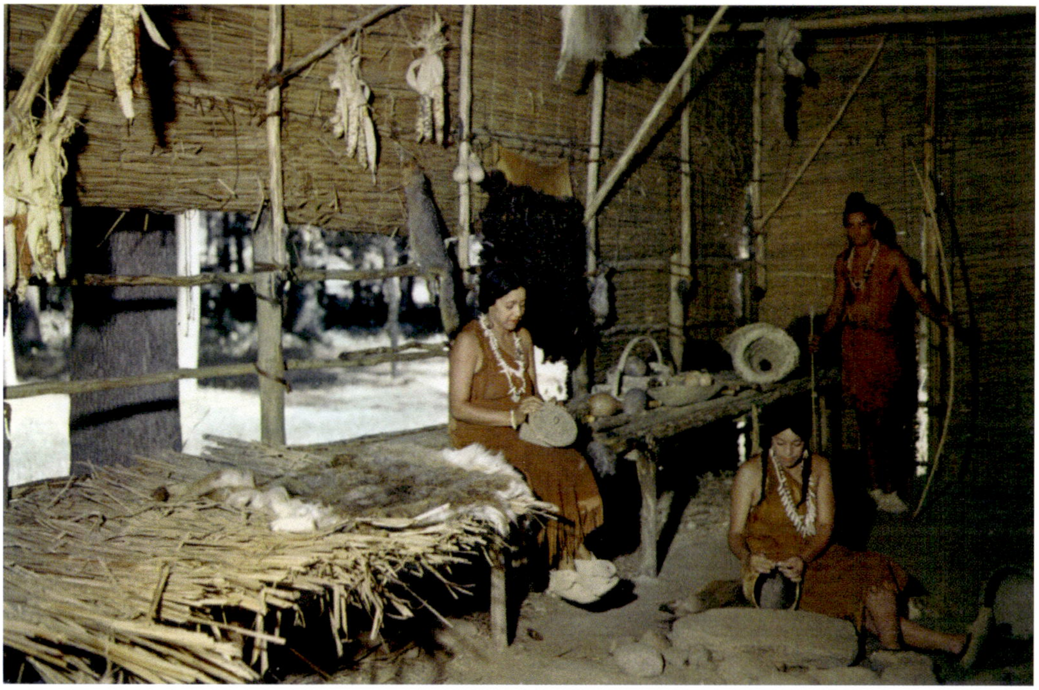

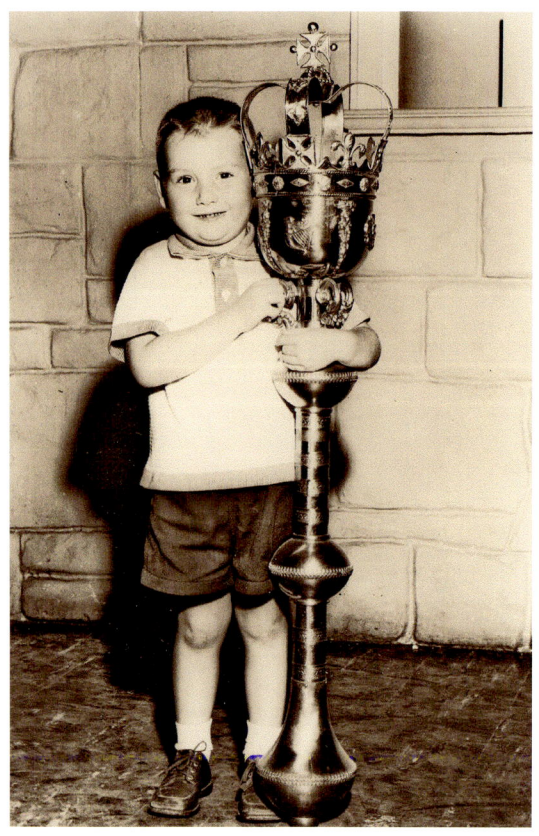

THE SPEAKER'S MACE: Taken on August 26, 1957, Christopher Butts of Westerfield, New Jersey, a four-year-old visitor to the Old World Pavilion, demonstrated that the replica of the speaker's mace, symbol of authority of Great Britain's House of Commons, is bigger than he. Dating from 1660, the speaker's mace is carried by the sergeant of arms in procession before the opening of every session of Commons; it rests on the table during the session.

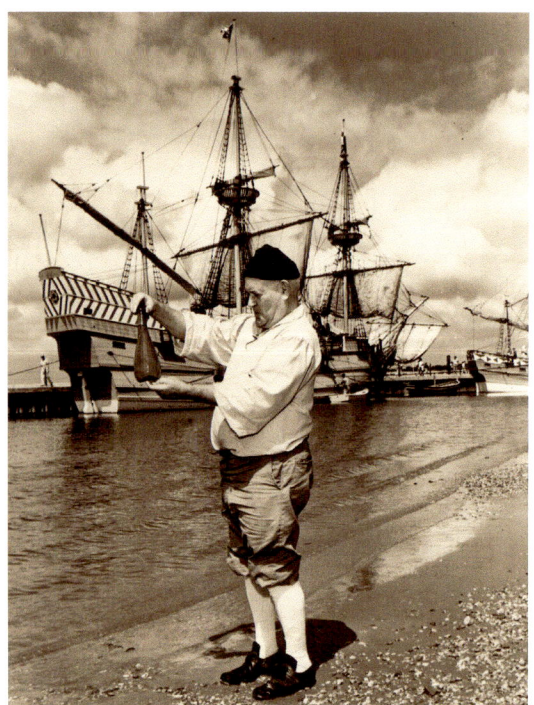

BLESSING IN A BOTTLE: Appropriately costumed Ernest Tomlinson fills a bottle he blew himself with water from the James River at Jamestown, Virginia, in answer to a request from England. The bottle of river water was later to play an important part in the Royal artillery's searchlight tattoo at Woolwich, England, where it was used to christen a small-scale replica of the *Susan Constant*. In the background is a full-scale replica of the *Susan Constant*, flagship of the fleet that brought the first permanent English settlers to the New World in 1607. The British military display has as its theme the 350th anniversary of the founding of Jamestown. Tomlinson was a worker at the reconstructed glasshouse, or glass factory, built at Jamestown in 1608. The picture was taken on August 28, 1957.

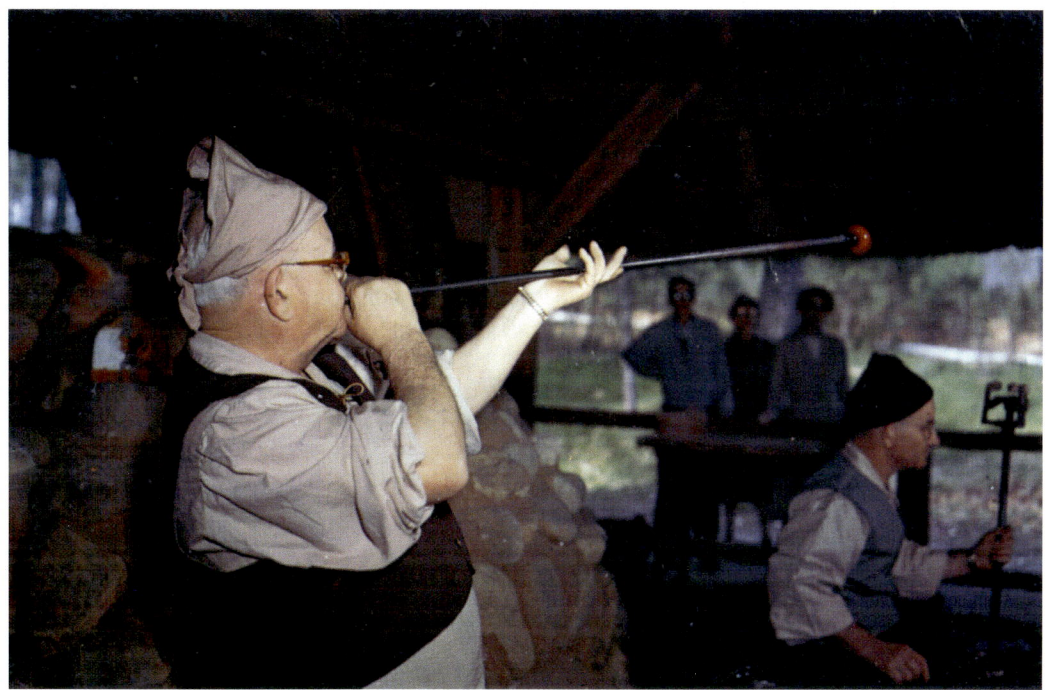

GLASSBLOWING: One of the first English attempts at industrialization and manufacturing in America was glassblowing. The Virginia Company of London hoped glass production might provide the profit that it was looking for. The New World abounded with raw materials -wood for fuel and ash, and sand (silica) for the glass. All that was needed were artisans and various laborers to produce the glass. Arriving with Captain Christopher Newport on the second resupply in early October 1608, the Virginia Company of London sent eight Dutchmen (Germans) and Poles to produce glass, pitch, tar, and soap ash. By early December, Newport departed for England with "trials of Pitch, Tarre, Glass, Frankincense, Sope ashes, with what Clapboard and Waynscot that could be provided." However, what type or form of glass and how much was actually produced is unknown. This first attempt at a full glass production facility in the New World would not be successful. At "glass point" near Jamestown, the glass furnaces were re-discovered and excavated in 1948. Today, in a reconstructed, interpretive facility, glassblowing is again performed at Jamestown. Modern artisans, in reproductive clothing, produce common glass objects very much as they must have done almost 400 years ago. The picture of the glassblower (shown here) was taken at Jamestown Festival Park during the 1957 celebration.

FOLLOWING PAGE:

THE QUEEN AND THE PRINCE (ABOVE): Queen Elizabeth II and Prince Philip appear amused by two "prisoners" in stocks during their tour of the Old Fort at Festival Park on October 16, 1957. Less than fifty years later, on May 4, 2007, the queen and Prince Philip would return to Jamestown to attend the ceremony commemorating the quatercentenary of the settlement. *Library of Congress.*

HIGHLIGHT OF THE CELEBRATION (BELOW): This general view of the crowd that awaited the arrival of Queen Elizabeth II on this October 16, 1957, was taken by the United Press International from the stand from which she was later scheduled to speak. The queen's speech was the highlight of the 350th Jamestown Celebration.

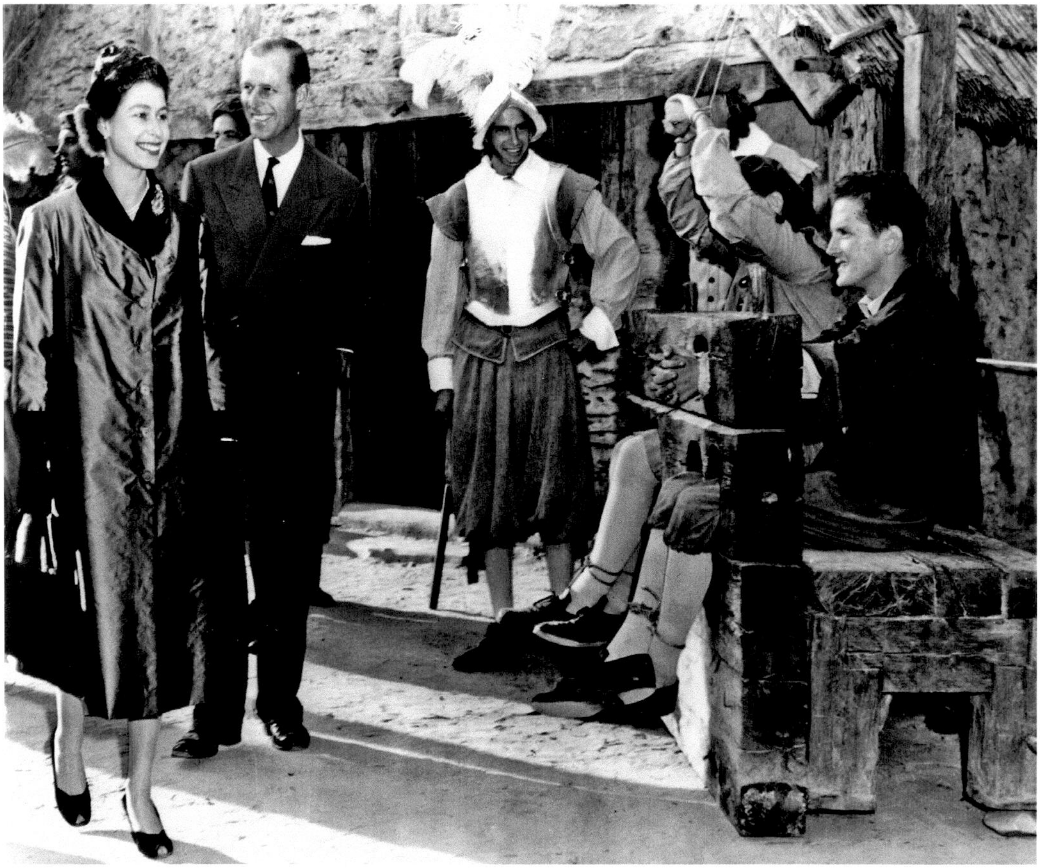

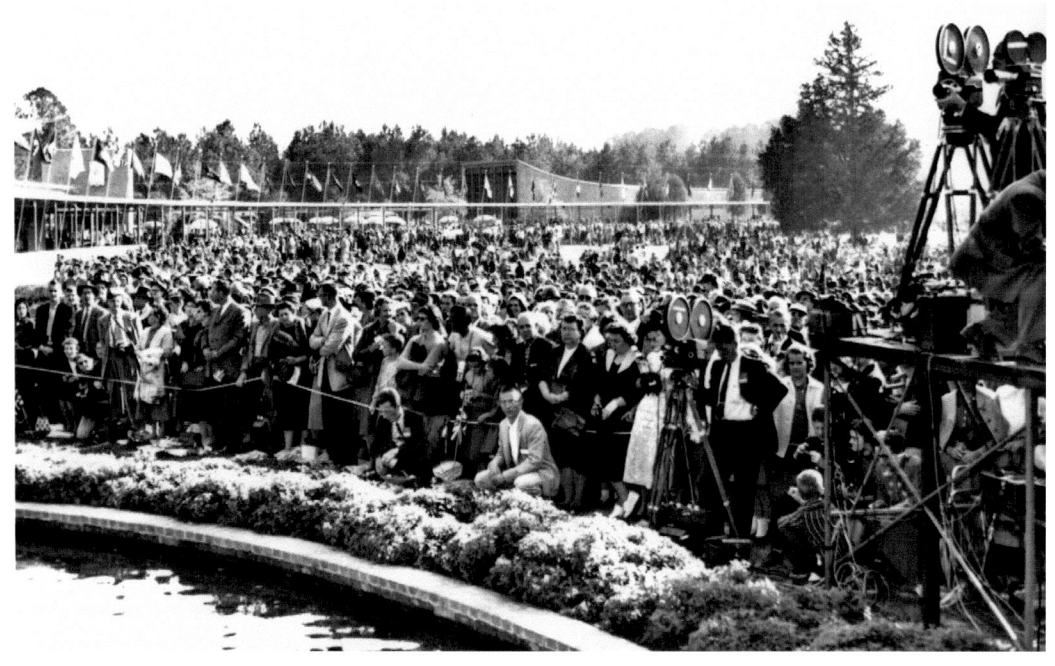

THE HALBERDIER AND THE CHICKEN (RIGHT): Robert Chandler of Richmond, Virginia, dressed in the garb of an eighteenth century halberdier, is shown here in April 21, 1959 United Press International photograph escorting a prize white silkie show chicken up the red carpet as part of a ceremony at Jamestown commemorating the arrival of the first chickens in 1607. Several hundred onlookers showed up for the event.

EARLY SHIP REPLICAS (BELOW): Jamestown's three replica ships—the *Susan Constant*, *Godspeed* and *Discovery*—are shown here as they looked on June 15, 1962, when Williamsburg photographer Thomas L. Williams took the picture.

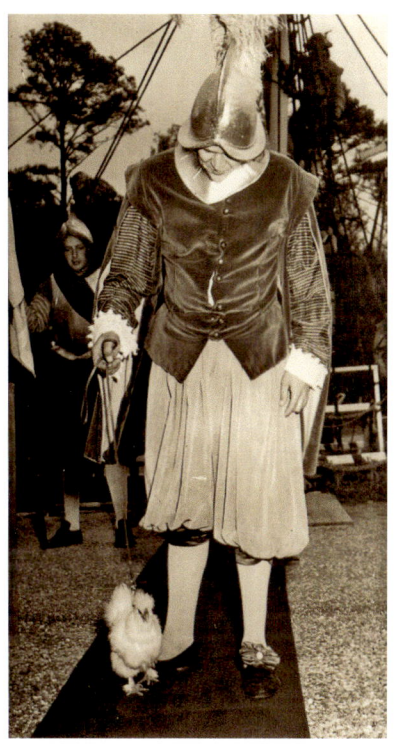

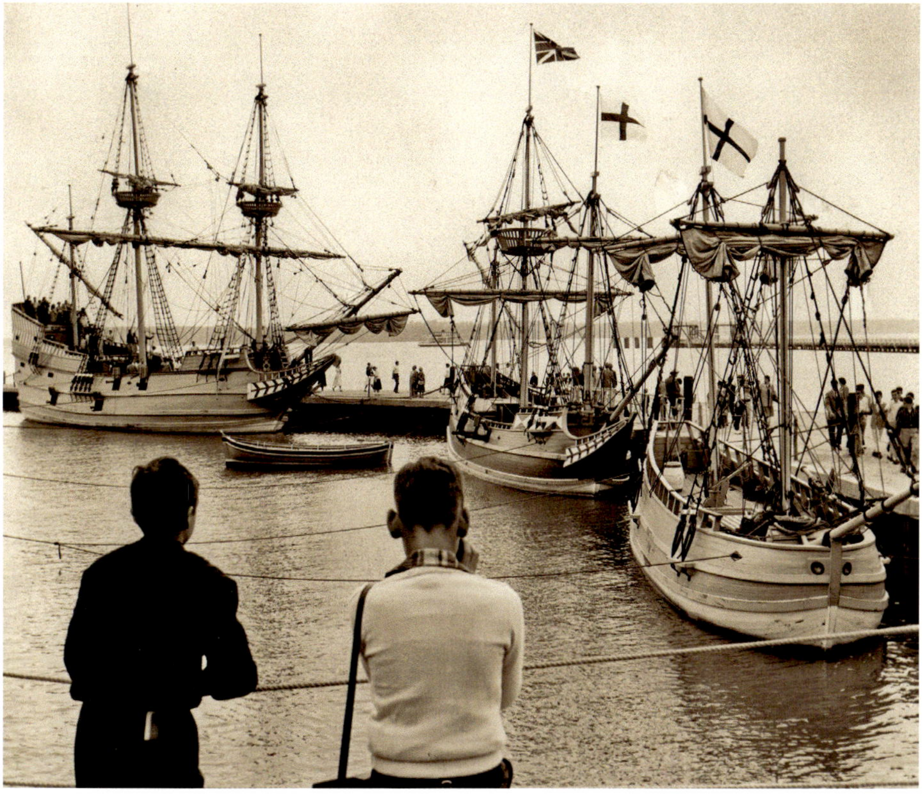

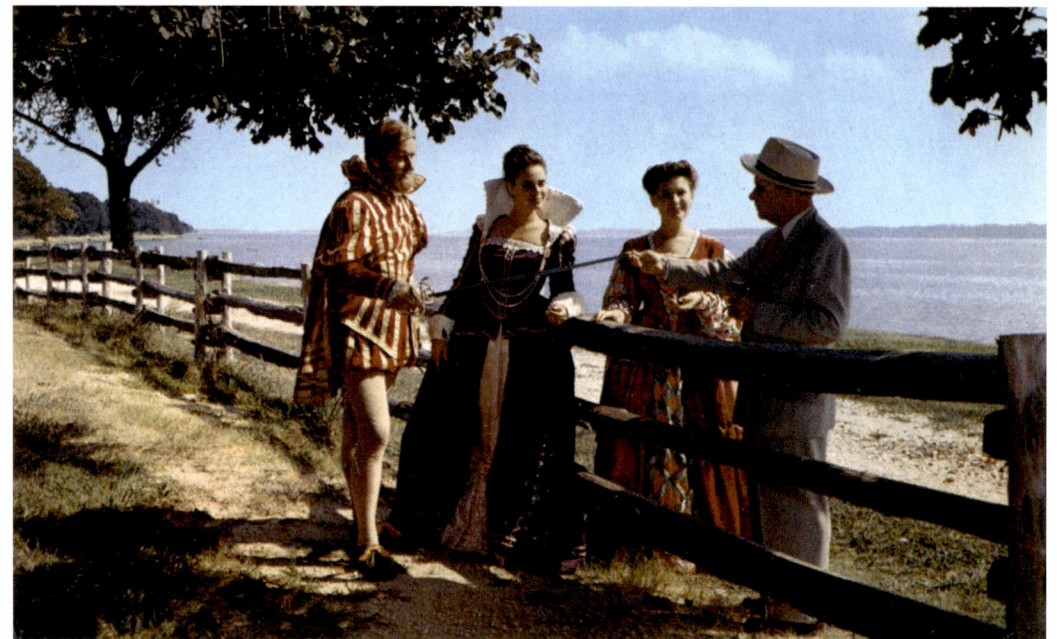

JAMESTOWN RE-ENACTORS: A visitor was photographed as he discussed an early seventeenth-century sword with a group of costumed re-enactors on the shore of the wide James River. The picture, taken by Thomas L. Williams, appeared on a postcard mailed on February 21, 1965.

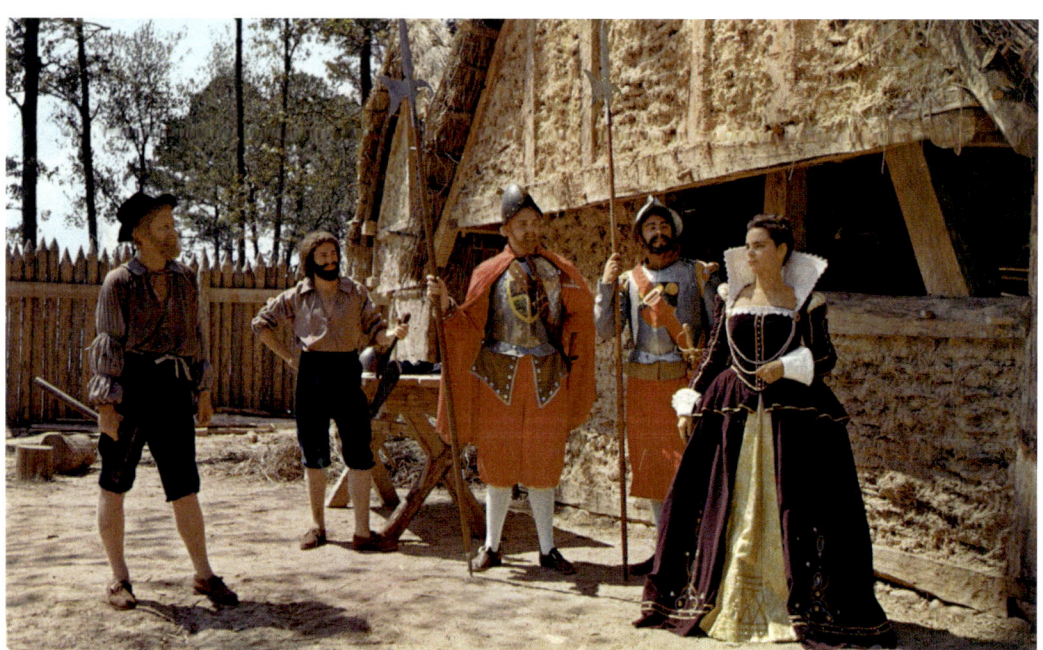

RECREATED JAMES FORT: Inside the recreated James Fort, this group of colorfully attired re-enactors is circa 1960. In 1619 "maids" were dispatched to Jamestown by the London Company to become the wives of the men sent to settle the Virginia Colony. Homes with wives and children were thought conducive to permanent residence; however, as early as 1608 women were part of the Jamestown settlement, established in 1607.

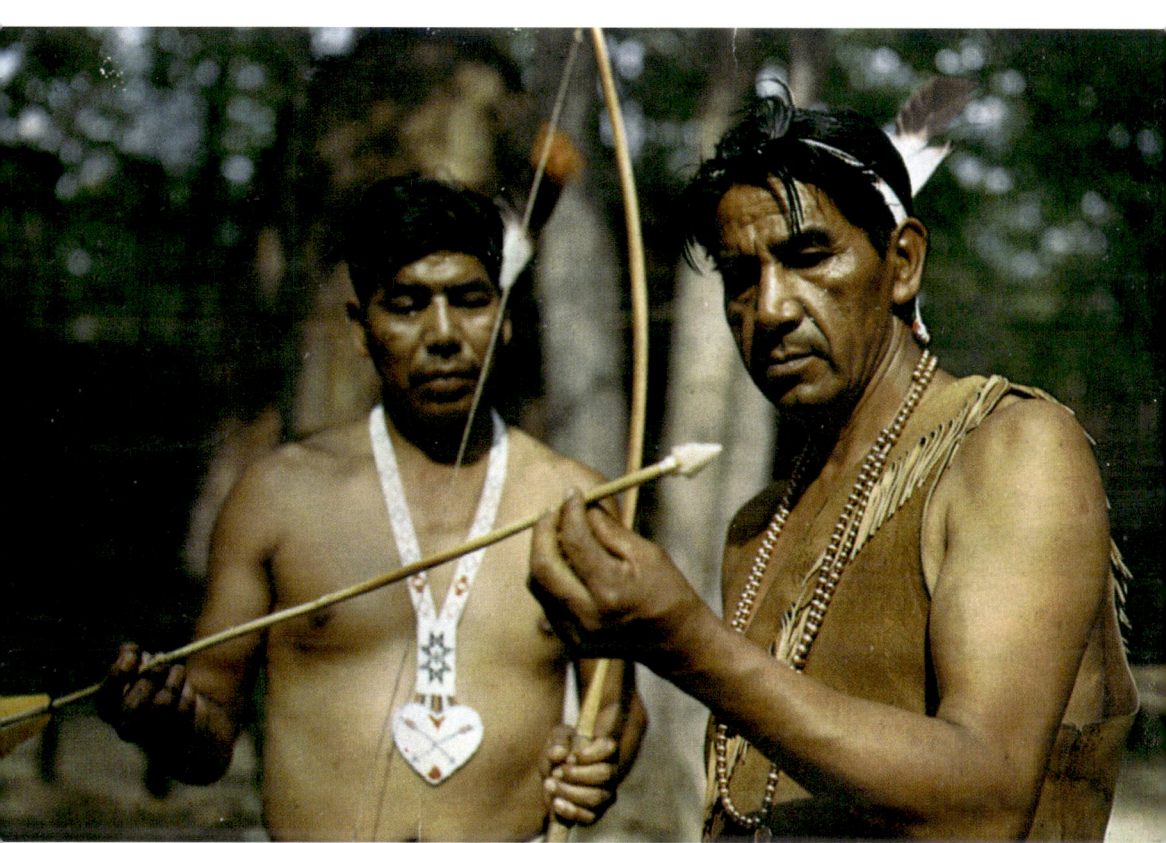

Powhatan Tribes: Powhatan Indian lands dwindled faster in the eighteenth century as many lost their reservations. The only Powhatan tribes that maintained their reservations were the Pamunkey, Mattaponi and the Gingaskin. Some traditional ways were still practiced, but, after decades of interactions with the English, many Powhatan Indians were identifying themselves as Christians and speaking English. By the end of the century, many of the native languages were no longer heard. In the nineteenth century, the Powhatan Indian tribes with reservations were pressured again for their lands and there was an aggressive effort to end Virginia Indians' legal status as tribes. Many of the tribes were quite poor and surrendered to legal pressure; they sold their reservation lands for profit. The Pamunkey and Mattaponi, though also poor, withstood termination attempts and refused to give up reservation land, which they still hold today. They also maintained their tribal structure and treaties with the Commonwealth of Virginia. Pamunkey descendants participated for decades in re-enactments of the first settlement at Jamestown and, later, at the reconstructed Powhatan village, shown on this 1960 period postcard.

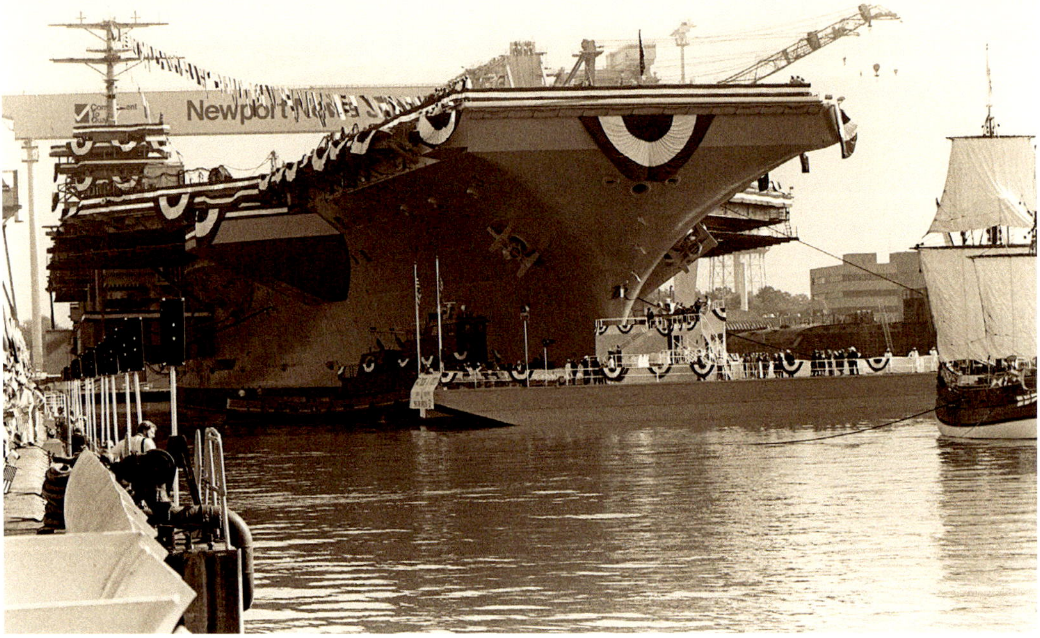

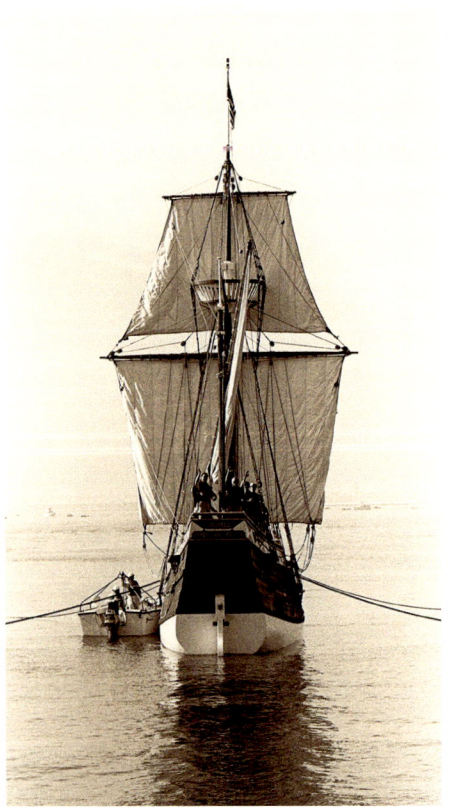

The Aircraft Carrier and the Bark (above):
This is a starboard bow view of the *Nimitz*-class nuclear-powered aircraft carrier USS *Theodore Roosevelt* (CVN 71), shown during its launching ceremony at Newport News Shipbuilding and Drydock Shipway 12; the speaker's podium and VIP seating area are located on the barge under the ship's bow. The replica of the sailing ship *Godspeed* is on the right. The picture was taken on October 27, 1984. *National Archives.*

Historic Launching Ceremony (left):
The Jamestown replica sailing ship *Godspeed*, on display for the launching ceremony of the nuclear-powered aircraft carrier USS *Theodore Roosevelt* (CVN 71), stern view, October 27, 1984. *National Archives.*

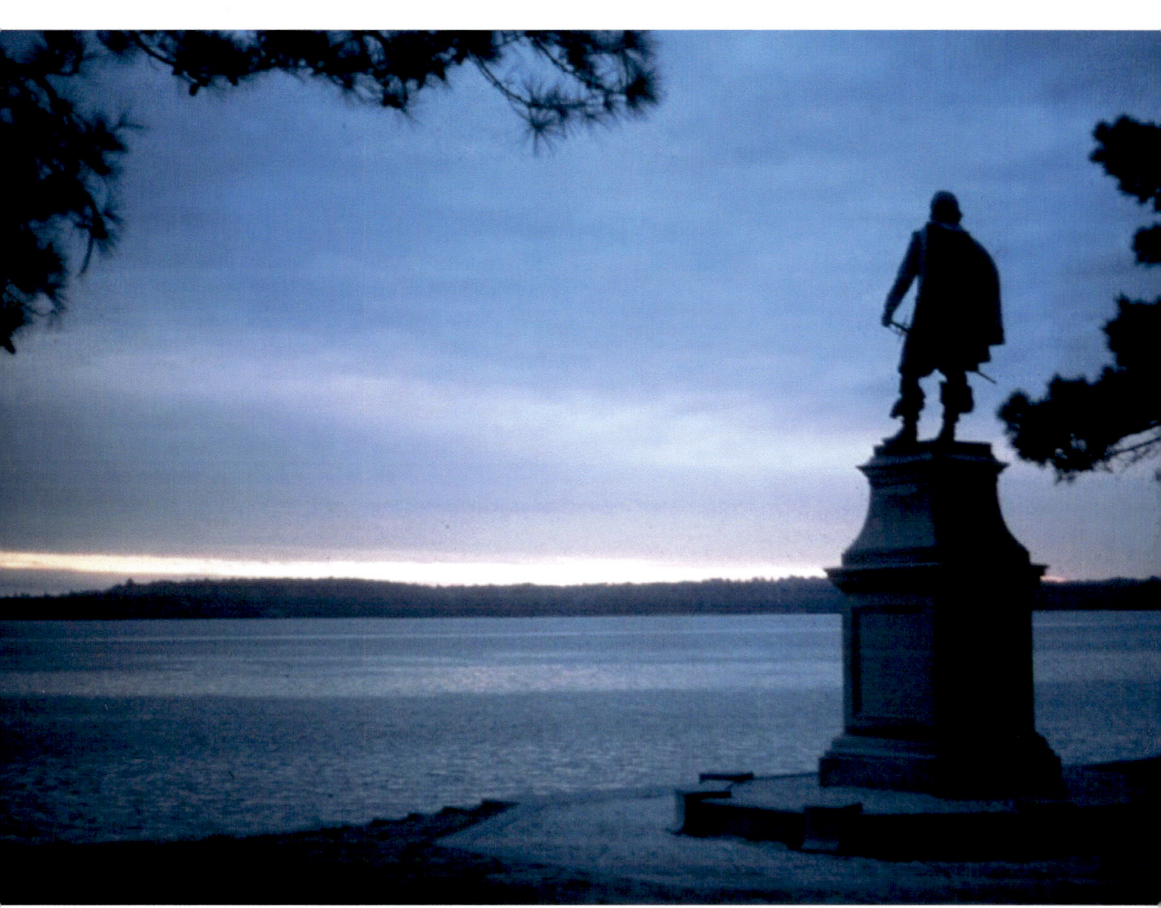

CAPTAIN JOHN SMITH STATUE: Dusky blues and purples paint the sky behind the statue of Captain John Smith, erected to commemorate the site of the first permanent English settlement in the New World at Jamestown, Virginia. This undated contemporary photograph was taken by the National Park Service, Colonial National Historical Park. *National Archives*.

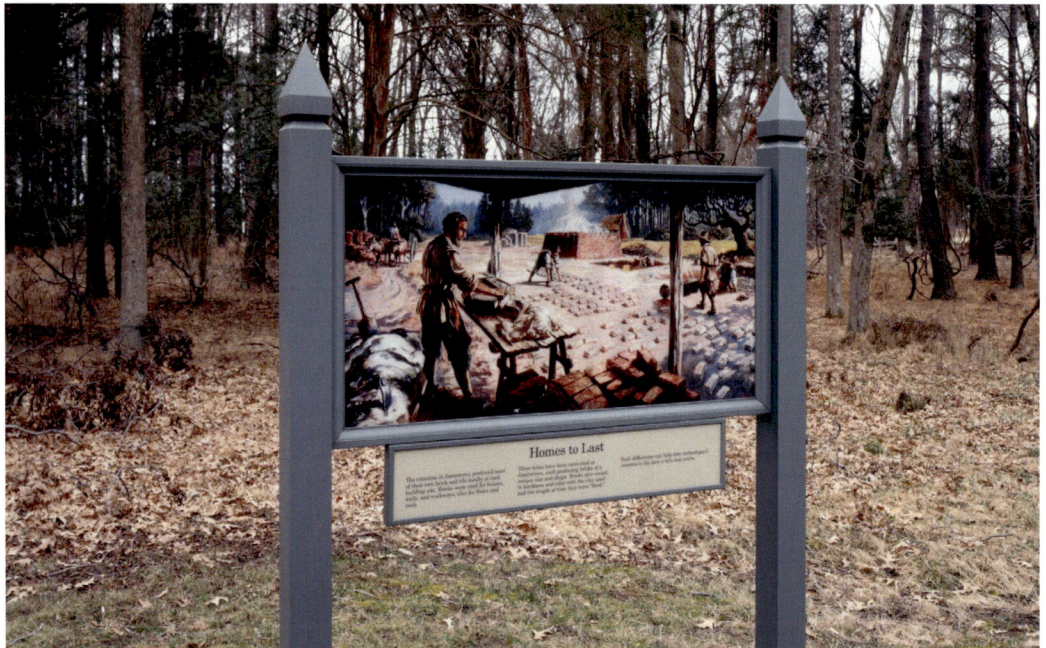

SIDNEY KING PAINTS JAMESTOWN: Completed in 1957, the Jamestown Island loop road was the last road-building contract associated with the completion of the Colonial Parkway. Along the short (three-mile) and full circuit (five-mile), interpretive paintings by Sidney E. King depict the first settlers' use and adaptation to the land. These paintings are representative of the 1950s interpretive programs of the National Park Service at the Colonial Historical National Park. Shown here are two examples: the brick making sign at stop one, and the boatbuilding sign, stop eleven, both photographed in 1995 as part of a park service documentation project. *Library of Congress.*

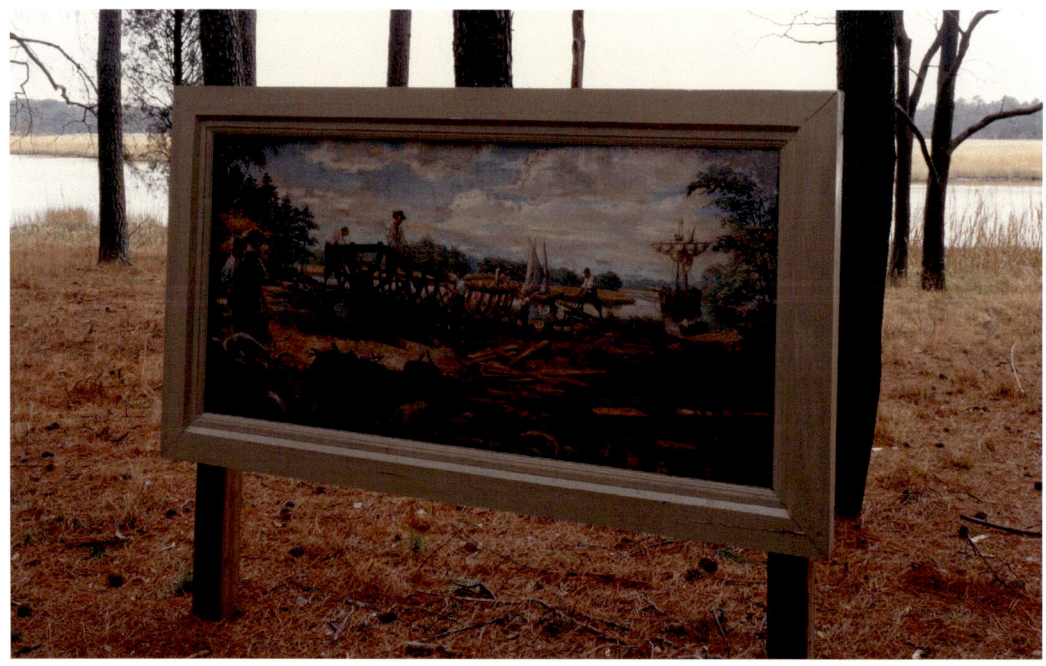

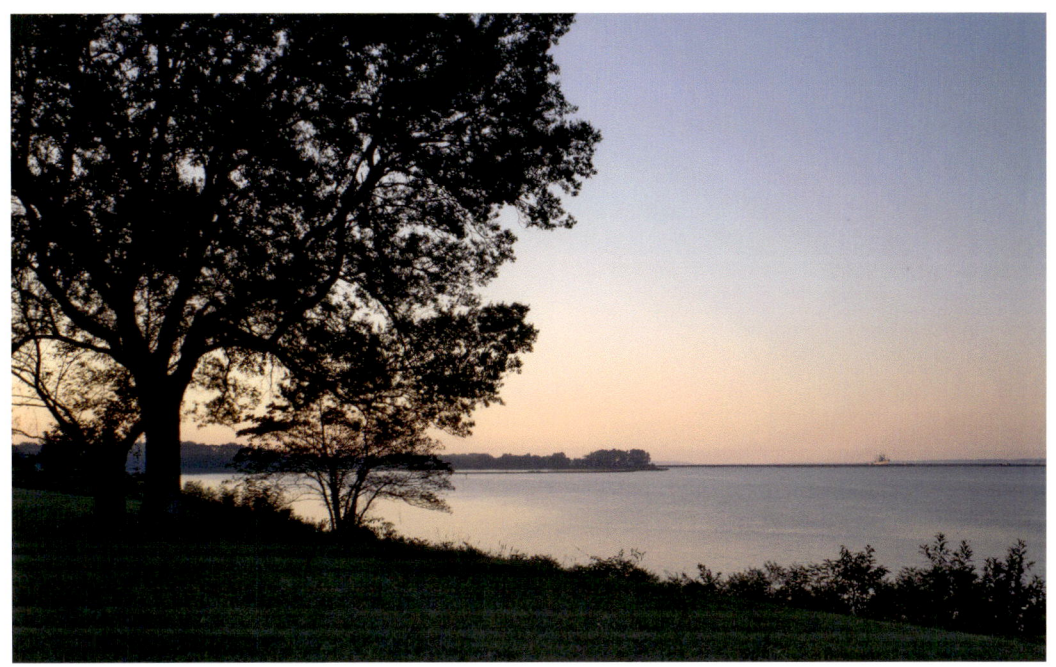

FROM BELLFIELD PLANTATION: This is a view from south of the York River at Bellfield Plantation, part of the collection of pictures taken by Jack E. Boucher in September 1995 of the Colonial Parkway, Yorktown to Jamestown Island, Yorktown vicinity, for the Historic American Buildings Survey/Historic American Engineering Record (HABS/HAER). *Library of Congress.*

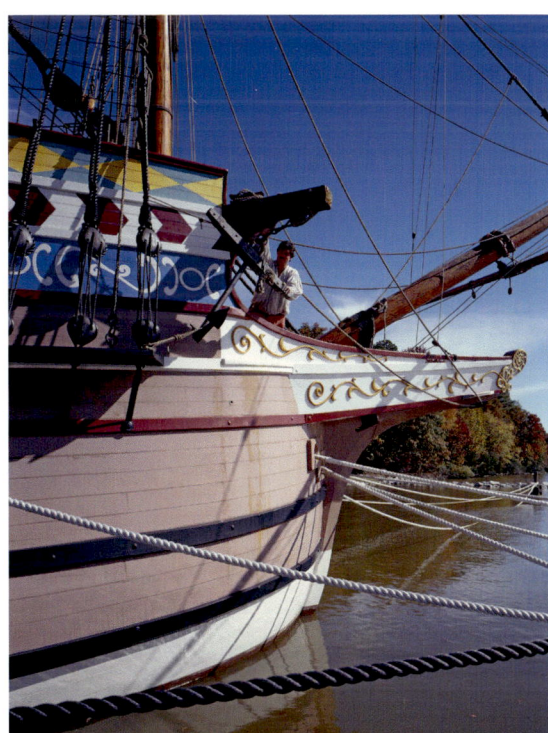

THE FLAGSHIP: One of the tall-masted ship replicas of the three English ships that sailed to Virginia in 1607, the flagship *Susan Constant* is shown at anchor in the James River at the settlement location. Carol M. Highsmith contemporary photograph. *Carol M. Highsmith Archive, Library of Congress.*

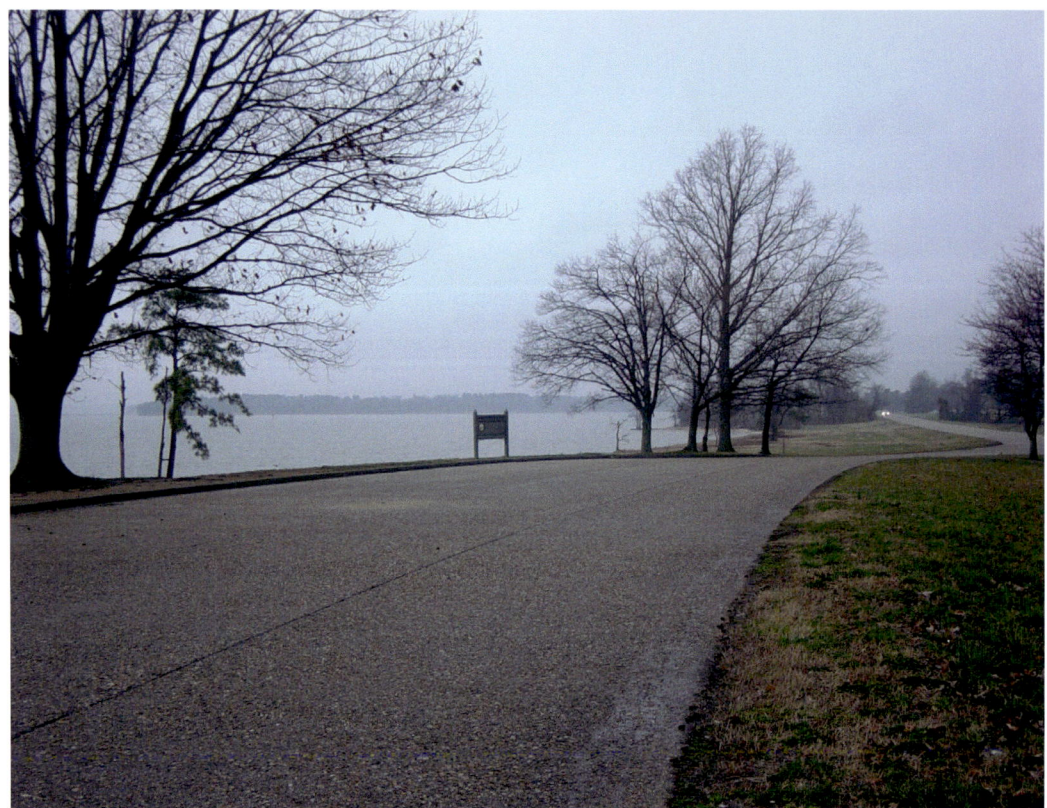

ARCHER'S HOPE CREEK: On May 12, 1607, a point of land at the mouth of Archer's Hope Creek (now College Creek), a little below Jamestown, was examined in detail. Captain Gabriel Archer was particularly impressed with this location and urged that it be the point of settlement. The soil seemed good, timber and wildlife were abundant, and it appeared adaptable for defensive measures if these should become necessary. It was not possible, however, to bring the ships close to the shore, and consequently Archer's Hope was rejected. From this site the ships moved directly to Jamestown, where they arrived May 13. Archer's Hope, shown in this contemporary photograph taken by the National Park Service, provides visitors with a panoramic view of the James River, of the western end of Jamestown Island and a sweeping vista of the Colonial Parkway. This area is located approximately five miles from the Jamestown gateway. *National Archives.*

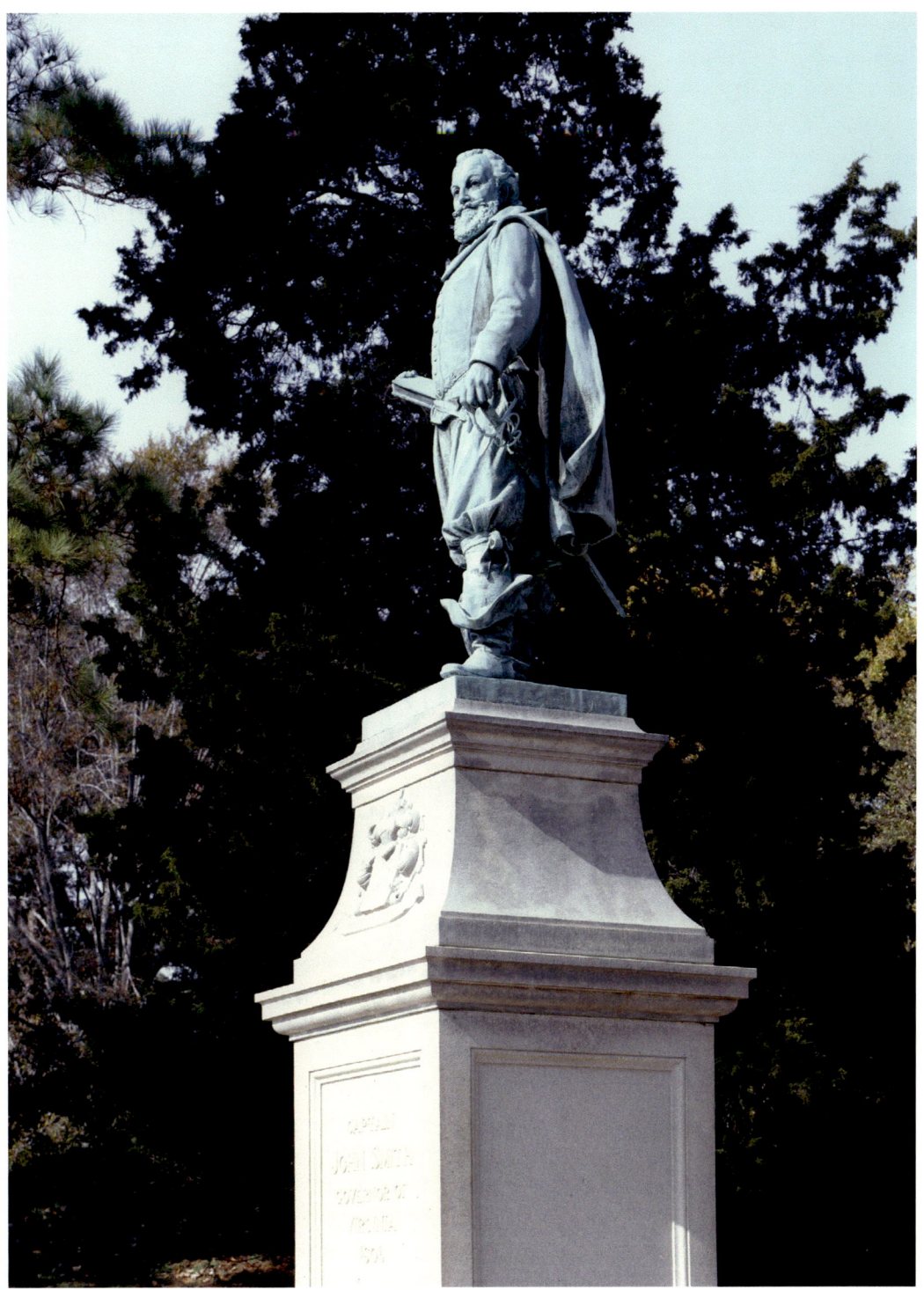

COUPER'S SMITH STATUE: The statue to Captain John Smith by William Couper was erected in 1909 on Jamestown Island, part of the Colonial National Historical Park in Jamestown, Virginia, photographed by Carol M. Highsmith. *Carol M. Highsmith Archive, Library of Congress*.

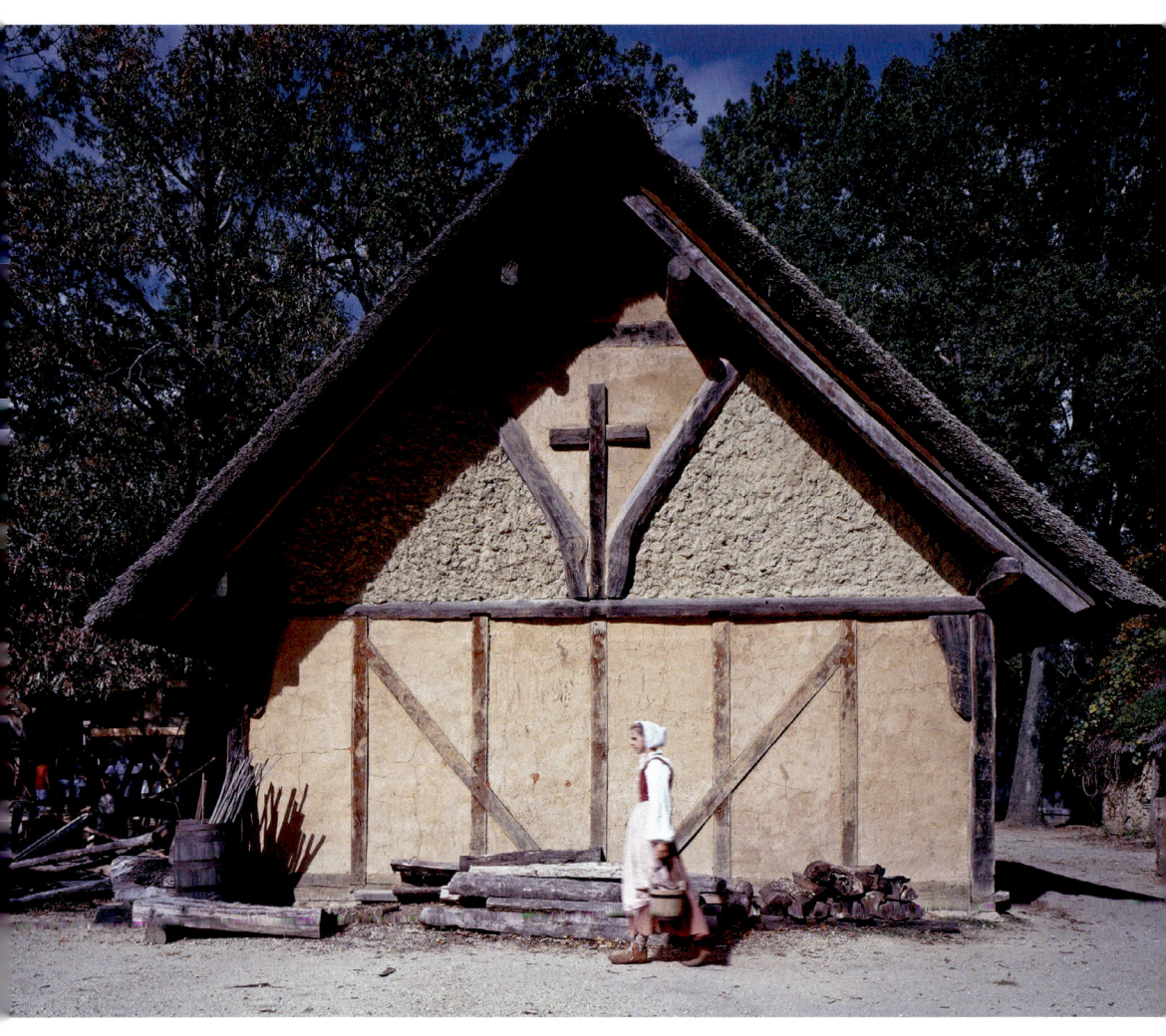

JAMES FORT RECONSTRUCTED: Carol Highsmith took this contemporary photograph inside the reconstructed James Fort. *Carol M. Highsmith Archive, Library of Congress.*

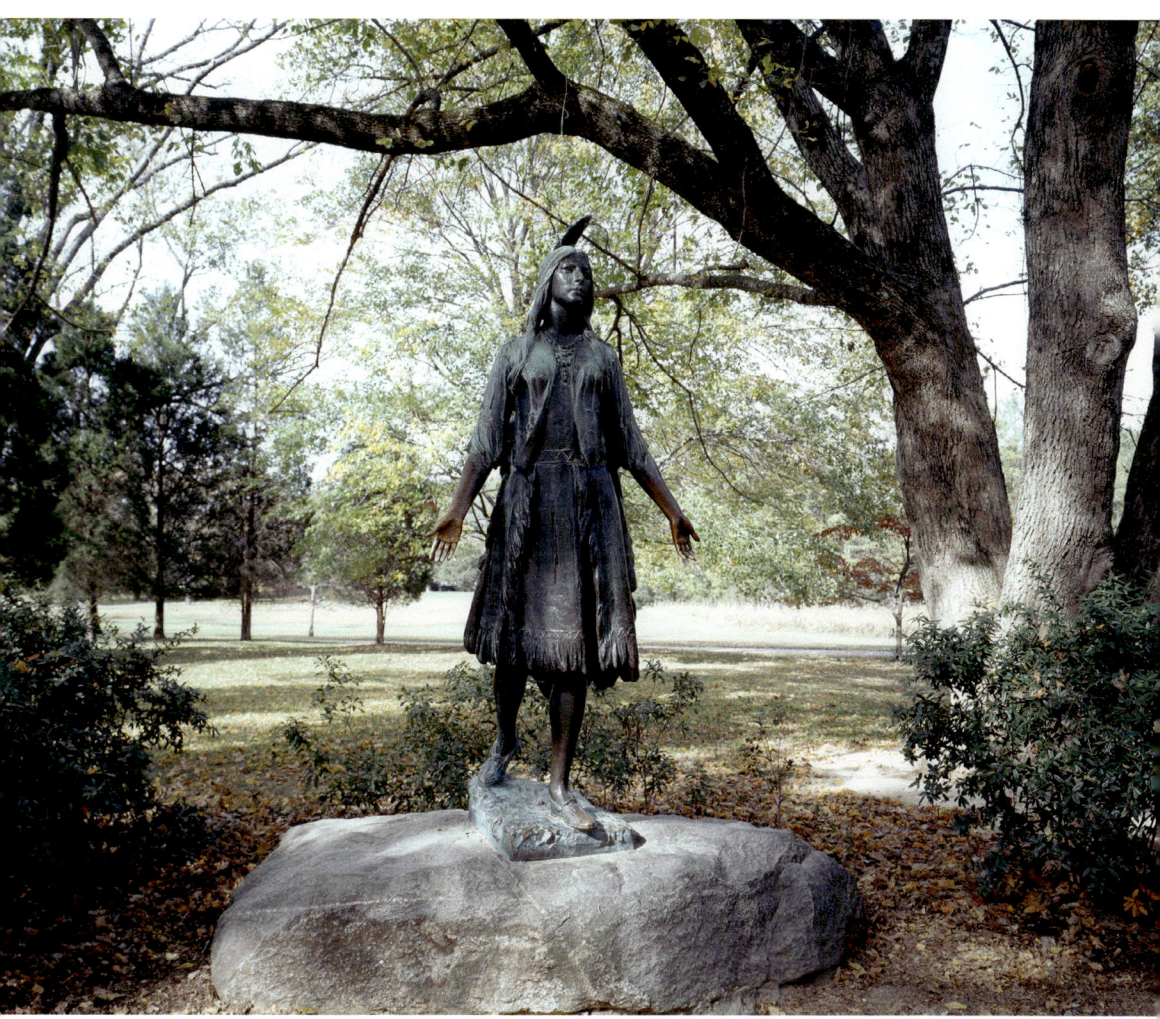

MOVING POCAHONTAS: William Ordway Partridge's statue of Pocahontas was removed from its original pedestal to a low rock base near the APVA entrance gate for the 350th celebration in 1957. The statue was moved again in 2014—this time just a few feet to the west—to accommodate ongoing archaeological work. After Pocahontas married John Rolfe in April 1614, she helped to establish peaceful relations between the Indians and the English. In 1616 she visited England with her husband and infant son, Thomas, and was presented to the court of King James. While returning to Virginia she died on March 21, 1617, and was buried in Saint George's Church in Gravesend, England. Virginia governor James Lindsay Almond Jr. presented a reproduction of this statue to the church in Gravesend in 1958. *Carol M. Highsmith Archive, Library of Congress.*

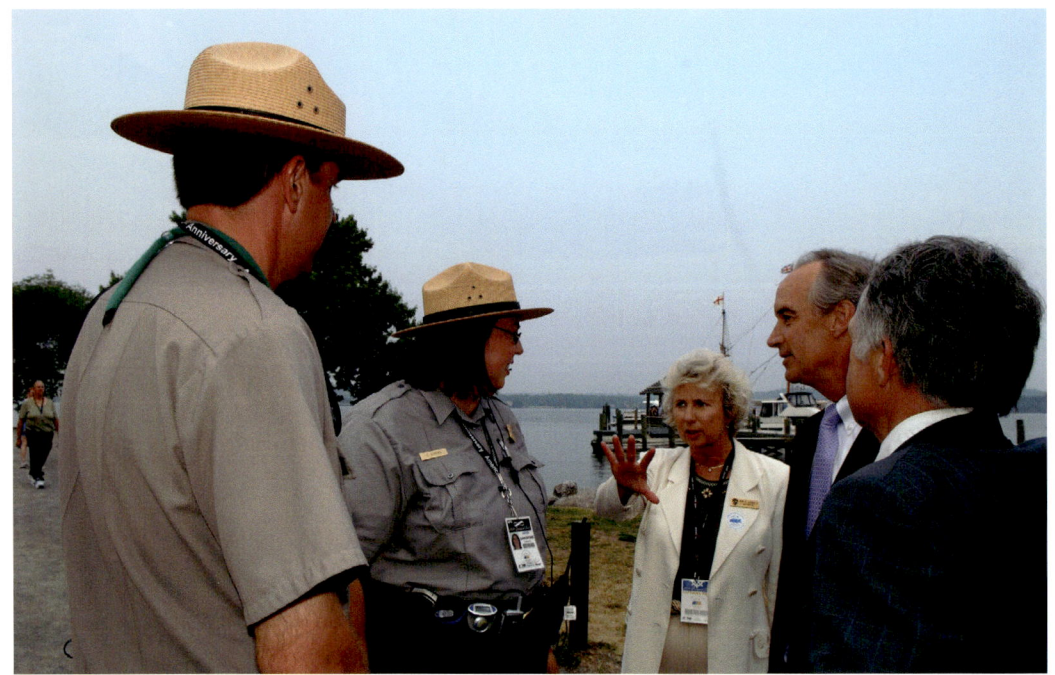

JAMESTOWN SETTLEMENT VISIT (ABOVE): Secretary of the Interior Dirk Kempthorne (right, purple tie) visited the Jamestown Settlement on June 1, 2006, with National Park Service director Frances P. Mainella (center, white jacket) and other officials for tours of the grounds and the replica seventeenth-century sailing ship *Godspeed*, as well as attend other events in conjunction with the 400th anniversary of the founding of Jamestown. The picture was taken by Interior staff photographer Tami Heilemann. The most recent replica of *Godspeed* (shown here) was built at Rockport Marine, Rockport, Maine, and completed in early 2006. *National Archives.*

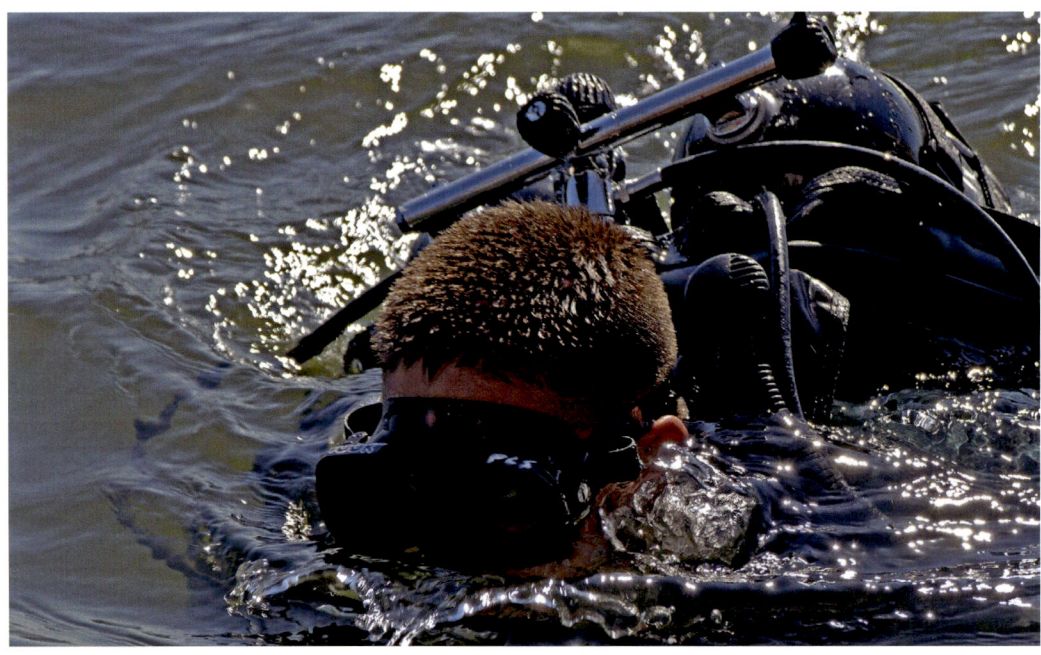

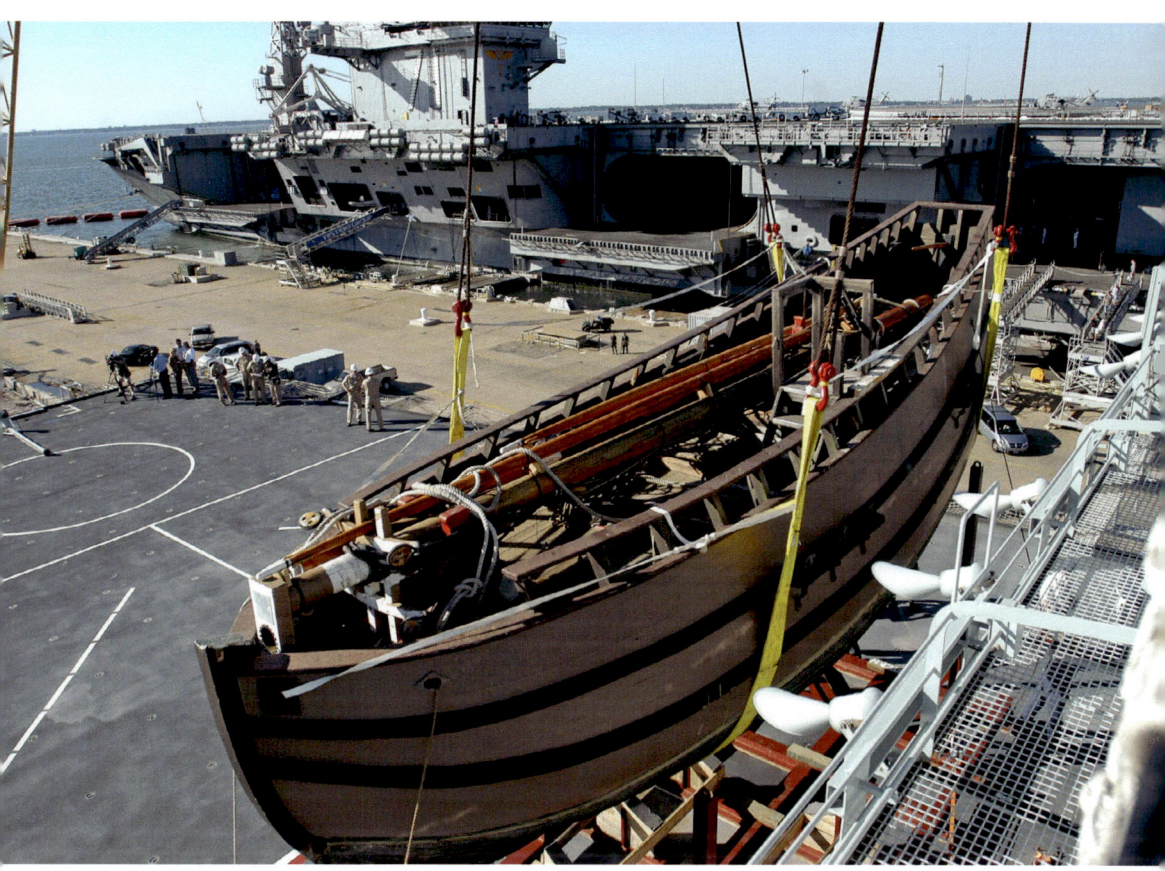

A NEW HOME: The replica ship *Discovery* is hoisted by crane aboard the British Royal Fleet Auxiliary *Fort Rosalie* at Naval Station Norfolk, Virginia, on October 2, 2006. In the background is the *Nimitz*-class nuclear aircraft carrier USS *Theodore Roosevelt* (CVN 71). The photograph was taken by Mass Communication Specialist Third Class Chad Hallford, USN. This is the *Discovery* replica built in 1984 at Jamestown. After its tour, which finished in September 2007, the ship was laid up in Ipswich Marina awaiting a move to a more permanent home. On December 19, 2008, 402 years to the day she left London docks bound for Virginia, this replica of *Discovery* was officially handed over to Westenhanger Castle by the Jamestown UK Foundation, which had brought it to England. The *Discovery* now on view at Jamestown (the replacement for the 1984 pinnace) was built in Boothbay Harbor, Maine, and launched in September 2006, a month before its predecessor headed overseas. *National Archives*.

OPPOSITE BELOW:

DISCOVERY GOES TO ENGLAND: Utilitiesman First Class Paul Sarniak, from the United States Navy's Underwater Construction Team 1, swims in the water during a dive at Naval Station Norfolk, Virginia, on October 2, 2006. Sarniak assisted in the delivery of the replica ship *Discovery* to the Royal Fleet Auxiliary (RFA) *Fort Rosalie* (A385), the ship that transported it to the United Kingdom. *Discovery* was the centerpiece of a major tour promoting the 400th anniversary of the settlement in Jamestown, Virginia. A "fly-boat" of the British East India Company, *Discovery* was the smallest of three ships that took part in the voyage from England to what would become the nascent Virginia colony. The picture was taken by Mass Communication Specialist Seaman Zach Hernandez, United States Navy. *National Archives*.

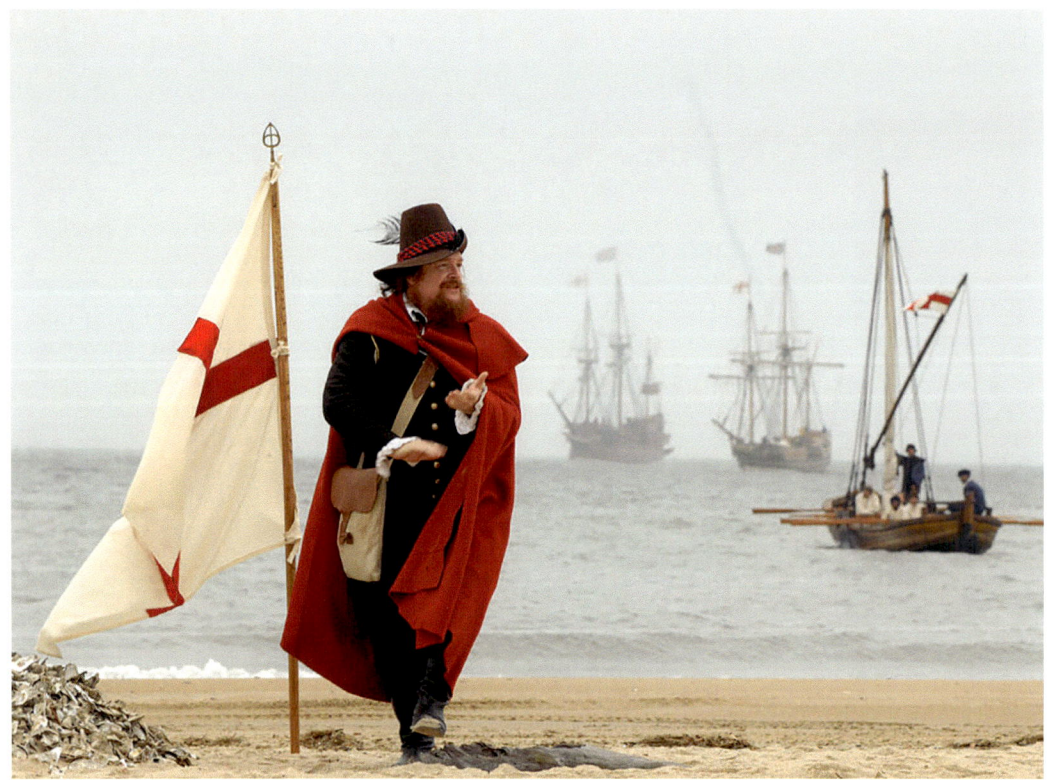

COMMEMORATING THE FIRST LANDING: Captain John Smith, played by Dennis Farmer, claims the beach for England during a re-enactment ceremony on the 400th anniversary of the First Landing in the New World. Settlers from the ships the *Godspeed*, *Discovery* and the *Susan Constant* landed at Cape Henry (now in Virginia Beach), and stayed four days before transiting to Jamestown. This United States Navy photograph was taken on April 26, 2007, by Mass Communication Specialist Seaman Matthew Bookwalter.

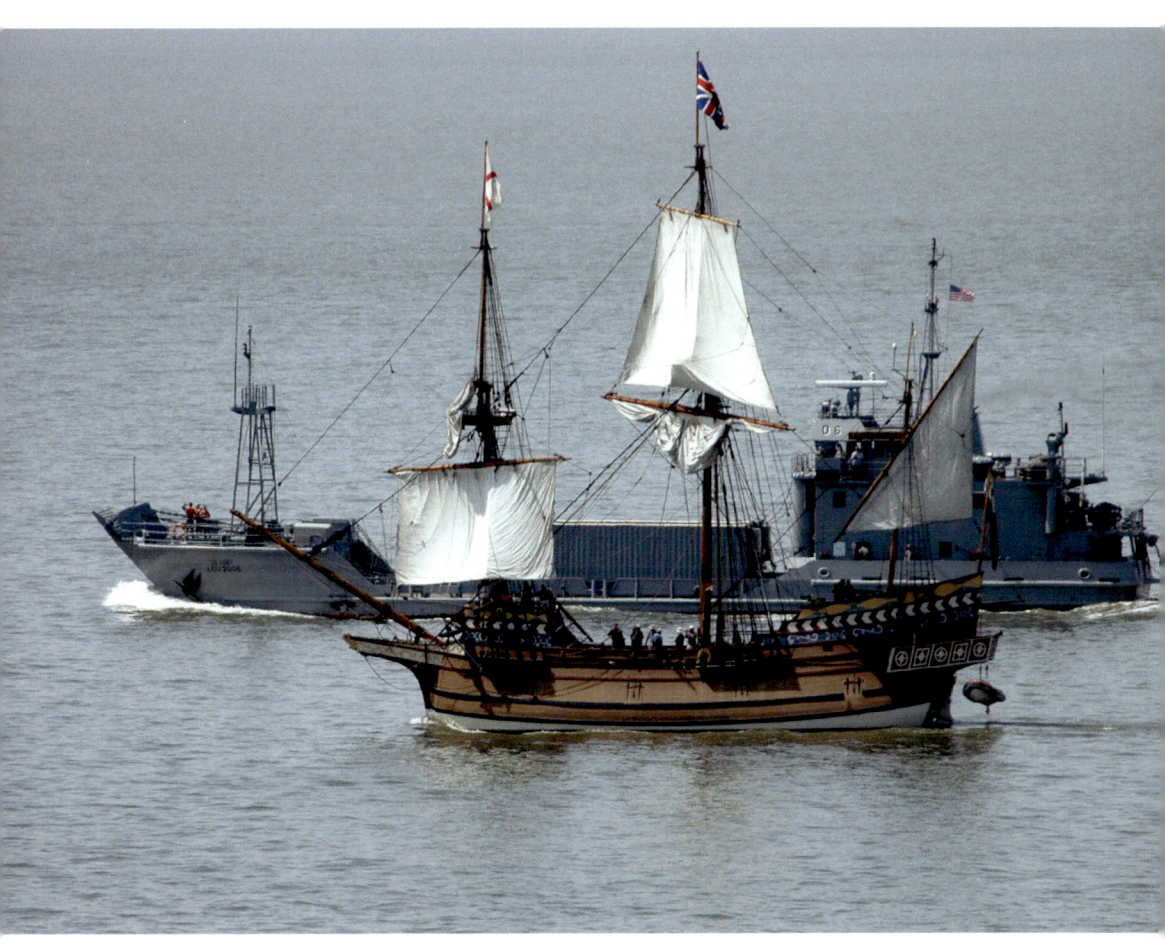

REPLICAS ON THE JAMES RIVER: The United States Army Landing Craft Utility *Bristoe Station* (LCU 2006) secures the water around one of the three replicas of the Jamestown Settlement ships, the *Susan Constant*, as the *Susan Constant*, *Godspeed*, and *Discovery* transited the James River on April 24, 2007. The full-scale replicas of the ships that brought America's first permanent English colonists to Virginia in 1607 were in Hampton Roads for the start of their journey up the James River to the site of the original settlement, a signature event of America's 400th Anniversary celebration. The picture was taken by navy photographer Mass Communication Specialist Seaman David Shen.

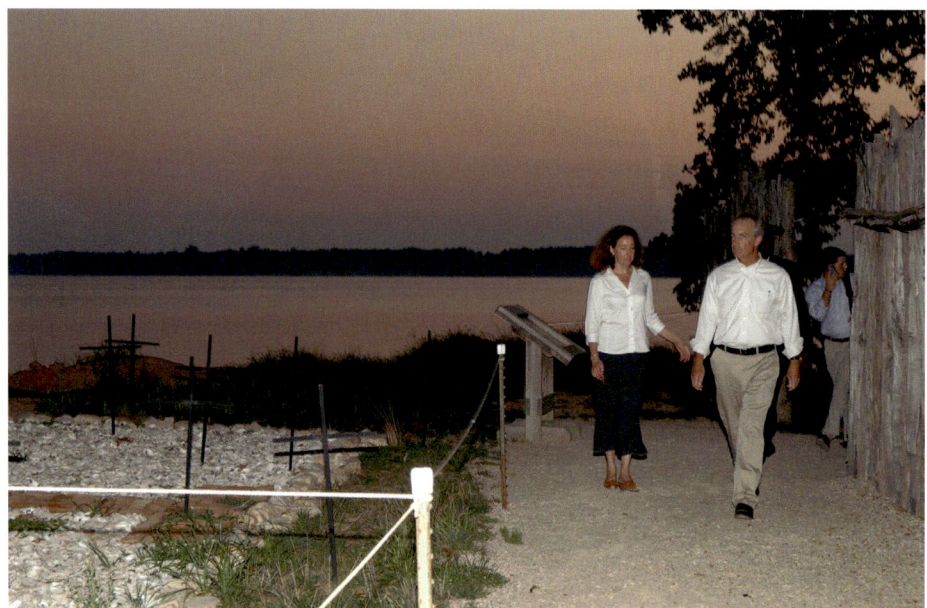

MASS GRAVES DISCOVERED: Secretary of the Interior Dirk Kempthorne visited the Colonial National Historical Park, holding discussions with National Park Service director Mary Bomar and park staff, and delivering the keynote address at the National Association of State Park Directors and National Park Service Leadership Council Conference; he is shown here (right, white shirt) touring a mass grave at Jamestown discovered by archaeologists beneath the foundations of one of the later capital buildings. Kempthorne was secretary of the Interior from 2006 to 2009. The picture was taken by Tami Heilemann, an Interior staff photographer, on September 4, 2007. *National Archives*.

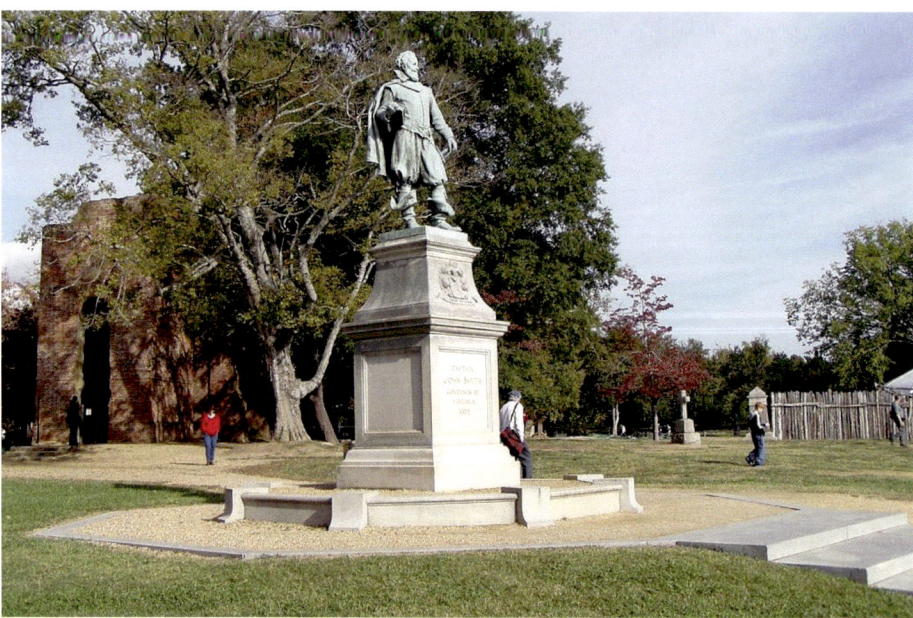

JAMESTOWN TODAY: This view of historic Jamestown today is looking toward the statue of Captain John Smith, erected in 1909. The Jamestown church is in the background. *United States Army*.

Select Bibliography

There were dozens of historical narratives, government documents and reports, programs, pamphlets and articles consulted in the crafting of the book. With limited space to convey a comprehensive bibliography, this is a select list of reference materials that were particularly helpful in the compiling of this pictorial history.

Books
Hutchins, Frank and Cortelle. *Houseboating on a Colonial Waterway*. Boston: L. C. Page, 1910.
Yarsinske, Amy Waters. *The Elizabeth River*. Charleston, South Carolina: The History Press, 2007.
Yonge, Samuel H. *The Site of Old 'James Towne' 1607–1698*. Richmond, Virginia: The Hermitage Press, 1907.

Documents
Day, H. Summerfield. *Preliminary Archeological Report of Excavations at Jamestown, Virginia*. Jamestown Archeological Project. July 1, 1935.
———. *Summary Status of Activities*. Jamestown Archeological Project. September 10, 1936.
Hatch Jr., Charles E. *Jamestown, Virginia: The Townsite and Its Story* (handbook). Washington, D.C.: National Park Service, 1957.
———. *James Towne in the Words of Contemporaries* (handbook). Washington, D.C.: National Park Service, 1955.
Rouse Jr., Parke, ed. The Jamestown Festival Program. Virginia 350th Anniversary Commission, 1957.

Web
Jamestown Rediscovery. Historic Jamestowne http://historicjamestowne.org
National Park Service, United States Department of the Interior. Historic Jamestowne http://www.nps.gov/jame/index.htm
- Colonial National Historical Park http://www.nps.gov/colo/index.htm
Preservation Virginia. Historic Jamestowne http://preservationvirginia.org/visit/historic-properties/historic-jamestowne
Virginia Foundation for the Humanities and Library of Virginia. *Encyclopedia Virginia*: http://www.encyclopediavirginia.org
Virtual Jamestown. http://www.virtualjamestown.org/

About the Author

To those who know Amy Waters Yarsinske, it's no surprise that this award-winning Renaissance woman became a writer. She learned at an early age that self-expression had to be forceful, accurate and relevant. This drive to document and investigate history-shaping stories and people has already led to over 70 nonfiction books, most of them spotlighting current affairs, the military, history and the environment. She is presently working on a multiple-book series documenting richly historic locations in the mid-Atlantic, as well as additional books with diverse subject matter from a world-famous aviator's biography to a whistleblower's true story of scientific misconduct that affects us all. The author of several best-selling, award-winning narratives, Amy graduated from Randolph-Macon Woman's 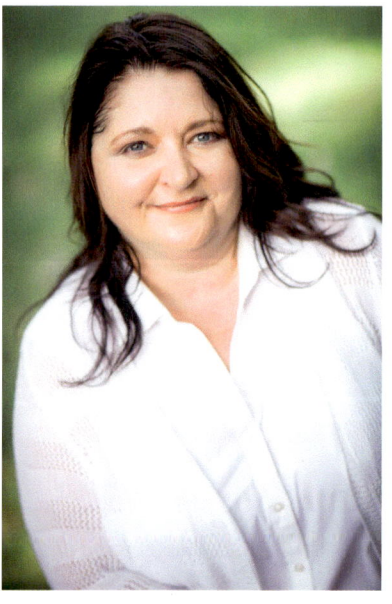 College in Lynchburg, Virginia, where she earned her Bachelor of Arts in English and Economics, and the University of Virginia School of Architecture in Charlottesville, Virginia, from which she earned a Master of Planning degree in Urban and Environmental Planning, was a DuPont Fellow and Lawn/Range resident. She also holds numerous graduate certificates, including from the CIVIC Leadership Institute and the Joint Forces Staff College, both headquartered in Norfolk, Virginia. She is a member of the American Society of Journalists and Authors (ASJA), Investigative Reporters and Editors (IRE), Authors Guild and the North Carolina Literary and Historical Association (NCLHA), among her many professional, civic and volunteer activities.

If you want to know more about Amy and her books, go to
www.amywatersyarsinske.com